Centerville Library
Washington-Centerville Public Library
Centerville, Ohio

DISCARD

P9-AQV-929

AMERICANWOODWORKER'S
Hand Tool
Fundamentals

Whether you are working with hand tools or machine tools or a combination of both, accurate layout is essential for excellent results.

AmericanWoodworker's

Hand Tool Fundamentals

Advice, Techniques & Projects to Build Your Skills

POPULAR WOODWORKING BOOKS
CINCINNATI, OHIO
www.popularwoodworking.com

Foreword

Woodworking with hand tools is alive and well, and in fact, despite reports to the contrary, the muscle-powered hand-tool approach never did fall before the onslaught of the machine. That's because most woodworkers embrace the best of both: machines for gross removal of material, precision, and repetitive, labor-intensive operations; hand tools for finesse, accuracy, and for singular operations that don't need to be repeated hundreds or thousands of times.

But there are more reasons to embrace working with hand tools, including these:

—it's direct. Your hands, and the simple tools you're holding, bear directly on the wood. There's no elaborate system of fences to control the workpiece and keep hands away from whirling cutters, no mandatory hearing protection and safety goggles to impair your senses.

—it's physical. For a terrific whole-body workout, try ripping planks with a hand saw and hand-planing a stack of boards to width and thickness. You won't need to go to the gym that day.

—it's quiet. In fact the gentle sounds that hand tools make are vital clues to what's happening at the cutting edge. The roar of the machine, on the other hand, drowns out subtlety and nuance.

—it's meditative. When it's going well, the work fully absorbs both mind and body, time flies by and crowds out distraction and turmoil. Many hand-tool aficionados report achieving a zen-like state of oneness with their work.

—and with just a little skill, hand work is surprisingly quick and efficient. Adept woodworkers often note that they can complete a task with hand tools in less time than it would take to set up a machine, and they are mostly correct. And even when they are wrong, the other benefits of hand-tool woodworking outweigh the little extra time it might take.

This volume presents a variety of hand tools and techniques, extracted from the archives of *American Woodworker* magazine, that most woodworkers will find useful and pertinent to their shop projects. It includes exercises in choosing, making and modifying hand tools, as well as techniques for using them. And it also includes a detailed section on sharpening, the essential skill that every hand-tool woodworker must master.

Planes and Chisels, 8

Hand Tools and Bench Aids, 56

Contents

Planes and Chisels

Hand Tools and Bench Aids

Joinery, 96

Sharpening, 130

Planecraft is the heart of handtool woodworking.
Planing wood smooth is a delight with tools you
have made yourself.

Planes and Chisels

by Tom Caspar

Planes: Match the Size to the Job

LENGTH, WIDTH AND HEFT ALL MAKE A DIFFERENCE

Pocket-Size

Low Angle

Standard Angle

Hand planes come in a bewildering variety of sizes. Why are there so many? I'll help explain this mystery by dividing the field into four groups, in order of size: block planes, smoothing planes, jack planes, and leveling planes. I'll show you what the planes in each group are used for, and recommend two different starter sets.

Each group best serves a particular purpose. Smoothing planes, for example, are specifically designed to make wood as smooth as silk, ready for a finish. In general, length is the key to understanding a group. Picking a plane at random, you could use it for most any task, but pick a plane that's the correct length and you'll get the job done much faster, with better results.

No. 3

No. 4

No. 4½

No. 5¼

No. 5

No. 5½

No. 6

No. 7

No. 8

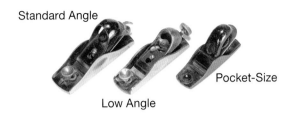

Standard Angle

Pocket-Size

Low Angle

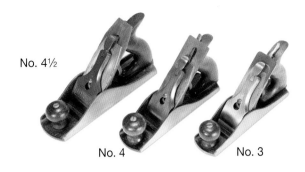

No. 4½

No. 4   No. 3

Block Planes

Block planes are often associated with carpenters and do-it-yourselfers because they're inexpensive and small enough to fit in a toolbox or toolbelt. They have important roles in the woodshop, too. A high-quality block plane can do amazing work, and may become one of your favorite tools.

Types. Standard-angle block planes are the most common. Their blades are bedded at about 20 degrees, with the bevel facing up. If the blade is sharpened at 25 degrees, its effective cutting angle is 45 degrees, which is similar to larger planes. In a low-angle block plane, the blade is bedded at about 12 degrees, resulting in a much lower cutting angle. Pocket-sized planes have a standard bedding angle; what distinguishes these planes is their ultra-small size and light weight.

Uses. Block planes are well-suited for planing end grain or for fitting drawers and doors, where part of the assembly is end grain. Planing end grain requires more force than planing face grain and puts more stress on the blade. Block plane blades chatter less because their bevels face up, not down, as is the case with most larger planes. Bevel up, the blade's tip has additional support from the plane's body. Planing end grain using a low-angle block plane requires less force than using a standard-angle block plane.

Block planes have more uses beyond planing end grain, though. They're very comfortable to hold in one hand for shaping parts and chamfering edges. A pocket plane is easy to carry around in your apron.

Smoothing Planes

A smoothing plane is a serious hand-tool user's best friend. Set to cut a tissue-thin shaving, it can make a board feel smooth as silk. The wood's grain will pop in a way that you can't achieve through sanding alone.

Types. The No. 4 size is the type most commonly used, although the larger No. 4½ is gaining in popularity. The 4½ is heavier than the 4, and that added mass makes it easier to maintain momentum while planing difficult woods. A No. 4 blade is 2". wide, while a No. 4½ blade is 2⅜" wide. A No. 3 smoothing plane is lighter and narrower than a No. 4. It's perfect for a user with less muscle power because its shavings are narrower. The blade of a No. 3 is 1¾" wide.

Uses. Smoothing planes prepare boards for finishing. Their relatively short length makes them ideal for planing a wide board or a glued-up top because they can follow slight irregularities in a board's surface and still make a long, continuous thin shaving, the gold standard in smoothing work. Longer planes require a board to be flatter in order to make continuous shavings (flatter than need be, quite often), so these planes are less practical to use in preparing wood for finishing. Fine-tuning a smoothing plane can really pay off: on many woods, you can make a surface so smooth that little or no scraping or sanding is required.

Block planes are designed for cutting end grain, such as the stile of this door frame. Their compact size also makes them perfect for planing with one hand.

Smoothing planes take the place of power sanders. They're used for making a surface ultra-smooth and ready for finishing.

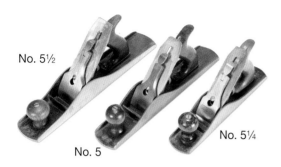

No. 5½
No. 5
No. 5¼

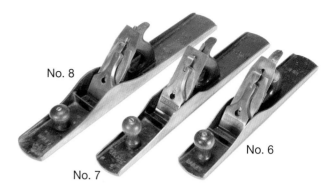

No. 8
No. 7
No. 6

Jack Planes

"He's a jack of all trades, but master of none." That expression perfectly describes a jack plane, and helps explain the origin of its name. A jack plane is longer than a smoothing plane, so it's not as efficient in smoothing a large top because it takes more strokes to cut down to the low spots. It's shorter than a leveling plane, so it's more difficult to use in making an edge straight or truing a large surface. But it can smooth or level reasonably well.

Types. The classic jack plane is a No. 5. Its blade is 2 in. wide, the same as a No. 4, but its body is about 5 in. longer. A No. 5½ is longer, wider, and heavier than a No. 5. Like a No. 4½, this additional mass makes it easier to plane difficult woods. The No. 5¼ is shorter, narrower and lighter than a No. 5. It was designed for youngsters learning to work wood in shop classes, and is often referred to as a manual-training plane or a junior jack.

Uses. You can smooth or level with a jack plane–it just takes a bit longer than using a more specialized smoothing or leveling plane. If you sharpen a jack plane's blade with a pronounced curve, this tool is perfect for hogging off a lot of wood fast, in any situation. A jack plane is also useful for evening joints, such as a table leg and rail, because this operation combines both leveling and smoothing.

Leveling Planes

Leveling planes are long, wide, and heavy. They have two specific purposes: straightening edges and flattening large surfaces. Accuracy is the goal in both situations, and that requires a plane with a long, flat sole.

Types. The leveling plane most often used these days is the No. 7, more commonly known as a jointer plane. As its name implies, a jointer is best suited for straightening edges prior to joining them together. A No. 6 plane is the same width as a No. 7, but about 4 in. shorter. The No. 6 is best suited for leveling the majority of a large surface. It's commonly known as a fore plane (because its used before a smoothing plane, which finishes the job) or a trying plane (because it makes a surface true and flat). A No. 8 plane is a behemoth: it's longer, wider, and heavier than a No. 7.

Uses. One plane, either a No. 6 or a No. 7, can be used for jointing and truing, although having both is ideal. If you have only one, it's best to have two blades. Jointing requires a blade that is sharpened dead straight across; truing is most efficiently done with a blade that's sharpened with a slight curve. A No. 8 is so large that it can be a bit unwieldy, but it's the perfect plane for jointing a long, wide edge, and useful for big jobs such as fitting an entryway door.

Jack planes can both level and smooth a surface. They're useful for evening up one piece with another, such as this breadboard end on a tabletop.

Leveling planes are used to make edges straight, such as these two boards, which will be glued together. Leveling planes are also used to make large surfaces flat and true.

Starter Set Recommendations

Journeyman Three-Plane Set

This is a good starter set for a woodworker who wants to really enjoy what hand planes can do. Each plane has a specialized purpose. The low angle block plane excels at cutting end grain; the leveling plane (which can be either a No. 6 or a No. 7) joints edges and flattens a large surface; the smoothing plane (either a No. 4 or a No. 4½) can make wood look so good that it hardly needs a finish.

Apprentice Two-Plane Set

A No. 5 jack plane and a standard-angle block plane will serve you well in most situations. You'll find dozens of uses for the block plane, taking off a little bit here or there on your projects. With the jack, you can do everything a smaller or larger plane can do, such as straightening an edge, smoothing a surface, or evening up a joint. The job will just take a bit longer.

Cutting Angles

Cutting angles affect the amount of effort it takes to push a plane. The lower the angle, the easier it is for a blade to cut wood fibers, particularly end grain.

Block planes are often touted as having lower cutting angles, but do they really? The answer for a standard block plane is, no. Even if you sharpen it at the fairly low angle of 25-degrees, it cuts at the same angle as a bench plane: 45-degrees. A low-angle block plane cuts at about 37-degrees, which is an improvement.

Why choose a block plane for end grain? Here's the real reason: its blade won't chatter, because it's supported right down to the tip.

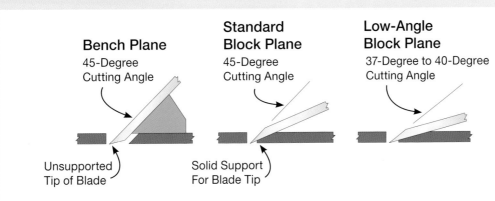

Bench Plane
45-Degree Cutting Angle

Standard Block Plane
45-Degree Cutting Angle

Low-Angle Block Plane
37-Degree to 40-Degree Cutting Angle

Unsupported Tip of Blade

Solid Support For Blade Tip

A standard block plane has the same cutting angle as a bench plane. That's because the block plane's blade is flipped over, with the bevel up.

There's extra support for the tip of a block plane blade. It's less likely to chatter than the blade of a bench plane when you're up against really tough wood, such as end grain.

Some block planes cut at a very low angle. They're easier to push through tough wood.

by Tom Caspar

Choosing a Block Plane

ADJUSTABILITY ENABLES FINE WORK

I love my power tools, but there's one old-fashioned hand tool that I turn to almost every day in my shop—a block plane.

When I need to soften the edges of a freshly milled board, I pick up a block plane.

If I must shave a miter that doesn't quite fit, I put a fresh edge on my block plane.

There's a block plane in my tool belt when I go to trim a sticky kitchen cabinet door in the summer.

It's clear: A block plane is a tool of a thousand uses.

Utility and Cabinetmaker's Block Planes

In the past, every carpenter and handyman owned a block plane. Dozens of models were readily available. Many were light weight, inexpensive utility planes designed to cut softwoods.

Veritas Low Angle Plane

Two innovations make the Veritas low-angle block plane from Lee Valley Tools stand out from the rest: a traditional English mechanism that's a combination lateral lever and depth-of-cut adjuster, and two setscrews that keep the blade from shifting side-to-side. Add to that an extra-thick blade with a huge bed for support and you've got one terrific tool!

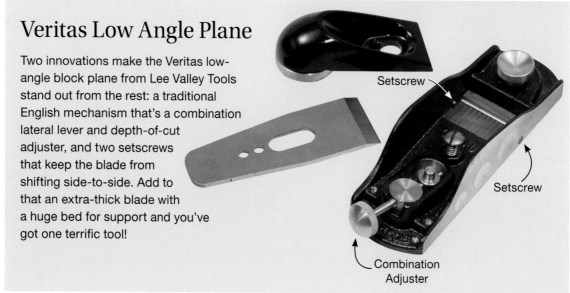

Setscrew

Setscrew

Combination Adjuster

These utility planes are what you're likely to find today at a hardware store. Uncomplicated in design, utility planes generally do not have a lateral lever or an adjustable mouth. They're OK for occasional use, but chances are the blade won't hold an edge as long as the blade in a more expensive plane.

A cabinetmaker working with hardwood needs a better block plane, one with a high-quality blade, heavier body and most of the features of a full-size bench plane. You'll find these premium block planes in tool catalogs and some hardware stores. They're divided into two types: standard-angle and low-angle.

The Standard-Angle Plane

The blade of a standard-angle block plane cuts at about 45 degrees, the same angle as a bench plane. But from the outside it looks like a block plane cuts at a lower angle. So what's going on? The answer lies in looking at how the blade is oriented. In a bench plane, the bevel goes down. In a block plane, the bevel goes up. Thus the block plane blade sits at a lower angle, but its effective cutting angle is about the same.

Despite the similarity in cutting angles, a block plane isn't a substitute for a bench plane. Its sole is too small to true a large surface and its body is too light to take big shavings.

Choose a standard block plane for common situations where you'll take small shavings, like easing edges, cutting chamfers and trimming the sides of cabinet doors.

The Low-Angle Plane

The blade of a low-angle plane is pitched about 8-degrees lower than a standard plane. It's easier to push a plane with a lower cutting angle, which comes in handy when dealing with the stiff grain of a miter or the end grain of a door's stile. Holding the plane askew actually lowers the cutting angle even more. To work best, the blade has to be super-sharp and precisely set.

Tearout may be more of a problem with a low-angle plane than with a standard-angle plane. Steeper cutting angles generally result in less tearout.

Reserve a low-angle plane for tricky situations where each shaving is critical. It's designed specifically for miters and end grain.

One-handed planing is a breeze with a standard-angle block plane. You can trim a sticky cabinet door without having to remove it.

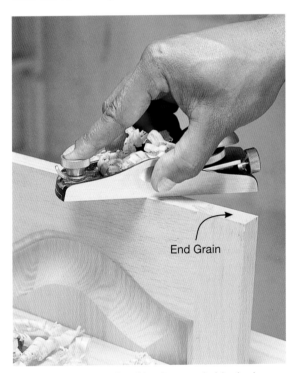

End Grain

Cut through end grain with a low-angle block plane. A sharp blade leaves a surface that hardly needs sanding.

Three Features to Look For

Adjustable Mouth

To minimize tearout in hardwoods, narrow the opening between the blade and sole. Pushing a lever moves the mouth plate in and out. You can easily reset the mouth to a large opening for thick shavings.

Softwoods rarely tear out, so a plane without an adjustable mouth works fine.

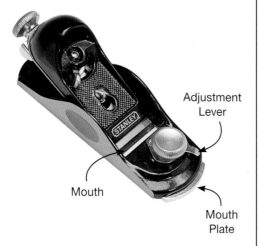

Adjustment Lever

Mouth

Mouth Plate

Lateral Lever

Swing this lever from side to side to set the blade parallel to the sole, a critical adjustment for any plane.

Block planes without lateral levers are fussier to adjust. You have to shift the blade itself by hand.

Lateral Lever

Extra Rigidity

You'll get better control using a plane with a blade that's firmly locked down. The best system combines a thick blade, a large bed, a large-diameter tightening screw and a long lever cap that pushes down directly above the bed.

Thick Blade

Large Tightening Screw

Large Bed

Long Lever Cap

Make a Rabbet Plane

Last year I made my wife a window bench that required 92 mortise and tenon joints. After fine-tuning two or three tenons with a chisel, I realized I needed a rabbet plane to speed up the process. Of course, I didn't have one.

Rabbet planes can be expensive, so I thought I'd make one. I know that sounds daunting, but I'm a mechanic and I had a $15 flea-market block plane that was begging to be transformed into a better tool.

To make a rabbet plane, I had to create an opening and move the blade to the block plane's outside edge. Fortunately, cast iron is very easy to work. I marked an opening on the plane's side, drilled out most of the waste and filed the edges smooth. Next, I modified the blade. It's hardened, of course, so I used my grinder to create a relief that allowed sliding the blade over 1/8" I also lengthened the blade's adjustor slots. Now the blade sits flush with the plane's side.

Converting my block plane to a rabbet plane was easy, but I still have 89 tenons to fit!

—Jon Brinkerhoff

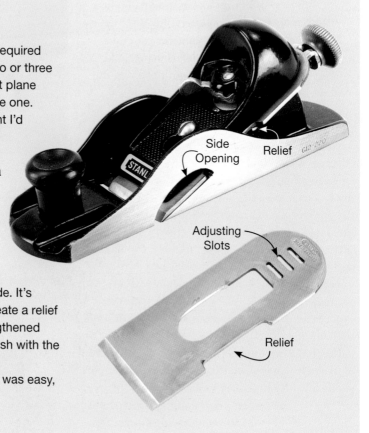

Side Opening

Relief

Adjusting Slots

Relief

by Tom Caspar

Tune Up an Old Chisel

POLISH BOTH BACK AND BEVEL

One of my favorite tools is a legendary Stanley No. 50 chisel. Made in the 1920s, it has seen hard times. Restoring it was a labor of love, and well worth the effort. Its steel holds a long-lasting, super-sharp edge. No doubt you've got some beat-up chisels in your toolbox that could be revived, too.

I'll take you through the complete process of restoring a chisel that's in tough shape. These steps are equally useful for a new tool, fresh from the box. Please notice that I put equal emphasis on the chisel's bevel and back. Both must be in perfect condition, for every sharp edge has two sides. Let's begin with the back.

Evaluate the Back

Inspect the back by sanding with fine paper (Photo 1). Put 220-grit pressure-sensitive-adhesive (PSA) sandpaper on a flat surface, such as a granite surface plate, ¼"-thick piece of glass, cast-iron tablesaw wing or jointer bed. Sand the back a few times using diagonal strokes.

Sanding reveals low spots. With an old tool, you'll probably find rust pits, large hollows or a dip at the leading end.

Flatten the Back

My chisel's back looked so bad that I began flattening with 60-grit paper (Photo 2). If the inspection sanding indicates few low spots, begin with a finer grit. The point is to avoid making unnecessarily deep scratches. Machinists call this process lapping. For the coarse work, I use premium-grade sanding belts stretched tightly on a shop-made jig. They can be reused many times, unlike PSA paper. Lapping a back in

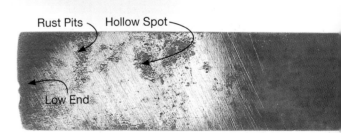

Rust Pits — Hollow Spot —

Low End

1 An old chisel usually needs lots of help. Lightly sanding the back reveals hollow spots, rust pits and a rounded-over or low leading end. This chisel's bevel is also chipped and uneven.

2 Flatten the back on sandpaper using heavy pressure and diagonal strokes. I prefer to work on a 6" x 48" sanding belt. It's easy to reuse and lasts a long time. The belt is stretched taut on a shop-made jig.

Unsanded End is OK

3 Sand until the back is level. You'll know you're done when all the rust pits and low spots are gone and the back is completely covered with scratches. If the leading end is low and unscratched, don't worry about it. You'll grind this off later.

4 Start smoothing the back with finer grits. Hold the chisel in an opposing diagonal direction on each grit. Keep sanding until all the scratches from the previous grit are gone. It's easy to distinguish new scratches from old ones because they run in opposite directions. Go up to a 120-grit belt.

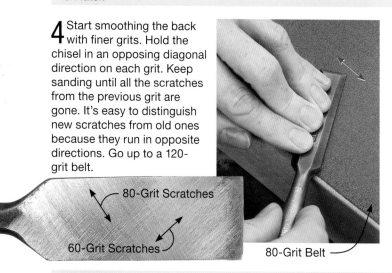

80-Grit Scratches

60-Grit Scratches

80-Grit Belt

Granite Surface Plate

5 Switch to 150-grit pressure-sensitive-adhesive (PSA) sandpaper and a flatter surface, such as a granite surface plate. Repeat the process with 220-grit paper. The back isn't fully polished yet, but it's time to take a break and go to the grinder.

poor condition may require many strokes, which is hard on your hands, so I often wear rubber-coated gardener's gloves and take frequent breaks.

Continue sanding until you reach the bottom of the low spots. How far up the back must you go? Two to three inches are minimum, but I usually lap the whole back. (A totally flat back enables me to use guide blocks when I pare mortises, tenons and dovetails.) If ¼" or less of the back's leading end is lower than the worst rust pits and hollows (and that's not unusual), don't worry about it (Photo 3). Let it go. It's too much work to lap the entire back down to this level. Instead, you'll grind off the leading end later.

Smooth the Back

Smoothing the back requires going through a series of finer grits (Photo 4). With each one, you must remove all traces of the scratches made by the previous grit. How can you tell when that happens? I change direction with each grit. This makes coarser scratches easy to distinguish from finer ones. On the 60-grit paper, for example, I held the chisel pointed right. On the 80-grit paper, I pointed it left. It doesn't pay to skip grits. If you start with 60-grit, continue with 80-, 100- and 120-grit papers.

Precision is critical as you continue to refine the back. After a 120-grit belt, I switch to 150- and 220-grit PSA paper (Photo 5). (Fine sanding belts won't work because their backing has too much give. This rounds over a chisel's sides.) Mount the PSA paper on an absolutely flat surface. I prefer a granite surface plate because, unlike glass, granite is virtually unbreakable. The granite also can be stored with sandpaper stuck to it, which you can't do when using your tablesaw or jointer bed as a flat reference surface. An inexpensive granite surface plate costs about $20.

Grind a New Bevel

Grind a blunt edge if the bevel requires major reshaping (Photo 6). This is the best strategy when the back's leading end is low or if the bevel is heavily nicked or out of square. The blunt edge should be square to the chisel's sides. Draw a pencil line across the back to guide your grinding. Continue to grind until you've removed all the low spots.

Adjust the tool rest and grind a 25-degree bevel (Photo 7). Go right up to the leading end. The bevel doesn't have to be perfectly straight, but a straight end is easier to hone than a crooked one.

Polish the Back

Continue lapping the back by polishing it on your sharpening stones (Photo 8). Your goal is to achieve a mirror surface, but you can't get there in one step. I use three waterstones: medium (800 or 1,000 grit), fine (1,200 or 2,000 grit) and super-fine (4,000, 6,000 or 8,000 grit).

Begin with a medium stone, but first make sure it's flat. A medium stone won't create visible scratches. Instead, you'll get a very dull shine. This should extend all the way across and 1½" to 2" up the chisel's back.

Hone the Bevel

Begin honing the bevel on the medium stone (Photo 9). I use a honing guide to maintain the angle; most guides can accept a variety of chisels. Place the chisel in the guide at the correct projection to hone a 30-degree bevel. This is 5 degrees steeper than the ground bevel, so you'll only be sharpening the leading edge. Creating two bevels saves time and effort.

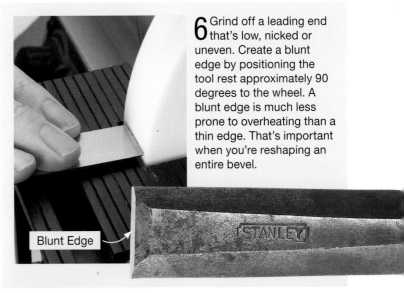

6 Grind off a leading end that's low, nicked or uneven. Create a blunt edge by positioning the tool rest approximately 90 degrees to the wheel. A blunt edge is much less prone to overheating than a thin edge. That's important when you're reshaping an entire bevel.

Blunt Edge

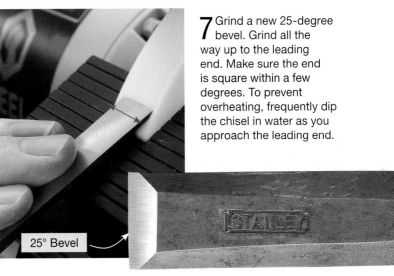

7 Grind a new 25-degree bevel. Grind all the way up to the leading end. Make sure the end is square within a few degrees. To prevent overheating, frequently dip the chisel in water as you approach the leading end.

25° Bevel

Lapping Jig

Opposed wedges tighten a sanding belt placed over this jig. Strike the wedges with a hammer to stretch the paper taut. This jig works for a belt of any size, though I prefer 6" x 48" belts for their huge surface area. Make the jig from three layers of ¾" MDF glued together. To round the ends, make two 45° crosscuts first, and then sand in between them.

8 Polish the back on a medium stone until all the 220-grit scratches are gone. A medium stone creates a dull grey finish. You only have to work the first two inches or so, not the entire back.

9 Hone the edge at 30 degrees to create a new, narrow bevel. I use a honing guide to ensure that each stroke follows precisely at the same angle.

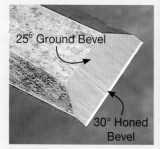

25° Ground Bevel

30° Honed Bevel

Medium Stone

Hone until you feel a wire edge along the chisel's back (Photo 10). This small metallic ridge must extend all the way across, from corner to corner. A wire edge is the best indication that the honed bevel and the back meet, creating a sharp edge.

Remove the wire edge on a fine stone (Photo 11). Polish the back until you can no longer feel a ridge. (After your tool has been restored, you should only remove its wire edge on your super-fine stone.) Keep polishing the back until it's evenly shiny.

Hone the bevel on a super-fine stone (Photo 12). Increase the bevel angle by 2 degrees to save time. This creates a narrow microbevel. A microbevel isn't necessary on a freshly ground chisel, but after a number of sharpenings, the 30-degree bevel will grow quite wide. At this point, honing a microbevel on the super-fine stone makes sharpening more efficient.

Most times, you won't be able to feel a wire edge develop while you're using a super-fine stone. The best strategy is to hone six strokes or so, flip the chisel and polish the back six strokes. Repeat this process three or four times.

Inspect the edge before you remove your chisel from the honing guide. Catch the reflection from a light or window. You should see a bright line extending to the leading end from tip to tip. If you see a dull line at the leading end, you haven't honed enough on the super-fine stone. If everything looks OK, remove the chisel from the guide and test it on the barrel of a pen (Photo 13). You should be able to hold the chisel at a very low angle and make a curl. Now that's sharp!

10 Feel for a wire edge. This small, raised ridge of metal on the back's leading end indicates it's time to stop honing. Be sure to check the corners. The wire edge must go all the way across.

11 Polish the back on a fine stone. Push down on the back with one finger to ensure the back stays flat to the stone. When the back is uniformly polished and the wire edge is gone, turn the chisel over. Hone on the same stone until you feel a new wire edge.

Fine Stone

12 Hone the edge and polish the back on a super-fine stone. A wire edge created by this stone is difficult to detect, so go back and forth between the bevel and the back a few times. Both surfaces will have a mirror polish—the key to an ultrasharp tool.

13 Test your edge on a plastic pen barrel. If you can push the chisel at a very low angle and create a long curl, the chisel is good to go. The ultimate test for a sharp chisel is paring end grain. After I lapped and honed my tool on an 8,000-grit stone, it passed with flying colors.

14 When I needed a very wide chisel for accurately paring some dovetails, I just removed the blade from a plane and added a handle to it. This massive chisel proved to be so easy to control that I use it for many other jobs, too.

Make the handle from ½" thick stock. Round the sides and top edge and chamfer the bottom edge of each piece. Fasten the two halves with 1" long ¼-20 machine screws and square nuts. Chop square recesses for the nuts so they sit flush with the surface.

Planecraft

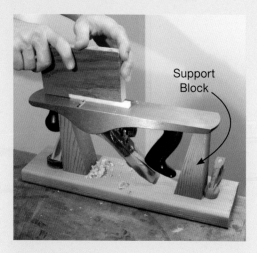

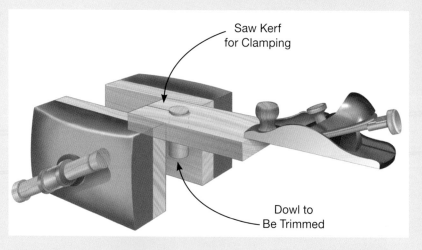

Plane Stand

Small pieces of wood can be difficult to plane accurately. To handle these small jobs, I devised a stand for my No. 5 Stanley jack plane. The plane rests upside down on two wood blocks that fit up between the ridges on the sides of the plane. This keeps the plane centered and also prevents sideways movement. The front knob pushes against the front wooden block and keeps the plane from moving backwards. With the use of a small push block, I can safely and accurately plane even tiny pieces of wood.

—*Jim Williams*

Chip-Free Planing of Round Stock

When making chairs I often need to plane the ends of dowels or other round parts. My method is to drill a hole the same diameter as the dowel (or slightly larger) in a piece of hardwood scrap. I cut a slot with the bandsaw, insert the stock, and put the whole assembly in a vise. Using a low-angle block plane, I get a very smooth cut with no chipping.

—*Yeung Chan*

The guide consists of four pieces of ⅛" MDF glued so one pair of pieces shoulders the sole of the plane (see photo, right). On the sole, this shoulder must extend slightly beyond the blade. The magnets are epoxied into their predrilled holes.

Right-Angle Guide for Jointing

Planing the edge of a long board perpendicular to its face is a real challenge. To make the job easier, I built a guide that attaches to the side of my plane with rare earth magnets. Now jointing an edge is much easier. I simply alter my grip to take full advantage of the square-cornered support that the fence offers.

—*Frank Penicka*

by Allen Snyder

Restoring an Old Plane

THE SECRET IS A STEP-BY-STEP PROCEDURE

I'll bet you've got an old, tarnished plane sitting somewhere in your shop. Maybe it was your grandfather's tool—one he lovingly used and cared for, now neglected. If the plane isn't heavily rusted, you'd be surprised how easy it is to return the plane to its former glory. I know, because I've restored over 500 of them.

I'm a dealer in antique tools as well as a woodworker. I restore every plane I sell, because I believe tools should be well-maintained, and look just the way they did when they were used every day.

With so many tools to refurbish, I've worked hard to develop an efficient, low-cost method for restoring them. It takes me only an hour or so to turn a pretty ugly plane into one that glows with a soft shine. Let me show you how to do it.

Frog
Cap Screw
Lever Cap

1 Completely disassemble your plane. To avoid damaging any parts, use a screwdriver with a large blade that perfectly fits the screw slots.

Lever Cap Screw

2 If a screw won't budge, use a brace and bit for added leverage. Secure the piece in a handscrew or vise.

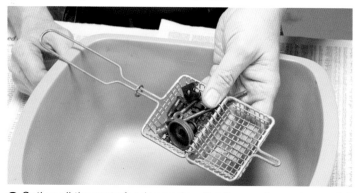

3 Gather all the parts for degreasing. Put the small ones in a metal container, so they don't get lost. Don't include the plane's frog or body. Degreaser may harm the black paint, also called japanning.

4 Spray degreaser on every surface. Removing oils with degreaser is an essential step. It prepares the parts for removing rust and tarnish.

Disassembly

First, take the plane completely apart. As you disassemble it, count and keep track of the parts—particularly the screws. They may have special threads, and often can't be replaced by hardware-store screws.

First, remove the lever cap and the plane iron assembly. Separate the iron from the chip breaker by unscrewing the cap screw. Next, remove the frog by loosening the two screws that fasten it to the plane's body (Photo 1). Each screw should be accompanied by a washer. Disassemble the frog by unscrewing the brass adjustment nut, then remove the lever cap screw (Photo 2) and the frog adjusting screw and tab.

Remove the knob and handle. They'll be fastened to the plane's body by a bolt and brass nut. To avoid damaging the nuts, use a screwdriver with a wide blade (you may have to shorten a screwdriver with a grinder to get a good fit). If possible, unthread the nuts from the bolts.

Degreasing

Next, clean the accumulated grease and grime from all the unpainted parts. I place the small ones in a wire basket that I found at a flea market (Photo 3), but a strainer—a kitchen utensil—would work just as well. Set aside the plane's body and frog for now, because degreasers usually soften their paint.

Degreasing agents are corrosive, so wear rubber gloves and work in a well-ventilated area. Spray all of the parts with degreaser and allow them to sit for a few minutes (Photo 4). Scrub the parts with a nylon brush to remove any stubborn grease deposits, then rinse the parts in hot water (Photo 5).

Dry the parts thoroughly with compressed air (Photo 6).

De-rusting

Now you're ready to treat corrosion on the plane's body and frog. You can use a knife or scraper to remove most of it, but I like to use a small pry bar on which I've freshly ground a sharp, 60° edge (Photo 7). Used carefully, this tool won't damage the cast iron. Alternatively, you can make a scraper from a hacksaw blade. Snap 6" off one end, then place this short piece on your bench and sand 1" of both faces on 120-grit paper. File or grind the end square. With this tool, pushing works better than pulling.

To remove the rest of the corrosion, I use a product called Rust Free. Again, wear rubber gloves and work in a well-ventilated area. Don't use Rust Free on a very old, plated tool, however. Its chemicals may damage the plating.

Spray the rust remover directly on the plane (Photo 8), but avoid getting it on the japanning (the black, enamel-like paint on the plane). Gently scrub the area with a fine abrasive pad (Photo 9). I use 3M Metal Finishing pads, cut into small pieces. 3M Scotch Brite 7447 pads are similar, and available in bulk quantity. I usually go through about one-half pad per plane.

While the treated surfaces are still wet, thoroughly dry them with paper towels. If you don't, the chemicals may continue to work after you are finished, producing an inconsistent appearance on the surface. After drying, the metal should appear dull and free of black corrosion. If rust remains in some spots, repeat the process, starting with the pry-bar scraper.

Polishing

Next, polish all of the plane's parts using a fine wire wheel (Photos 10 and 11). Begin by using the edge of the wheel, then the flat side. The wheel shouldn't leave any marks, but if it does, remove them using 0000 steel wool.

It's pretty hard to get inside the brass adjusting nut with a large wire wheel, however. For this part, and other similar items, use a small wire wheel mounted on a rotary tool, such as a Dremel (Photo 12). Be careful when polishing brass parts—you don't want to dig in and texture their surface.

The stud for the adjusting nut is also hard to get to with a wire wheel. Clean this by hand with a wire brush (Photo 13).

Do not use a wire wheel or steel wool on a highly polished surface. They will dull it, and you'll have to buff the surface to restore its shine.

Immediately after cleaning and polishing, treat all the parts with a preservative to ensure that they do not begin to rust (Photo 14), which can happen right away. I use Boeshield T-9. Allow the T-9 to dry for at least one hour (overnight is best), then remove the excess with a paper towel and buff with a cotton rag.

5 Scrub the parts with plain water and a nylon brush to wash off the degreaser.

6 Thoroughly dry each part with compressed air. This removes moisture from every nook and cranny.

7 Turning to the plane's body, scrape off rust and tarnish with a de-scaling tool. I use a hardware-store pry bar whose end is beveled and sharpened.

8 Spray Rust Free on the body to help remove the rust that you can't get to with the de-scaling tool. Avoid getting rust remover on the japanning.

9 Scrub with a fine abrasive pad. Wipe off the residue with paper towels before it dries. You may have to repeat this a few times. Use the same procedure on all of the other parts.

10 Polish the body, and all the other parts, with a fine wire wheel chucked in your drill press.

11 Tip: If your wire wheel becomes contaminated with oil or dirt, run it against the corner of a 2x4. This transfers the oil from the wheel to the wood.

12 Use a small wire wheel mounted in a rotary tool, such as a Dremel, to polish the inside of the brass adjusting nut.

Cleaning

Clean the japanned parts of the plane—and any other painted parts—with Natchez Solution (Photo 15). Scrub with a toothbrush. If the grime residue is especially stiff, scrub it lightly with 0000 steel wool.

Wipe the parts dry with a paper towel, then polish with a cotton rag. Natchez Solution leaves a clear waxy finish on the japanning. It should be shiny—if the finish appears dull, then a grime residue remains. Repeat the process until the shine lasts.

I also apply Natchez solution to all the unpainted parts, too, because it leaves such a nice, soft luster.

Treat the knob and handle with Natchez Solution (Photo 16). Remove dirty solution with a paper towel. Apply an additional coat and allow the solution to remain overnight, so that the wood will absorb it. (If the wood's color has faded, repeat this process several times. Staining shouldn't be necessary.) Polish with a clean cotton rag.

Reassemble your plane. For further protection, add a drop of 3-In-One oil to all the screws and under the frog. You may have to reapply Natchez solution to the knob and handle every three months or so to retain the luster.

13 If the threads on the adjusting-nut stud are rusty, clean them with a wire brush.

14 Immediately after polishing the plane body and all other parts, apply Boeshield T-9 to protect them from tarnishing.

15 Clean the japanning on the plane's body and frog with Natchez solution, a mixture of light oils and beeswax.

16 Clean the handles with 0000 steel wool and Natchez solution. to bring back the finish's luster.

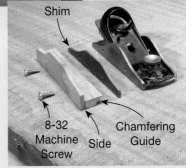

Shim
8-32 Machine Screw Side Chamfering Guide

Custom Chamfering Plane

Chamfering an edge with a block plane is often easier, faster and safer than using a router or tablesaw—particularly on a small part. I do it so often that I've dedicated one of my planes for the job.

To modify your plane, make two 3/16" thick hardwood sides, two 3/8" thick chamfering guides and shims of various thicknesses. Shape the sides and shims to fit your plane. Bevel the guides at 45° and glue them to the sides.

The space between the guides determines the width of the chamfer. I made my guides wide enough to make a 1/8" chamfer, then add shims between the sides and the plane to make larger chamfers.

To attach the guides, drill mounting holes in the sides for 8-32 machine screws. Position the guides on the plane and mark the holes' locations with a center punch. Drill and tap the holes.

When you start planing, hold the tool at approximately 45°. It will automatically adjust itself to the correct angle as you go. When the plane bottoms out against the guides, you're done.
—*Doug Perlick*

by Tom Caspar

Troubleshoot Your Plane

PRACTICAL SOLUTIONS TO 6 COMMON PROBLEMS

When a plane is working right, it can produce a silky-smooth surface that absolutely glistens. When it doesn't work, you get an ugly surface covered with blemishes. The problem can be your sharpening, your technique, or the plane itself. Quite often, it's the plane.

A handplane can be a mysterious tool. These troubleshooting tips should go a long way to clearing up how a plane works and how to tune it up. Most Stanley, Record and similar types of planes certainly require a tune-up. You'll probably encounter every problem addressed here. Premium planes, such as a Lie-Nielsen, Veritas or Clifton, usually don't need much tuning at all.

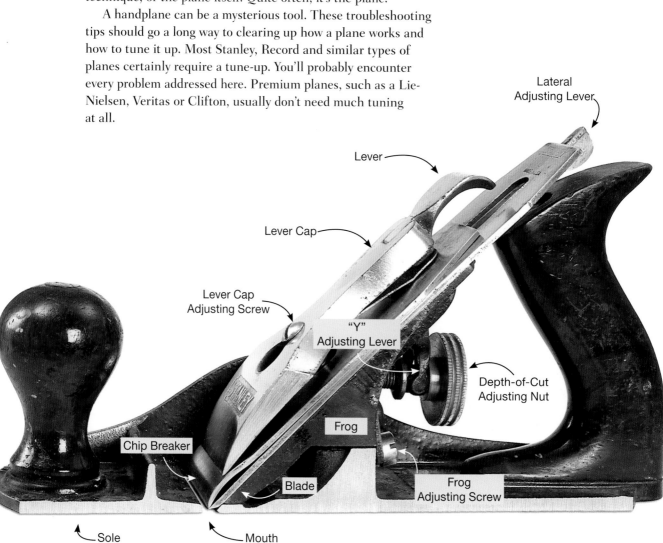

Lateral Adjusting Lever

Lever

Lever Cap

Lever Cap Adjusting Screw

"Y" Adjusting Lever

Depth-of-Cut Adjusting Nut

Frog

Chip Breaker

Blade

Frog Adjusting Screw

Sole

Mouth

You retract the blade to take a lighter cut. The plane works fine for a while, then suddenly stops cutting.

Cause: There's backlash (play) in the plane's adjustment mechanism.

Solution: Always set a blade's final depth of cut by adjusting the blade downwards, deeper into the wood. If your blade cuts too deep, back it out until it cuts a very thin shaving or not at all. Then advance the blade bit by bit until the shaving is the thickness you want. If you overshoot, start over again.

To understand the "why" behind this procedure, let's back up to the original problem. You've retracted the blade, and eventually it stops cutting. What's happened is that the blade has slowly crept back up the frog. If you remove your plane's lever cap, you can see how this works.

Turn the adjusting nut clockwise to advance the blade, then counterclockwise two turns to retract it. Hold the blade with your fingers and push it up the frog (photo). It will move by at least ⅟₃₂". That's why the blade stopped cutting.

Now turn the adjusting nut clockwise again, two full turns, to advance the blade. Try moving the blade up the frog with your fingers again. It shouldn't budge.

Backlash is the problem. ("Backlash" is the play between mechanical parts.) In a plane,

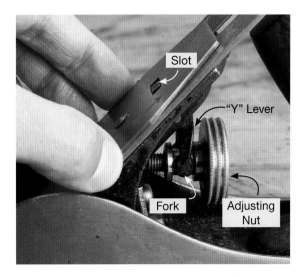

there's often significant play in two places. First, there's play between the adjusting nut and the "Y" adjusting lever's fork. Second, there's play between the top of the "Y" lever and the slot in the chip breaker. Some planes have more play than others, but there must be some play in any plane or the parts won't move. It's usually impractical to alter the plane to remove backlash, so the best strategy is to learn to live with it.

Plane Talk

Before launching into troubleshooting, let's identify a plane's basic parts. I cut open one of my No. 3 Stanley planes to give you a better look at how the parts fit together. We'll start at the bottom and work our way up.

- **The sole** is the full length of the plane's bottom.
- The **frog** holds the blade assembly at a 45-degree angle to the sole.
- The **frog adjusting screw** moves the frog forwards or backwards.
- Moving the frog effectively opens or closes the plane's **mouth**, the gap in front of the **blade**.
- The uppermost part of the blade assembly is the **lever cap**.

- The middle part of the blade assembly is the **chip breaker**. It's screwed to the blade.
- Pushing down on the **lever** clamps the blade assembly to the frog.
- This clamping pressure is regulated by the **lever cap adjusting screw**.
- Turning the **depth-of-cut adjusting nut** rocks the "Y" **adjusting lever**, which slides the blade and chip breaker up or down the frog.
- Pushing the **lateral adjusting lever** side-to-side levels the blade with the sole.

Your plane cuts at the beginning or end of a board, but not in the middle.

Cause: The plane's sole may not be flat.

Solution: Rule out some simpler causes first. Test the board's flatness with a long straightedge. If it's hollow in the middle, the problem is with the board, not your plane. Similarly, test the flatness of your bench. If it's hollow, the board will bend as you plane. Time to flatten the bench. But if your board and bench are just fine, and this mysterious behavior persists, chances are the sole of your plane isn't flat.

A plane's sole must be extremely flat for the blade to remove continuous, thin shavings the full length of the board, your ultimate goal. Test your sole by placing the plane on a very flat surface, such as a tablesaw's cast iron wing. Try to slide a thin strip of paper underneath it at various places. If it slips under at any point, the sole isn't flat enough. It needs lapping (a machinist's term for flattening).

The easiest way to lap is using self-adhesive sandpaper on a rigid, flat surface, such as a tablesaw's cast iron wing, a jointer bed, or a long piece of ¼" plate glass. (You can also use regular sandpaper and a low-tack spray adhesive.) You may have to remove a lot of metal, so it helps to have a variety of grits available, from 80 to 220. The surface and paper should be at least twice as long as the plane's sole.

Retract the blade and start lapping with 120 or 150-grit paper (photo). If the sole is convex, grip the plane as shown to avoid rocking it. Inspect the bottom after a few strokes (photo). The newly sanded areas should be easy to see. If there are lots of low spots, switch to coarser paper.

Whichever grit you start with, keep sanding until the entire bottom is scratched with sanding marks. The area right in front of the mouth is very important; it must be flat to prevent tearout. Don't worry about the sole's extreme ends, though, or old scratches from previous use. Once the sole is flat, work up to 220 grit or more to polish it.

Flatten your plane's sole using sandpaper. A flat sole enables a plane to make long, thin shavings.

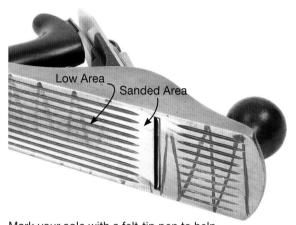

Mark your sole with a felt-tip pen to help reveal the low spots. Planes with corrugated (grooved) soles have less metal to remove than planes with smooth-bottomed soles, so they're easier to flatten.

Tip
• •
Rub your plane's sole with a few squiggles of paraffin or canning wax every ten strokes or so. This helps your plane glide much more smoothly.

Your plane suddenly stops cutting. When you take it apart, you find shavings wedged between the blade and chip breaker.

Cause: There's a gap between the blade and chip breaker.

Solution: First, lap the chip breaker's bevel, located under the breaker's leading edge (photo, left). The angle of this bevel is important. It must be steep enough so that the bevel's point, not its heel, touches the blade. With most chip breakers, if you keep the screw hole aligned with the sandpaper's edge, the bevel's angle will be just fine. Keep lapping until you feel a wire edge develop along the chip breaker's entire width, just as in sharpening a blade.

The second step is to round the top of the chip breaker. You can use a file if the chip breaker is quite blunt, but sandpaper usually works well enough. Use a rolling motion to create a rounded edge, ending up at about 45 degrees (middle photo). Keep sanding until the wire edge you formed earlier is gone, then alternately sand both the bevel and the top until the chip breaker is sharp.

When you're done, hold the chip breaker firmly against the blade, as if it the two were clamped together by the lever cap (right photo). Sight from behind the chip breaker. There should be a slight gap at the heel, but no light showing between the chip breaker and blade.

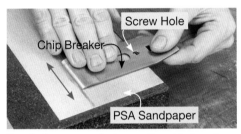

To eliminate gaps between the chip breaker and blade, begin by lapping the bevel underneath the chip breaker's leading edge. Keep the chip breaker's screw hole aligned with the sandpaper's edge to form the bevel at the correct angle.

Round the top of the chip breaker to create a sharp edge. Lift the cap iron up as you drag it across the sandpaper.

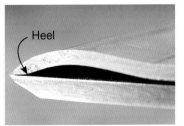

Squeeze the blade and chip breaker together to inspect for gaps. No light should be visible between them. In addition, the chip breaker's heel shouldn't be touching the blade.

Your blade chatters. It feels like its bouncing up and down as it cuts.

Cause: Your blade may not be clamped down tight enough, or your frog may not be flat.

Solution: Try simple fixes first. Your blade may be dull, or set too deep, or your chip breaker may have slipped over the blade's edge, so it's trying to do the cutting. If you rule out these causes, try the following:

First, increase the clamping pressure on the blade. This is controlled by the lever cap adjusting screw (photo). This screw isn't something you fiddle with every time you plane, though. Adjusting it is a matter of finding the sweet spot that puts lots of pressure on the blade, but not too much. If you overtighten the screw, applying too much pressure, you won't be able to turn the large brass wheel that controls the depth-of-cut.

To find the sweet spot, loosen the lever cap and tighten the screw 1/8 turn. Re-tighten the lever cap. Turn the brass adjusting nut to move the blade up and down the frog. If it moves very freely, loosen the lever cap again and tighten the lever cap screw another 1/8 turn. Re-fasten the lever cap. Repeat this procedure until the adjusting nut is somewhat hard to turn with two fingers, but not too

Your blade will also chatter if your frog's top surface isn't flat. Flatten the frog with sandpaper adhered to a flat surface.

hard. Once you've found the best setting for the screw, leave it there. You should rarely have to re-adjust it.

A second cause of blade chatter may be a frog that's not flat (photo). To check your frog, unscrew it from the plane's body and remove the lever cap screw. Lap the frog on sandpaper. You won't be able to lap the entire surface because the Y lever sticks out the top, but that's OK. Flattening the first two to three inches is good enough.

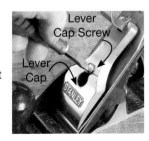

Your blade will chatter if the lever cap doesn't provide enough pressure to clamp the blade tight to the frog. Adjust the lever cap screw to provide more pressure, if needed.

Your smoothing plane leaves tracks on a board's surface.

Cause: The blade isn't level, or its corners are too square.

Solution: First, make sure the tracks you see aren't ridges caused by a nick in the blade. If the tracks look like shallow steps (drawing), one side of the blade is cutting deeper than the other. Raking light or chalk used flat-side down clearly reveals these tracks.

You'll have more success avoiding track marks and leveling your blade if you round it. This prevents the corners from digging in. Rounding a smoothing blade's profile one way or another is an old tradition. Here's how I go about it. First, I round over the blade's corners on the grinder. I do the rest of the rounding work when I hone, by rocking the honing jig to one side or the other on the pull stroke (photo). This creates a cambered edge and a transition to the rounded corner.

If you're new to planes, I recommend you camber the blade's full width. The amount of curvature to aim for is very small. To check it, I hold the blade upright and lay the fat side of a small square on the blade's edge. The blade's center should be higher than the edges by about the thickness of one or two pieces of paper.

If you're more experienced with a smoothing plane, it's better to leave the majority of the edge straight across, and only camber the outer edges; that is, round ⅛" to ¼" of each side. This will create a flatter surface than the previous method, but the blade will be more difficult to level.

To level your blade, make a narrow shaving using the outer ½" of the blade's left side. Make another shaving using the right side (photo). Compare the thickness of the two shavings. Adjust the lateral lever until the shavings are equally thick. Back off the blade, re-adjust its depth of cut, and you're good to go.

Round a blade's profile by rolling the jig sideways as you hone. Favor the right side, then the left side on alternate pull strokes to produce a curved profile.

Level your blade by comparing shavings made with each side. Hang the plane off the edge of a board and make a narrow shaving using only the blade's left side. Turn the plane around and make another narrow shaving using the blade's right side. Adjust the lateral lever until these shavings are equally thick.

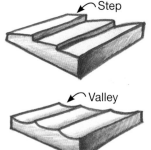

Shallow steps are caused by a plane blade that's not set perfectly level. One corner is digging in. A commonly used method to minimize this problem is to round the blade's corners, and maybe its entire profile. This produces a surface with extremely shallow valleys which can be leveled by scraping or sanding. Some makers prefer to leave these marks as subtle evidence of being worked by hand.

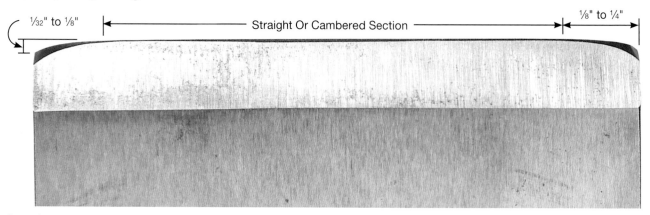

Round a smoothing plane blade to avoid making steps on a board's surface. The corners of this blade are rounded off, and the area in between is cambered (that is, very slightly curved), or left straight.

You get tearout, even though the blade is sharp.

Cause: The chip breaker is set too far back, or the plane's mouth is too large.

Solution: First, adjust the chip breaker closer to the end of the blade (photo). Second, move the frog forward to close the plane's mouth (photo).

In general, the finer the shaving you're trying to cut, the closer the chip breaker should be to the blade's edge. A $1/32$" setback is ideal for most hardwoods, but when you get tearout, try moving the chip breaker to within $1/64$" or less of the blade's end. This will make the plane harder to push, however. (In soft woods, like pine, where tearout isn't an issue, you can adjust the chip breaker up to $1/16$" back from the blade to make the plane easier to push.)

To move the frog, remove the lever cap, blade and chip breaker. Slightly loosen the two bolts that hold the frog to the sole. Reinstall the blade assembly and adjust the blade until it barely sticks out of the plane's sole. Turn the frog adjusting screw with a long screwdriver to close the plane's mouth. Once you have created the desired opening, remove the blade assembly and tighten the bolts that secure the frog. Tighten each one a little bit at a time, like a car's lug nuts.

Moving the frog may skew it, however. On most planes, you can only eyeball the frog to make sure it's front end remains parallel to the plane's mouth. Frogs on Stanley planes manufactured in the Sweetheart Era, roughly 1920 to 1935, are self-aligning, so skewing isn't a problem (photo).

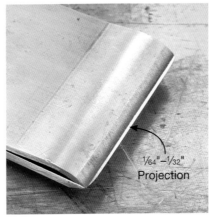

To reduce tearout, adjust the chip breaker closer to the blade's edge. A projection of $1/32$" is normal for most hardwoods, but to beat tearout you may have to go down to $1/64$" or less.

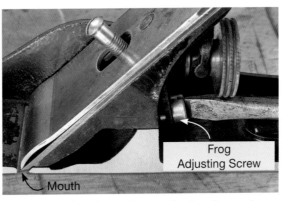

To further reduce tearout, move the frog forward by turning the frog adjusting screw. This closes the plane's mouth. Normally, the mouth should be about $1/16$" wide. You can reduce it down to $1/64$".

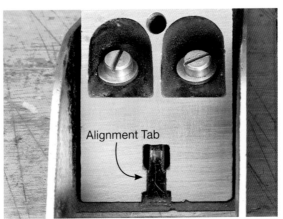

If you move the frog forward, you must double-check that it hasn't wiggled side-to-side and become skewed. Many older Stanley planes have an alignment tab to prevent skewing, which is an excellent feature.

Preventing Tearout

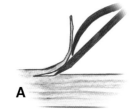

A

When the chip breaker is set back more than $1/32$" from the blade's edge, fibers may break out ahead of the blade, causing tearout.

B

Moving the chip breaker closer to the blade's end forces a shaving to rise at a steeper angle. This reduces tearout.

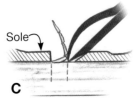

C

When the plane's mouth is wide open, with a large gap in front of the blade, fibers may split out between the blade and the sole.

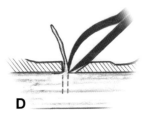

D

Closing the plane's mouth by moving the frog forward allows the plane's sole to push down on the fibers, which helps prevent tearout.

by Tim Heil

Handles for Socket Chisels

HOW TO TURN A PERFECT FIT

High-quality socket chisels—such as the Stanley Sweathearts and Lie-Nielsens—are making a big comeback. Why would these companies choose the socket style? Well, it's all about you, the user. If you're not satisfied with a handle's shape, you can change it. If you want a different wood—no problem. The handle of a socket chisel isn't glued or fastened to the tool, so you just remove it and make your own.

Truth is, woodworkers have been doing this for years. In the age before plastics, when a wood handle on a socket chisel split or mushroomed, replacing it was easy. But not all were fixed. Today, there are loads of wonderful old socket chisels going for a song, merely because they have busted or missing handles.

I'm a turner with a thing about handles—I just love making them. Screwdrivers, awls, ice cream scoops: If it's got a handle, I've got to make my own.

When I first turned handles for socket chisels, I would make a few crude measurements of the socket and just go at it. If the taper on the handle's shank wasn't quite right, I guessed where it was off and tried again. While this method works OK, I've since found a measuring system that's much more reliable. Following these steps, your shank should fit tight right away.

First, turn a cylinder that's an inch or two longer than the length of the handle you're going to make (of course, the full length includes the shank). The narrow end of the shank will most likely be a small diameter (anywhere from ¼" to ⅜"), so I prefer using a cone-shaped revolving center in the lathe's tailstock. This gives me more room to maneuver the parting tool when cutting the shank's taper.

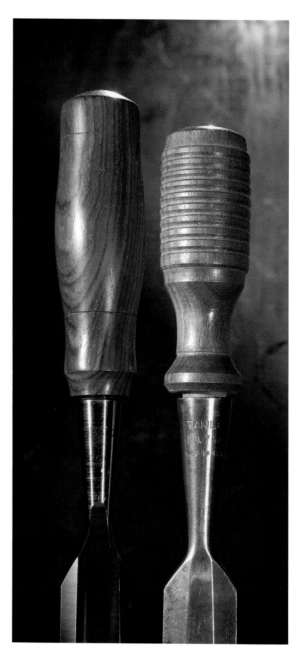

1 Chisel sockets come in many different sizes, so you'll need to take some measurements before turning the handle. Start by cutting a piece of notebook paper about 4" square. Roll it up around a pencil.

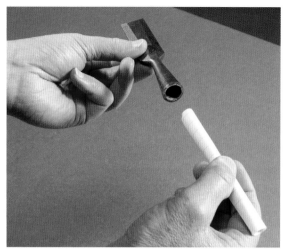

2 Push the paper cylinder all the way into the chisel's socket. Let go of the paper—it will unroll to form a cone. The cone will be exactly the same shape as the socket.

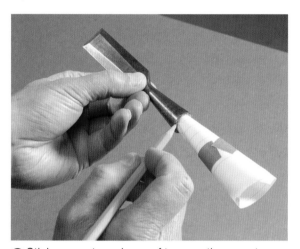

3 Stick one or two pieces of tape on the cone to hold its shape. Mark the cone at the end of the socket. Remove the cone from the chisel.

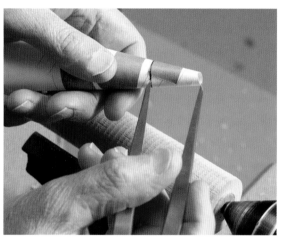

4 Set a divider to the distance between the pencil mark and the end of the cone.

Measure the Socket

Start by wrapping a small piece of notebook paper around a pencil, forming a cylinder (Photo 1). Push the cylinder all the way down into the chisel's socket (Photo 2) and let the paper unroll into a cone. You may have to help it a little bit. Once the paper has fully conformed to the socket's taper, put a couple of pieces of tape on the paper, to hold its shape. Then draw a line on the cone, following the top of the chisel's socket (Photo 3). Remove the cone—you're all set to take three measurements.

First, set a divider to the distance between the pencil mark you made and the end of the cone (Photo 4). Transfer that distance to the handle blank (Photo 5). Second, set a caliper to the diameter of the cone at the pencil mark (Photo

6). Turn the blank to this diameter, immediately to the right of the mark indicating the shank's length (Photo 7). I find it easier to do this if I start roughing out the shank at the same time. Third, reset the caliper to the diameter of the cone's end (Photo 8). Turn the end of the shank to this diameter (Photo 9), then form a straight taper up to the end of the shank.

Test the Fit

If all has gone well, the shank should perfectly fit the socket. Just to be sure, perform a simple test. Rub a piece of chalk on the inside of the socket (Photo 10). Turn off the lathe, pull away the headstock and push the socket onto the shank. Twist the chisel a few times and remove it (Photo

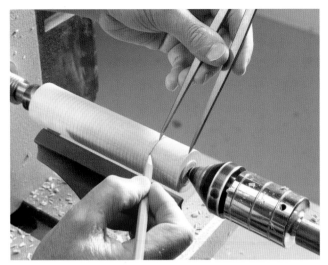

5 Mark this distance from the tailstock end of a blank you've roughed out.

6 Set a caliper to fit the cone at the mark you drew at the end of the chisel's socket. This will be the major diameter of the handle's shank (the part that fits into the socket).

Shank

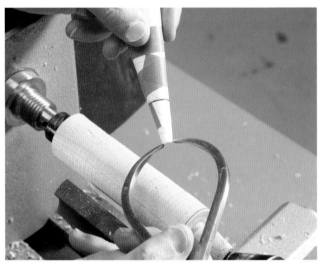

7 Turn the blank to the major diameter, just to the right of the pencil line. Rough out the rest of the shank's taper.

8 Reset the caliper to fit the end of the cone. This will be the shank's minor diameter.

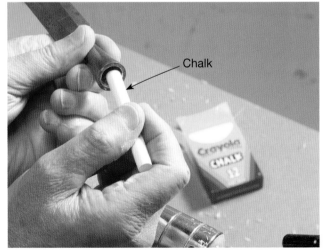

Chalk

9 Turn the end of the shank to the minor diameter, leaning the parting tool at about the same angle as the rough taper. Cut a straight taper between the major and minor diameters.

10 Check the fit of the shank in the chisel's socket. First, coat the inside of the socket with chalk dust. Then turn off the lathe and pull away the tailstock.

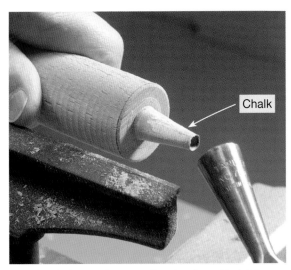

11 Push the socket onto the shank and twist it a few times. If its taper is correct, the full length of the shank will be coated with chalk. If it's not correct, only the high spots will be coated.

12 Once the taper is correct, lengthen the shank about ⅛" to the left.

13 Shape the rest of the handle as you wish. Stop the lathe and remove the handle from time to time to test how it feels.

14 Part the handle from the blank using a spindle gouge. (My gouge is very short, from turning so many handles!)

11). If the fit is correct, most of the shank will be coated with chalk; if it's not, the chalk will show you the high spots that need to be removed. If the fit is too loose, your best bet is to cut off part of the shank and start over from the beginning.

Once the fit is OK, lengthen the shank by about ⅛" (Photo 12) to create a small gap between the socket and shank. This gap allows you to drive the shank tight into the socket. The end of the handle shouldn't butt up against the top of the socket. If it does, the handle could split when you strike the chisel.

Turn the handle to any shape you wish (Photo 13). There's really no right or wrong here; traditionally, chisel handles came in many different shapes and sizes. If your work requires you to strike the chisel hard, you may want to put a ferrule on one or both ends of the handle to prevent it from splitting. Turn off the lathe from time to time and test how the handle feels. When you're done, part off (Photo 14). To install your handle, just drive it into the socket with a mallet. With a tight fit, there's no need for glue. When you apply finish to the handle, don't put any on the shank. If the shank is too slippery, it won't stay seated in the socket.

by Robert Ferencsik

Using a Chisel

TECHNIQUE BUILDS FROM BODY AND STANCE

The chisel is one of the most basic woodworking tools, and paring is one of the most basic chiseling techniques. By taking small shavings with a chisel, but without a hammer or mallet, you can fine-tune your joints for a perfect fit. And you can pare simple decorative edge treatments in less time than it takes to say "power tool." I'll show you how to get control over the chisel, for perfect cuts every time. We'll review some basic rules that apply to all paring operations, then I'll demonstrate the best hand and body positions for horizontal, vertical, and angled paring.

General Paring Guidelines

Hand and body positions are necessary for good paring, but they're not sufficient. Before we discuss the proper posture, here are four general guidelines for more precise paring:

Lay out first. You need reference lines to pare accurately. For rabbets, mortises and tenons, and other square shapes, lay out with a knife. By tapping lightly along the knife line, you can form a little shelf to support the chisel and keep it from jumping out of the cut. For curves or bevels, lay out with a pencil, not a knife—the cut lines will show in the finished surface.

Face the chisel in the right direction. It's usually best to face the bevel up away from the work. In this position, the bevel helps force the back of the chisel against the wood as you cut. Occasionally, when you pare in a tight spot such as a mortise, the back of the chisel can't reach the work surface. In this case, face the bevel down.

Pare across the grain when you can. When you pare along the grain, you have to fight the interlocked wood fibers. You also risk tearout. Cross-grain paring decreases the risk of tearout. Paring cross-grain is easy if you remember this rule:

Workbench workout. With the right hand and body position and a sharp chisel, you can pare your way to perfect-fitting joints, elegant decorative edges, and more.

Take light cuts. This is one of the most overlooked—and important—rules of chisel work. Light cuts give the smoothest results with the most precision. The heavier the cut, the harder the bevel will push against the back of the chisel, encouraging it to dive into the wood. If the chisel tends to slip on light cuts, you can press down on its face with your thumb or fingers.

Poised for Success

When you pare wood, the cutting force comes from the motion of your body, and it's channeled through your hands. Your ideal hand and body position depends on whether you're paring horizontally, vertically, or at an angle. The drawings show each hand and body position in detail. But here are a few posture guidelines for all paring situations.

Always hold the chisel with both hands. You won't believe the difference two hands make. The action of one hand opposes and limits the action

A Shelf to Guide Your Chisel

When paring straight, square cuts such as rabbets or tenons, you can widen your layout line into a shelf that guides and supports the chisel.

1 Lay out your lines with a sharp knife or gauge. Chisel into the line at exactly 90° to the work surface, tapping lightly with a mallet.

2 Pare at 45° to form a V-shaped shelf across the top of the workpiece. This shelf will guide your chisel neatly along the shoulder.

3 Pare down to the tenon cheek. An identical V-shaped cut along the side of the work will help guide your final paring cuts.

of the other—giving you much more control over the cut. Use your rear hand to transmit power and steer the chisel, and use your front hand to apply pressure to the cutting edge, so it moves through the wood in a controlled manner.

Keep your hands behind the cutting edge at all times. You might be inclined to wrap your fingers around the workpiece to get leverage and support. But one slip of the chisel, and your finger can get stabbed. It's better to clamp the workpiece in a vise or between bench dogs.

Push with your body, not your arms. Think of your body as a motor that powers the chisel; think of your arms and hands as micro-adjustable fixtures that hold the chisel in place. This gives you the ultimate combination of power and precision. Lock your elbows—this helps transmit power from your legs, hips, and torso to your hands. You can swing your arms from the shoulder if you need to.

Put your best foot forward. If your left hand is forward on the chisel, your left foot should

Controlling the Cut

You can orient the chisel two different ways for different paring circumstances.

Bevel away from work
This orientation is best for most paring situations. It yields the smoothest surface. Keep the back of the chisel pressed flat against the workpiece.

Bevel down toward work
This orientation is good for paring tight spots that the back of the chisel can't reach, such as mortises. But it yields a choppier surface.

be forward too—and vice versa. You provide the power and range of motion for each cut by shifting your weight onto your forward foot and driving the chisel from your hips.

Use your eyes. Look at your workpiece, but watch adjacent flat surfaces to gauge squareness. For vertical paring, keep your chisel square to the bench. Set a try square on your bench for reference. For horizontal paring, as on a tenon cheek, keep your chisel square to a vertical surface such as an adjacent shoulder.

Practice Makes Perfect

Now that you have learned basic paring techniques, all you need is practice. Following these rules and paving attention to hand and body position will lead you to paring proficiency.

Horizontal Paring

Horizontal paring is the most commonly used paring technique. Trimming tenons and making rabbets are only two of numerous applications.

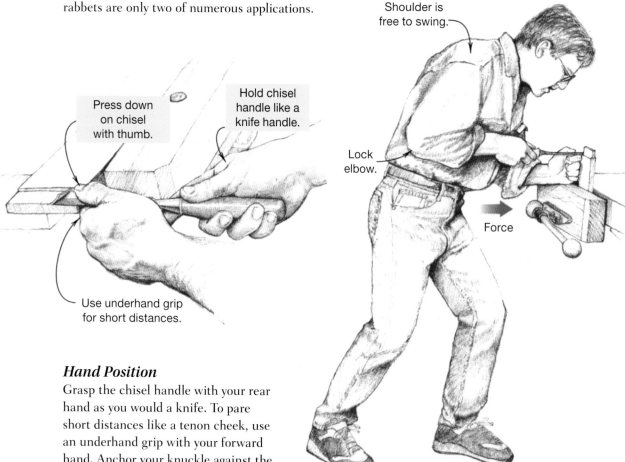

Press down on chisel with thumb.

Hold chisel handle like a knife handle.

Use underhand grip for short distances.

Shoulder is free to swing.

Lock elbow.

Force

Hand Position

Grasp the chisel handle with your rear hand as you would a knife. To pare short distances like a tenon cheek, use an underhand grip with your forward hand. Anchor your knuckle against the workpiece if you can. Support the blade from underneath with your index finger. To help control the cut, press down on the blade with your thumb. To pare long distances like a chamfer along a long board, use the overhand grip shown with angled paring. The overhand grip is also good for paring in the middle of a board.

Body Position

Your upper body—not your hands—powers the cut, as you shift your weight from your back foot to your forward foot. Position your legs to match your hands: If your right hand is back, so is your right leg. Keep your back elbow locked and tucked close to your body. Let your shoulder swing, so your forearm can transmit the forward force from your torso out to the chisel.

Vertical Paring

Good vertical paring technique helps you make smooth tenon shoulders and mortise walls.

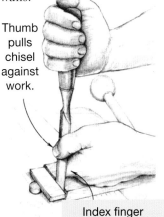

Put thumb on butt of chisel handle.

Thumb pulls chisel against work.

Index finger supports chisel.

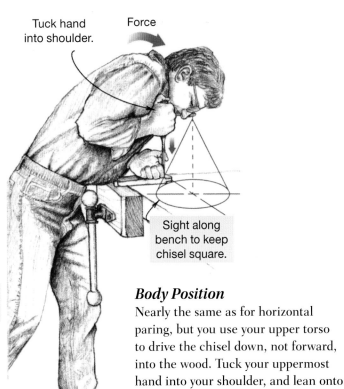

Tuck hand into shoulder.

Force

Sight along bench to keep chisel square.

Hand Position

Place your lower hand in an underhand grip. Plant the thumb of your uppermost hand on the butt of the handle, with the fingers wrapped over the handle. Pull the chisel against the work with your lower hand. Use the thumb and index finger of your lower hand to help control the cut.

Body Position

Nearly the same as for horizontal paring, but you use your upper torso to drive the chisel down, not forward, into the wood. Tuck your uppermost hand into your shoulder, and lean onto the butt of the chisel. Bend at your hips, and rotate your weight onto your forward leg to power the cut through the wood.

Angled Paring

This powerful paring technique is ideal for making miters and bevels on end grain.

Hand Position

For angled paring, you'll need to change your grip for comfort as you move to different parts of the workpiece. Initially, position your rear hand as you would for horizontal paring. Put your forward hand in an overhand grip. To control the cut, press down on the chisel with your forward hand. The ball, wrist, or elbow of your forward hand supports your weight and controls the chisel's motion. Increase your leverage by keeping your rear hand and forearm close to your side.

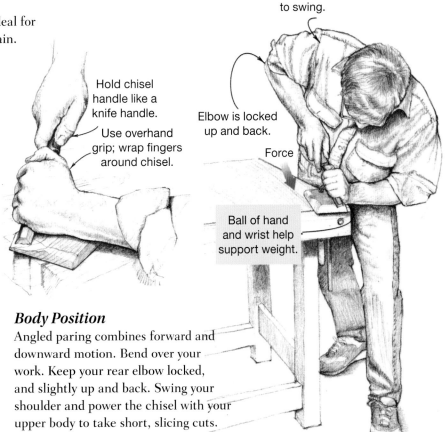

Hold chisel handle like a knife handle.

Use overhand grip; wrap fingers around chisel.

Shoulder is free to swing.

Elbow is locked up and back.

Force

Ball of hand and wrist help support weight.

Body Position

Angled paring combines forward and downward motion. Bend over your work. Keep your rear elbow locked, and slightly up and back. Swing your shoulder and power the chisel with your upper body to take short, slicing cuts.

by Mario Rodriquez

Make a Smooth Plane

AN ANTIQUE BEAUTY YOU'LL USE EVERY DAY

Recently I came across an engraving of a beautiful coffin-shaped smooth plane with a closed handle and a back end that was cut down razee style.

It looked substantial and solid, but sleek with an appealing 19th-century character. Though such planes were traditionally intended for producing the final smooth finish on a piece. they also were commonly used for more general planing tasks.

I called Tom Witte, an antique-tools dealer, to inquire about obtaining this kind of smooth plane. Tom told me there weren't many around and that I'd have to pay hundreds of dollars to get one. At that point I figured I'd try to make

one. I've made planes before but I've usually had an example to work from. This time I had only overall dimensions

I already had a thick antique iron 2-1/4 in wide with a chip breaker that I'd picked up from Tom. If you can't locate an antique iron, look on the Internet for thick and heavy replacement irons to match the old style. Planes of this type were commonly made of beech, apple, boxwood, or rosewood. I chose to make mine of rosewood because of its weight and looks. The wood you select should be stable and dense.

I modified the original plane design in two ways. My first modification was to laminate the plane from two blocks of wood (after making all the interior cuts) instead of working from a single block. I did this because I didn't have a piece of rosewood wide enough for a solid block. Also, laminating made hollowing out the cavity an easy task.

The second design modification was to mortise a full handle into the back of the plane instead of gluing a closed handle onto the top and bottom of the razee cut. Since many antique planes have broken handles, I figured I'd make the handle more durable. Also, a full handle helps hide the lamination seam on the back of the plane.

Special Tools

There are three special tools that are useful in plane-making. They're not necessary but they will make certain operations easier. The first tool is a pair of single-cut files or rasps. Planemakers call them floats. These floats are used almost exclusively in plane-making for flattening the bed and cleaning up the abutment (see Fig. 1). I made my own floats, and if you're serious about plane-making, you should too.

Another useful tool is a detailing file. This file is handy for finishing the handle and removing chisel marks on both the inside and outside of the plane.

The third tool is a pair of ½" wide skew chisels (one skewed left, the other skewed right) for getting into the corners. You can make a skew chisel by regrinding the angle of a spare straight chisel, or you can buy one.

Making the Plane Body

Choose two pieces of wood that are straight-grained and stable measuring 1½" by 2¾" by 10¼" To align the two halves of the plane while you shape it. mark out and drill two ¼" holes in each half for registration dowels (see Fig. 2). Fit these holes with dowels. These dowels will also help register the two sides during glue-up. You won't see these registration holes in the photos because I drilled them after I shaped the cavity.

Next, with a marking knife and a sliding bevel, lay out the body halves as shown in Fig. 2, with the grain running front to back. Try to match the pieces for grain pattern and color to minimize the visibility of the glue line.

To lay out the halves, start by marking out the bed at 45° 2½" from the front end, or toe, of the plane. A bed angled 45°—the common pitch for a bench plane—is thought to be best for planing softwoods; angling the bed to 50°—the York pitch—is considered better for planing hardwoods. I've found my plane works well on both.

Next, mark the lower and upper breast line, leaving the mouth ³⁄₁₆" in front of the bed cut (see Fig. 2). Keep the mouth small—it can easily be enlarged later. Mark the cut where the abutment and the gain meet. To remove the waste between the marked lines, saw along the lines with a dovetail saw. Next make several saw cuts between the lines, and chip the waste out with chisels. File the surfaces smooth. It's important that the saw cuts be perpendicular to the plane sides. I used a guide block to ensure that the cuts were perpendicular.

It is equally important that these cuts be made to the correct depth. The cuts that make up the gain (see Figs. 1 and 2) will be the deepest—1¹⁄₁₆" deep (or barely half the width of the iron. The wall of each gain is parallel to the outside face of each plane side. Using a small adjustable square, check the depth of the gain frequently. Remember, it's best to keep your cuts on the shallow side. You can deepen them later if you need to.

Unlike the gain, the wall of the abutment is not parallel, but instead is at an angle to the outside face of the plane. (See Figs. 1 and 2.) The abutment is ¼" thicker than the gain at the top, and it tapers to the same thickness as the gain at the bottom, down by the mouth. It's important that the abutment tapers because any protrusion into the mouth opening hinders the evacuation of shavings and causes the plane to choke. Check frequently that the two halves match up.

Remove the waste and clean up the saw cuts with chisels and files; the floats work well for this. Work on each abutment first and then each

Fig. 1: Smooth-Plane Anatomy

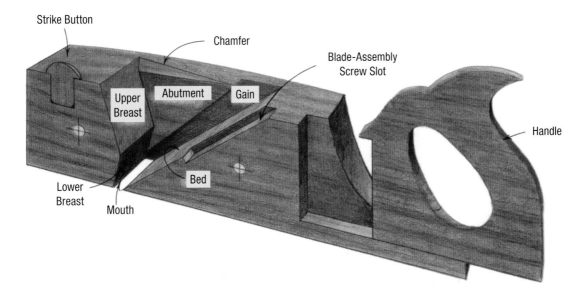

Fig. 2: Smooth-Plane Body

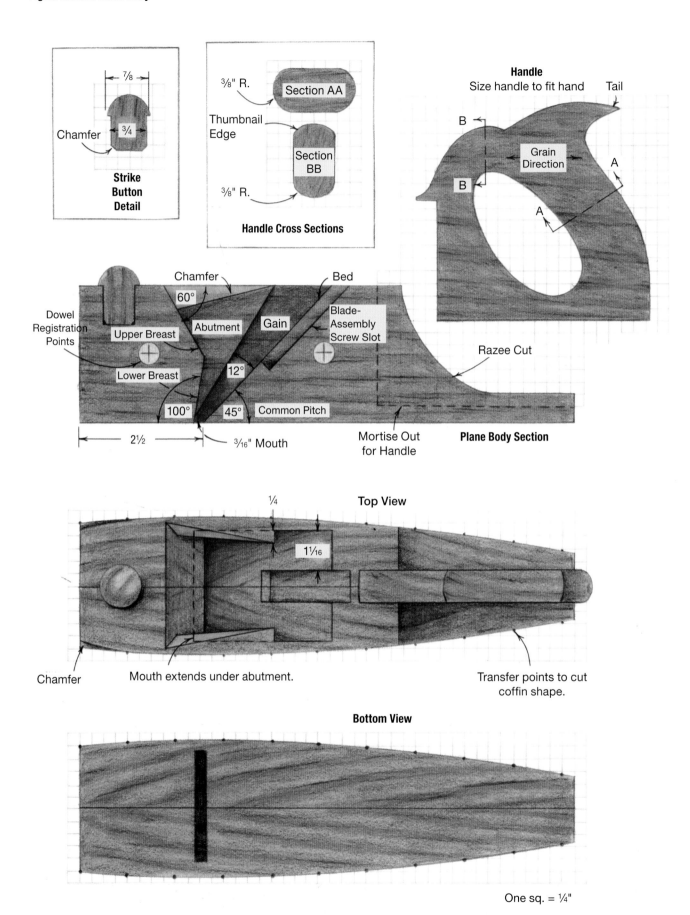

Chamfer

7/8

3/4

Strike Button Detail

3/8" R.

Section AA

Thumbnail Edge

Section BB

3/8" R.

Handle Cross Sections

Handle
Size handle to fit hand

Tail

B

Grain Direction

A

B

A

Chamfer

Bed

60°

Dowel Registration Points

Upper Breast

Abutment

Gain

Blade-Assembly Screw Slot

Razee Cut

Lower Breast

12°

100°

45°

Common Pitch

2½

3/16" Mouth

Mortise Out for Handle

Plane Body Section

Top View

¼

1 1/16

Chamfer

Mouth extends under abutment.

Transfer points to cut coffin shape.

Bottom View

One sq. = ¼"

gain. Leave the gains on the fat side since it's easy to bring them down to their final thicknesses after the plane has been glued and you're fitting the blade.

Make a mock-up of the wedge and check the fit of the blade with the mock-up wedge in each half. Make sure the gain on each side is properly sized so the blade and the wedge fit with no gaps. If it's too small to fit a wedge tightly, adjust the gain.

Mortising for the Handle

Before you cut the mortise for the handle, tape the two halves of the body together and handsaw the razee cut on the back end of the plane. (See Fig. 2.) With the body still taped together, file, sand, and scrape the curve smooth.

To cut the handle mortise, remove the tape from the two halves and with a dovetail saw and paring chisels work on each half of the mortise separately. (See photo and Fig. 2.) Make sure the mortise is square because the handle fits directly into this mortise without any shoulders to hide gaps.

This is a good time to lay out and cut the slot in the plane halves for the blade assembly's protruding screw. (See Fig. 2.) Using the dovetail saw and chisels, be sure to cut the slot wide enough to allow some lateral adjustment of the blade.

Gluing Up the Body

Since rosewood is resinous, I glued up the body with epoxy to insure a good bond. Be sure the clamps are spaced to apply even pressure. Though I didn't use the glue blocks, you might try placing them, one on each side of the plane, between the plane and the clamps to evenly distribute the pressure.

Once the glue has completely dried, try fitting the iron in the cavity. You may need to file the gains a bit for the blade to slide in. Once the iron slides in, you'll need to ensure it sits flat against the bed. If it rocks, the plane will chatter. Use files and chisels to flatten the bed.

Making the Handle

Cut the handle from solid ⅞" stock with the grain running horizontally. The dimensions of my handle are shown in Fig. 2. You can adjust these dimensions to fit your hand size.

To remove the waste from the center of the handle, drill out two ¾" holes to establish the inside ends of the grip. Use a jig saw or coping saw

Lay out the cuts on the two halves of the plane body with a pencil and sliding bevel. Remove the waste from the iron cavity with a dovetail saw and chisels.

Check to see that the cuts are perpendicular to the plane sides and that they are the correct depth.

Cut the mortise for the handle while the plane is still in two halves. Do this with a dovetail saw and paring chisels.

Glue up the two halves of the plane, making sure the clamps are spaced to apply even pressure.

to finish the interior cut. You can use a router with a ⅜" roundover bit to round the grip part of the handle. (See Fig. 2, Section AA.)

The contour of the tail on the handle is not half-round, but instead is more of a subtle thumbnail shape (see Fig. 2. Section BB). Shape this tail by hand. Use a fine-detail file or rasp to keep your shaping crisp and clean, then finish up the handle with fine sandpaper.

Make sure both the razee cut and the handle are sanded smooth. Glue the handle in the mortise.

Making the Wedge

There are two important things a wedge must do. First, it must fit well between the abutments and the blade to hold the blade solidly to the bed. Second, it must provide easy and smooth clearance for shavings or the plane will choke. Shape the wedge so the prongs flare out slightly at their ends. (See Fig. 3.) When you insert the wedge into the plane, first place one prong in and pull the other prong inward slightly to fit within

To cut the hole in the handle, first drill out two holes to establish the inside ends of the grip, then use a jig saw or coping saw to finish the interior cut. Shape the grip and round its edges by filing and sanding.

the opening. This ensures that the wedge fits snugly against the gains and prevents shavings from getting behind the prongs and clogging the mouth. Some antique blades will require a slot cut into the underside of the wedge to provide additional clearance for the blade-assembly screw.

To cut the hole in the handle, first drill out two holes to establish the inside ends of the grip, then use a jig saw or coping saw to finish the interior cut. Shape the grip and round its edges by routing or by filing and sanding.

Fig. 3: Plane Wedge

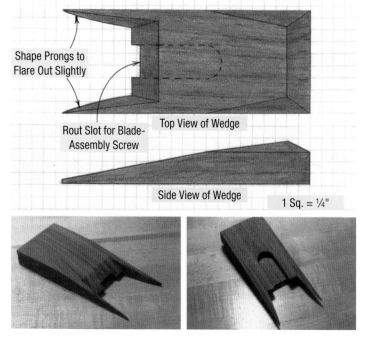

Shape Prongs to Flare Out Slightly

Rout Slot for Blade-Assembly Screw

Top View of Wedge

Side View of Wedge

1 Sq. = ¼"

The Strike Button

The purpose of the strike button (see Fig. 2) is to provide a single point of contact for the occasional hammer blow necessary to loosen the wedge. First, drill a ¼" dia. hole ¾" deep at the front end of the plane. (See Fig. 2.) Turn the strike button on a lathe, sand it, and glue it in place with epoxy. I made the strike button from rosewood but you can substitute a small, bronze roundhead bolt.

Cutting the Coffin Shape

To cut the coffin shape in the plane, use the pattern provided in Fig. 2, transferring the points to the top of the plane. Cut out the coffin shape on the handsaw, using the points as a guide. Make sure you cut on the outside of the line. Next, file and scrape down to the line, checking with a square to make sure the sides remain perpendicular to the sole.

Finishing the Sole

Now it's time to open the mouth to get the space between the mouth and the iron just right. To open the mouth, first mark and score the opening on the lower breast side. With files and skew chisels, slowly open the mouth, leaving a ¹⁄₁₆" to a tight ⅛" opening just in front of the blade.

To true up the sole of the plane, sand it down on a piece of sandpaper glued to a flat surface or piece of plate glass. Pass the plane over the paper until the sole is flat and evenly sanded, then progress to finer grits. Keep sanding until the sole is glassy smooth.

Finishing the Plane

The plane will require nothing more than a coat of 50/50 boiled linseed oil and some turpentine. Apply the finish with a rag and then wet-sand with

400-grit wet/dry paper. After the finish on the plane dries, apply a good coat of paste wax. After time and with plenty of use the plane will develop a beautiful patina.

Testing the Plane

The blade profile on a smooth plane should be honed flat though you may wish to round the corners a bit to prevent the blade from leaving ridges at the edge of the cut. Set your chip breaker approximately $1/16''$ behind the cutting edge of the blade. I find that it needs to be set back this far on most wooden planes. Make sure the blade assembly is bedded down well and is making solid contact, or the plane will chatter and choke. Set your blade to project slightly past the sole with a small mouth opening before the blade. You can fine tune the extension of the blade by lightly lapping the back of the blade with a mallet. You can back it off by tapping the strike button.

I find my plane works best if I shoot it straight ahead. It's more apt to choke if I angle it. If the plane does choke or cut unevenly, try backing the iron off a bit. If that doesn't work, try moving the chip breaker a little farther back. As a last resort, open the mouth slightly with files, then try it again. Keep making small adjustments until the plane produces a clean, full width shaving.

I thought that my finished smooth plane would end up as part plaything and part showpiece. However I find myself reaching for it each working day.

Making Planemaker's Floats

If you're going to get serious about plane-making, I recommend that you make a pair of planemakers floats. Floats are single-cut files designed to remove wood rapidly. If kept sharp, they leave a smooth, flat surface. This is what you need on the inside surfaces of your plane to guarantee a good bed for the blade and a tight fit for the wedge.

You'll need one edge float (the teeth are along the edge of the file) and one flat-sided float (the teeth are on a flat side of the file). Both floats are about $3/16''$ thick and are tapered for an easier fit into the inner surfaces of the plane.

Any small scrap of unhardened tool steel will work. An old fine file also work, but you must anneal or soften the steel to cut the teeth. Lav out the teeth about $3/16''$ apart. Secure the float blank in a vise so the top edge (the edge in which you will cut the teeth) is horizontal. Using a triangular mill file, cut V-shaped grooves of equal depth along

the length of the float from tip to tang. As you work backward toward the tang, be sure to cut the back edge of each groove so it's vertical (perpendicular to the floor), as the drawing shows. Your angles can be a bit off and your spacing erratic, but keep all the teeth the same height.

The completed float is not hardened, but is instead kept soft. Add a handle if you like and sharpen regularly with a mill file. I can make about two planes before I need to resharpen a float.

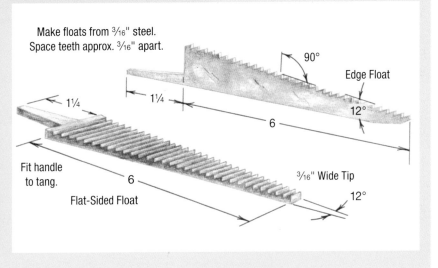

Make floats from $3/16''$ steel.
Space teeth approx. $3/16''$ apart.

90°

Edge Float

12°

$1 1/4$

$1 1/4$

6

Fit handle to tang.

6

Flat-Sided Float

$3/16''$ Wide Tip

12°

by Brad Holden

Make a Router Plane

A VERY USEFUL AND PRECISE TOOL

The modern router didn't arrive on the scene fully evolved; it descended from a hand-powered tool called the router plane. A quick glance at the router plane's handles—and the tasks for which it was used—makes the family resemblance clear.

The wooden router plane went out of favor in the woodworking trades long ago. It was replaced by the modern router because it couldn't match the production speed of an electric machine. However, a finely tuned router plane is anything but a relic. It still has a special place in my shop.

A router plane is my go-to tool for trimming any small surface that needs to be in the same plane as its surrounding surface, such as making a final adjustment to a dado or rabbet's depth, or trimming a tenon's cheeks.

Making this plane is a great introduction to tool-making, and it's really quite simple. As you become more adept with your router plane, you'll reach for it more and more, in many cases finding it faster than setting up a power tool. And there really is nothing more satisfying than using a tool that you've made yourself.

Make the Body

You can use any tough, hard-wearing species to make this plane. Hard maple is a classic choice. Start with a block that's a little oversize, and then mill it to final dimensions—1½" x 3½" x 9½".

The router plane's blades can be made from standard hex keys for Allen-head screws, 5/16" is a good size. Make the adjusting mechanism from a ⅜" shoulderless spade-style thumbscrew, with a ⅜" iron wingnut and washer to fit. The thumbscrew's oversize spade is perfect for holding the cutter. Drill the hole for the thumbscrew in the back edge of the body (Photo 1; Fig. A and B). Next, drill the 2" dia. throat opening (Photo 2; Fig. A), followed by the two 1" dia. holes (Photo 3).

1 Drill a hole on the back edge of the plane body's blank for the cutter holder, which is made from a large thumbscrew.

2 Drill the plane's large throat opening using a Forstner bit. Make sure your bit is sharp, so it doesn't burn the inside of the throat.

3 Drill the two smaller holes that define the insides of the handles, also using a Forstner bit. While you could drill these holes by hand, the drill press is likely to be more accurate.

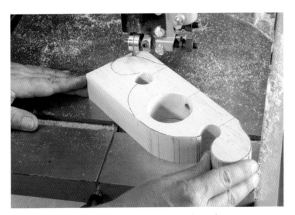

4 Saw the body's shape using the bandsaw, a jigsaw, or a coping saw.

Use the pattern (Fig. A) to draw the plane's shape on your blank, then cut it out on the bandsaw (Photo 4). Sand the plane's body and round over the corners of the top edges, so it's comfortable in your hands. Don't round over the bottom edges though, just ease them a bit.

Make the Cutter's Holder

The cutter holder is made by drilling a hole in a beefy iron thumbscrew. To hold the thumbscrew for drilling and filing, drill an $^{11}/_{32}$" x 2" deep hole in the end of a wood block. Thread the thumbscrew into the hole. It'll be tight, but that's what you want. When you can't turn the thumbscrew by hand anymore, stick the thumbscrew's spade in your vise jaws and turn the block.

Drill the hole in the thumbscrew using cutting oil so you don't overheat your drill bit (Photo 5). Using a square file, shape the hole to fit the hex key's cross-section (Photo 6). This sounds more difficult than it is, so don't sweat it. Perfection isn't necessary and the malleable iron thumbscrew files easily.

To make it even easier, tuse a ¼" square American-pattern file and start by by filing one flat on the side of the hole opposite the threads. Do your best to make sure this first flat is square to the threads, as this is what holds the cutter square. Once you've made the first flat, roll the file one file's-width either left or right and file the adjacent flat. Continue in this manner until you've come all the way around. Check the hex key's fit often so that you don't file more than necessary. The fit should be snug, so the cutter doesn't move during use.

Make the Cutter

Make another block to hold the hex key for cutting and grinding. Drill a $^5/_{16}$" hole in the end, and then use a mallet to drive the hex key into the hole. Again, it'll be a tight fit, but that's what you want. Hold the block in your vise to cut the 30° bevel angle (Photo 7; Fig. B). The hex key is hardened steel, so you can't cut it with a hack-saw. A rotary tool with a cutoff wheel works well. **Caution: There will be lots of sparks, so make sure there's nothing flammable nearby.** Cut off the

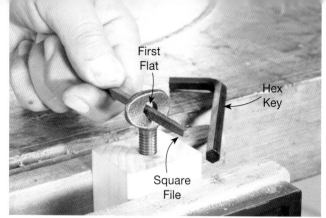

5 Drill a hole in the thumbscrew to hold the plane's cutter. Use a wooden block to hold the thumbscrew securely, and cutting oil to keep from overheating your drill bit.

6 File flats in the thumbscrew's hole to match the cross-section of a hex key, which will become the cutter. The first flat determines the cutter's alignment; be sure to make it square to the threads.

Fig. A: Plan View

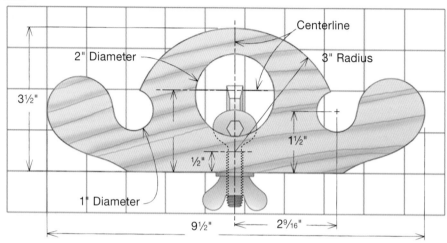

Fig. B: Section View

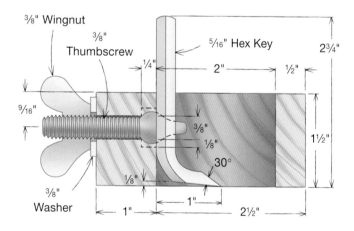

waste at the 30° bevel angle. The short end of the hex key should end up about 1" long.

Once you've made the bevel, cut off the bottom edge of the hex key (Photo 8). There are two things to consider when making this cut. First, the cutting edge needs to be at the widest part of the hex key (from point to point, not flat to flat). Second, the cut must angle up away from the cutting edge (Fig. B). This relief angle ensures that in use, the only part of the cutter that contacts the work is the actual cutting edge. Cut off the long end of the hex key so that the cutter is about 2¾" tall.

Sharpening a small, L-shaped cutter like this is tricky, so I made a guide block to ensure a flat, square cutting edge (Photo 9). To make the guide block, cut a shallow groove in the block that's just wide enough to firmly hold the cutter. Cut a 30° bevel on the block's front edge. Insert the cutter and slide it forward until it protrudes just slightly beyond the block's bevel.

Diamond paddles work really well for sharpening small, odd shapes; they're easy to control, and give fast results. Start with coarse grit, and work your way up to super-fine. Depending on how accurately you

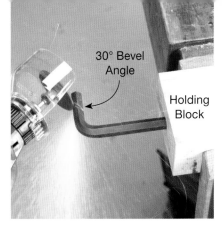

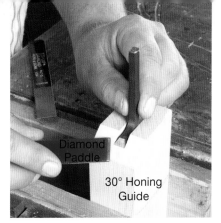

7 Form the cutter's bevel angle by cutting off the waste at 30° using a rotary tool outfitted with an abrasive wheel.

8 Cut the bottom off of the hex key so that the cutting edge is the widest point.

9 Sharpen the cutter using a guide beveled at 30° to ensure a flat, square cutting edge.

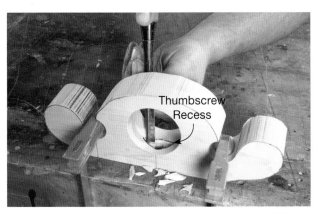

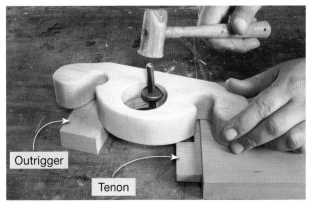

10 Excavate a recess for the thumbscrew's head. The recess has to be deep enough to allow the cutter to bear against the body when you tighten the thumbscrew.

11 Tap the cutter's end to increase the cutting depth. With the thumbscrew tight, a sharp whack will deepen the cut by a few thousandths of an inch.

cut the bevel, sharpening should take less than fifteen minutes.

The last step before assembling your plane is to chisel out a recess for the thumbscrew's head (Photo 10). Cut the recess deep enough so that when you tighten the thumbscrew, it pulls the cutter firmly against the plane's body. It's a tight spot, but with a little patience, you'll be done before you know it and ready to put your new creation to work.

Using the Router Plane

A router plane isn't meant to hog off ¼" of material in one pass. Instead, you'll take a light pass, reset the depth and take another pass, repeating as many times as necessary.

Assemble all the parts, with the cutting edge slightly above the plane's sole, so it doesn't make a cut, and then tighten the thumbscrew. Use a mallet to tap the cutter until it just takes a shaving. As you gain experience, you'll be amazed at how precise your mallet-driven adjustments become.

Tip

For trimming tenons, I used to reach for a shoulder plane until I learned the router plane method (Photo 11). The fundamental difference between the two methods is that a shoulder plane rides on the surface being trimmed whereas a router plane rides on the surrounding surface. With a shoulder plane, it's easy to cut too deep, or not in the same plane as the face of your workpiece.

Here's how the router plane method works to solve both of those issues. Fasten a piece of scrap the same thickness as your workpiece to the plane's sole. It works as an outrigger, supporting the plane's end as you trim. Because you're planing from the workpiece's surface, the tenon is guaranteed to be co-planar. Since the cutter is suspended, it's impossible to shave off any deeper than your last setting.

by Ernie Conover

Make a Tool Till

TRADITIONAL DRAWERS STORE SMALL HAND TOOLS

In the 18th and 19th centuries, a woodworker completed his apprenticeship by building his own tool chest. This "master's thesis" included making many of the planes, saws and chisels that the journeyman would need to ply his trade. An important part of the chest was its tool till, a smaller, multidrawered toolbox that rested on cleats within the main chest. A beautiful and functional toolbox in its own right, the till held smaller tools such as chisels, spokeshaves, marking gauges and shoulder planes.

The tool till shown here is my adaptation of an 18th-century till made by Benjamin Seaton of Rochester, England. The case is black walnut and the drawers are poplar, with walnut fronts and turned maple knobs. I sized the till and its drawers to house my collection of hand tools. You can alter the dimensions, if necessary, to suit your own.

Building a tool till can he a good lesson in solid-wood construction. It includes skills such as through dovetails and traditional drawer construction. And since all the parts are solid wood, you'll need to make the necessary allowances tor seasonal wood movement, such as orienting the grain of the case parts in the same direction and allowing room tor parts to expand and contract at different rates. The reward is a chest that will look and work great in your shop and that you can proudly hand down to future generations.

Making the Cases

Although it might appear to be a solid box, the till is actually two cases screwed together. (See Fig. 1.) The top case has four sides and a hinged lid, but no bottom. Inside this shallow case are cradles that organize your chisels and protect their edges. (See Cradles sidebar.) The lower case contains nine drawers, carefully sized to accommodate a broad range of small tools. I seem to be a magnet for hand tools, so I sized my till to allow for a few future acquisitions.

The lower case, as shown in Fig. 1, consists of four ¾"-thick boards joined with through dovetails. The back is ⅜"-thick solid wood, rabbeted to fit into ¼"-wide grooves in the case

Chest in a chest. The walnut tool till sits inside a larger poplar chest that also holds saws, planes and other large tools.

Fig. 1: Tool Till

The tool till has an upper and a lower case. Cradles in the upper case hold chisels (see Cradles sidebar).

Custom-sized drawers in the lower case accommodate small files, screwdrivers, wrenches, etc. Pocket screws hold the cases together (see Pocket Screws sidebar).

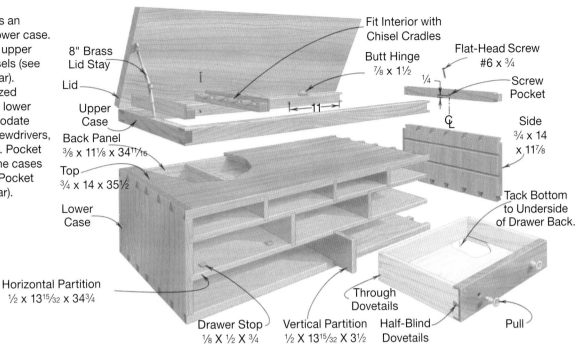

Fit Interior with Chisel Cradles

8" Brass Lid Stay

Butt Hinge
7/8 x 1 1/2

Flat-Head Screw
#6 x 3/4

Screw Pocket

Lid

Upper Case

11

Side
3/4 x 14
x 11 7/8

Back Panel
3/8 x 11 1/8 x 34 11/16

Top
3/4 x 14 x 35 1/2

Lower Case

Tack Bottom to Underside of Drawer Back.

Horizontal Partition
1/2 x 13 15/32 x 34 3/4

Through Dovetails

Drawer Stop
1/8 X 1/2 X 3/4

Vertical Partition
1/2 X 13 15/32 X 3 1/2

Half-Blind Dovetails

Pull

sides, top and bottom. The case is divided by 1/2"-thick horizontal and vertical partitions glued into dadoes. The upper case is much simpler: just four sides joined together with through dovetails and topped with a hinged lid. Here are an overview of the construction sequence and a few tips to help you build the cases.

Start by cutting the top, bottom and sides to their finished dimensions. Lay out the dovetails for the corner joints and the dadoes for the partitions, then cut the joints. (See Fig. 2.) I cut the dovetails by hand, sawing the pins first and using them to lay out the tails. I routed the dadoes for the partitions using a 1/2"-dia. spiral upcut bit, guiding the router with a fence clamped to the workpiece. Last, groove all four case pieces for the back panel. I made this groove 1/4" wide and 3/8" deep. (See Fig. 2.)

Next, thickness-plane your partition stock for a snug fit in the dadoes. Rip it to finished width, but don't cut it to length yet. You'll do that after you assemble the rest of the case. Note that the grain of all the partitions, including the short vertical ones, runs parallel to the length of the case.

The last case piece to make is the back panel. Be sure to allow enough headroom in the top and bottom grooves for the panel to expand across its width. I made mine in summer, when the relative humidity—and the moisture content of the wood—was high, so I allowed only about 1/16" for expansion. If your wood is very dry, allow-

about 3/16" for expansion. Quartersawn or riftsawn material will move less than flatsawn wood.

Now you're ready to assemble the case. First, glue and clamp the top, bottom and sides together around the back, which needs to float unglued in its grooves. I use bar clamps for this. To assure that the sides clamp tightly to the top and bottom, I make up notched cauls to use as clamping blocks at the four corners of the case. I saw the notches in the cauls so the pins can protrude through the tails as pressure is applied. It's critical that the cases are square when you clamp them up. Otherwise you'll have trouble fitting the partitions and drawers.

With the case glued up, you can now cut the partitions to exact finished length. It's important to fit them exactly between the dadoes. Cut the horizontal partitions to length first, then cut the dadoes for the vertical partitions. I slipped the partitions most of the way into their dadoes, then applied a dab of glue to the bottom of each partition before sliding it home. This allows any dissimilar expansion and contraction between the partitions and the case to work itself out at the back of the box. Attach the upper case to the lower case with pocket screws. (See Pocket Screw sidebar.) To attach the case, I clamped it in place, drilled pilot holes into the lower case through the pocket holes, then drove in the screws.

Last, make the lid as shown in Fig. 2. To minimize the possibility of warping, use quartersawn or riftsawn material.

Making and Fitting the Drawers

Many woodworkers overbuild drawers. I kept the thickness of the drawer fronts, sides and hacks to a minimum, and made the small drawers in the top row of even thinner material than the others. (See Fig. 2.) I cut all the drawer fronts from a single walnut board, arranging them in sequence on the face of the till. The drawer sides, backs and bottoms are poplar.

I made my drawers the traditional way. The sides are joined to the fronts with half-blind dovetails and to the backs with through dovetails. The bottoms are solid wood.

Here's how I make the drawers: I rip the fronts, sides and backs about $\frac{1}{32}$" narrower than the height of the openings. Then I crosscut each front and back to finished length—about $1\frac{1}{32}$" less than the width of the opening—and rip each drawer back to its finished width.

Years ago, I learned that if you taper a drawer to make it slightly narrower at the back, it will slide very easily into its opening even if the drawer front is snug across its width.

To taper the drawer, make the dovetail pins of the drawer backs slightly long, so they project about $\frac{1}{64}$" through the sides. Then, after gluing up the drawer, pare the pins flush to the drawer side.

Now install the drawer bottom. Because its grain runs parallel to the drawer front, the bottom will only expand and contract front-to-back in the drawer. So size it to fit exactly between the grooves in the drawer sides. I use quartersawn wood to minimize back-to-front movement. Slide the bottom into the grooves in the sides and tack it into the drawer back. (See Fig. 1.) Allow a little room for expansion in the groove at the front of the drawer.

Fit each drawer into its opening, planing the top edges of the back and sides if necessary to create about $\frac{1}{16}$" clearance in the opening and sides, and a little less than that at the top of the drawer front. I made drawer stops as shown in Fig. 1, and glued them in place with hide glue.

I turned my own pulls for this project (see Pull Detail, Fig. 2), but you could just as easily use store-bought versions.

Finishing Up

After planing all of the surfaces, I gave my box a final hand-sanding with 220-grit paper. Then my wife, Susan, finished it with four coats of Minwax Antique Oil finish. She wet-sanded the first coat with 320-grit, the second coal with 400-grit, and the last two with 600-grit. The final step was to install the lid stay and the butt hinges.

Easy Pocket-Screw Joints Without a Jig

Pocket-screw joinery was around long before commercial pocket-hole jigs were available. Tabletops were routinely attached this way, and it's the method I used to fasten the upper case to my tool till. An oversized screw hole allows for considerable cross-grain wood movement. All it takes to make the joint is a drill and an in-cannel gouge to cut a clean wall in the pocket.

To create a pocket hole, first scribe a centerline on the underside edge of the piece to be drilled. Then select a drill bit that's halfway between the diameter of the screw head and the screw shank. Drill through the underside edge of the piece, entering a little to the inside of your scribe line and angling the drill about 70° toward the inside face of the piece.

Next, carve out the wall of the pocket using an in-cannel gouge as shown in the photo. I used a $\frac{3}{8}$"-wide gouge for the #6 screws in this chisel tray. Clean up the floor of the pocket with a narrow flat chisel.

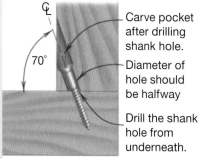

Section Through Pocket-Screw Joint

70°

Carve pocket after drilling shank hole.

Diameter of hole should be halfway

Drill the shank hole from underneath.

Carving the pocket. Use an in-cannel gouge to carve the wall of the screw pocket. Clean up the bottom of the pocket with a straight-edged chisel.

Fig. 2: Tool Till Dimensions
This tool till has a variety of drawer sizes to accommodate most common hand tools and layout devices. You can modify these sizes to suit your own tools.

Front Elevation

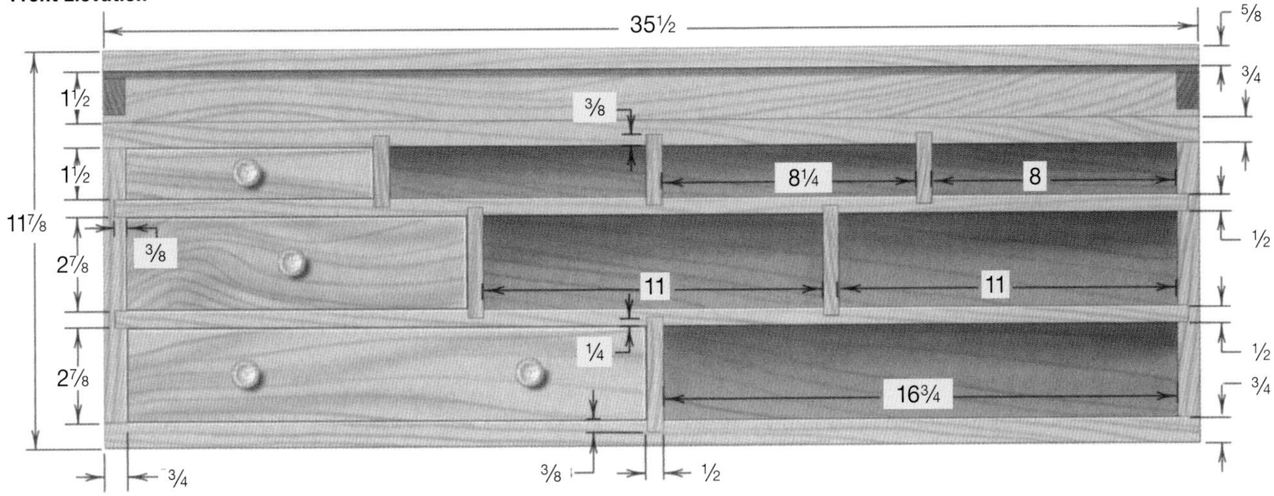
35 1/2
5/8
3/4
1 1/2
1 1/2
11 7/8
2 7/8
2 7/8
3/8
3/8
8 1/4
8
11
11
1/2
1/2
3/4
1/4
16 3/4
3/4
3/8
1/2

Side Elevation

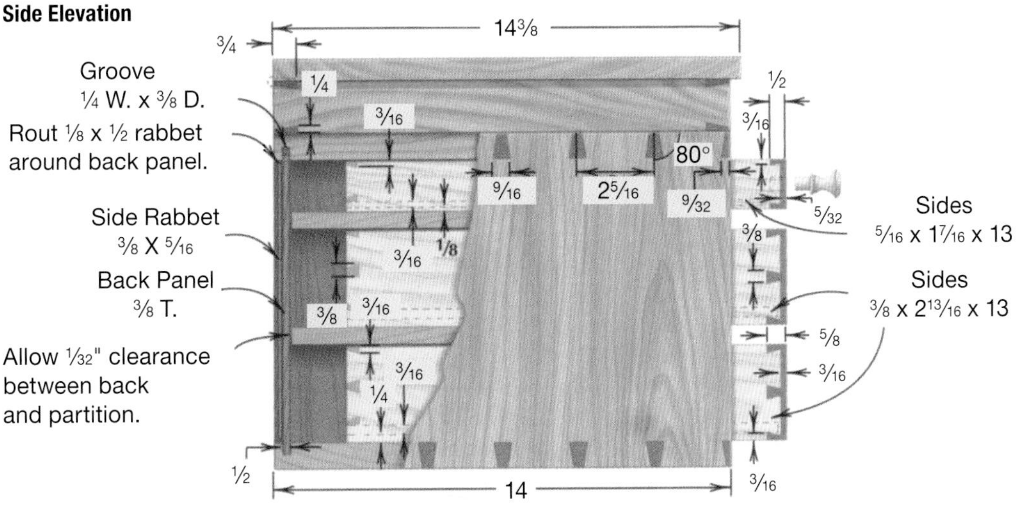
14 3/8
3/4
Groove
1/4 W. x 3/8 D.
Rout 1/8 x 1/2 rabbet
around back panel.
Side Rabbet
3/8 X 5/16
Back Panel
3/8 T.
Allow 1/32" clearance
between back
and partition.
1/4
3/16
9/16
2 5/16
80°
9/32
1/2
3/16
5/32
Sides
5/16 x 1 7/16 x 13
Sides
3/8 x 2 13/16 x 13
3/8
1/8
3/16
3/8
3/16
5/8
3/16
1/4
1/2
14
3/16

Pull Detail

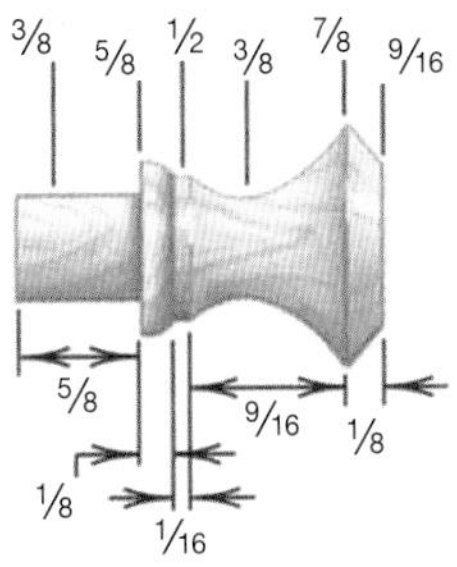
3/8
5/8
1/2
3/8
7/8
9/16
5/8
9/16
1/8
1/8
1/16

Making the Cradles

These easy-to-make cradles organize and protect sets of chisels. To cradle a flat blade just chisel a notch in the strip. To cradle the cutting ends of gouges, drill curved notches with the appropriate Forstner bit.

Cradle Construction

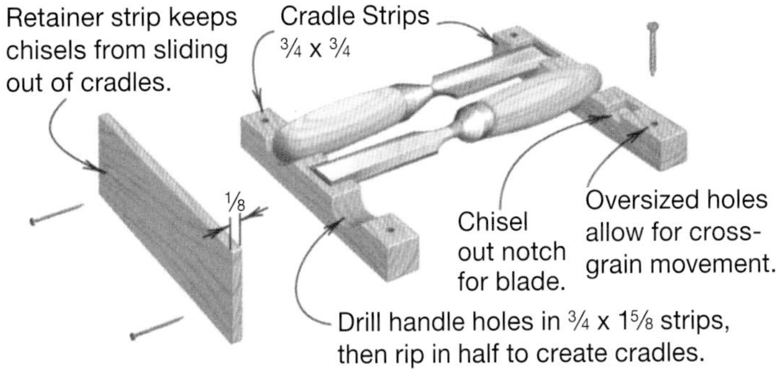
Retainer strip keeps chisels from sliding out of cradles.
Cradle Strips
3/4 x 3/4
1/8
Chisel out notch for blade.
Oversized holes allow for cross-grain movement.
Drill handle holes in 3/4 x 1 5/8 strips, then rip in half to create cradles.

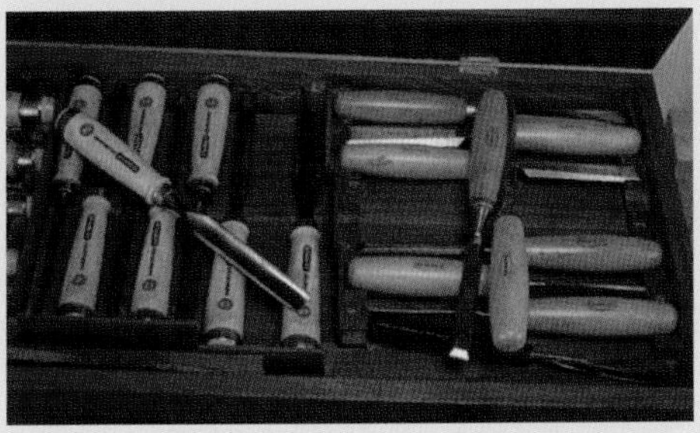

Chisel cradles. Wooden cradles keep chisels organized and protected from each other.

The shave horse holds the work for whittling to size and shape with
a drawknife. This is as close as we get to working wood purely by hand.

Hand Tools
and Bench Aids

by George Vondriska

Great Little Tools

TIME-TESTED AND WOODWORKER-APPROVED

What tools do I need for my shop? This has to be one of the most common question in woodworking. The answer usually starts with the big power tools: tablesaw, jointer, router, planer. But what about those everyday tools we take for granted? You know, the kind that cause you to turn to a shopmate and say, "This is a great little tool."

I polled several woodworking friends and compiled a list of some of our favorite tools. All the picks inexpensive. Here, in no particular order, is a short list of time-tested, woodworker-approved, great little tools.

Marking Gauge

Marking gauges are handy for all kinds of marking needs. Use one to scribe a line on a drawer side to locate mechanical slides or mark the depth of dovetails. I also use a marking gauge to lay out a board for resawing. After setting the gauge by eye to approximately the middle of the board, scribe a line with the gauge indexed off of one face and then scribe a second line with the gauge indexed off the opposite face. This almost always gives me a pair of lines that form a perfect track for my bandsaw blade to travel in as I resaw. If my eyes are really on the money, I get a single fat line to follow.

Rabbet Plane

A rabbet plane has an iron that goes all the way to the edge of the body so you can plane up to a shoulder. It's the perfect choice to shave down a tenon for a snug fit. The Stanley 93 shown here is actually two planes in one. Loosen the knurled knob at the top and the lower unit drops out as a chisel plane. On a chisel plane, the blade sticks out the front, which makes it ideal for removing glue, cleaning up the corners in a hinge mortise or trimming plugs. This tool may not fall into your daily-use category, but when you need it, you can't beat it.

Chisel Plane

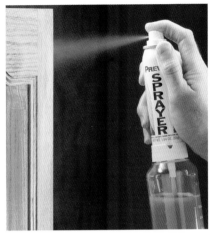

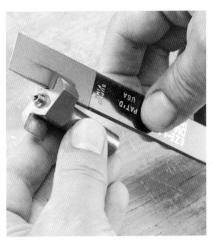

Flush-Cut Saw

A flush-cut pull saw is great for trimming off dowels you've left proud. The blade bends enough that you can keep it flat on your work while bringing the handle up to a comfortable angle. The fine teeth leave a smooth cut and won't score your work. Still, I recommend laying down a playing card just in case.

Pocket-Size Sprayer

Use a pocket-size sprayer when just a little dab will do ya. Got a touch-up to do? Fill the jar with finish, screw on the aerosol can, and let it fly. One can will spray about 16 oz. of liquid. This is also an easy way to make samples with different stains and finishes before you do the real thing. Sure beats cleaning out a whole spray-gun assembly for each sample.

Diamond Paddle

Diamond paddles can help you touch up an edge on a tired router bit. The paddles are embedded with industrial diamonds—abrasives that can sharpen carbide. The Hone and Stone paddle shown is small enough to fit under the flutes of a router bit and in your pocket. You can also use the paddles to freshen the edges on drill bits, hone scrapers, sharpen your pocket knife—you'll find many uses for this handy little tool.

Card Scraper

A card scraper may not be much to look at, but it provides an indispensable way to remove tissue-paper-thin shavings. Worried about sanding through a veneer? Try a scraper. Tired of sanders that are noisy and raise lots of dust? Try a scraper. There's an art to sharpening it, but once you master that, you'll reach for this tool often.

Paint Scraper

A 1" paint scraper may not be considered a traditional woodworking tool, but it can't be beat for scraping a glue joint. Grind or file a burr edge on the blade and this little paint scraper is capable of much more than simply scraping glue. Use it to shave hardwood edge banding or face frames flush with veneered panels. Its size makes it easy to control and the flared blade allows you to get right into corners.

by Tom Caspar

Make a Scratch Stock

THIS OLD TOOL GOES WHERE ROUTERS CAN'T

Need a molding your router can't make? Get out your hacksaw, find an old handsaw, and make a scratch stock.

A scratch stock is simply a scraper with a handle. You can make your own cutters from a variety of materials you've probably got kicking around the shop. The body can be made from any hardwood, using basic tools, and should take no more than an hour to complete.

You can also buy a new scratch stock instead of making one. Blank cutters are available, as well as sets of shaped cutters that are difficult to make in your shop.

With a scratch stock as part of your tool kit you can reproduce almost any molding profile. Your work won't be limited by the shapes of modern router bits. And you can shape compoundcurved furniture parts that a router can't manage, like the cabriole leg.

You'll find a lot of uses for your scratch stock. You can flute a tapered leg, bead a drawer edge, or cut a groove for inlay. Because it's so versatile, the scratch stock is an indispensable tool for anyone repairing old furniture.

However, a scratch stock does have limitations. Using it is hard work. This is not the tool for making long runs of molding. It doesn't cut well in softer woods, like pine. And the small waves it creates leave behind a tell-tale handmade look to a molding. But that might be just what you're looking for.

Making the Body

There are two types of scratch stock bodies. One is a solid block of wood with a saw kerf down the middle that holds the cutter. The second kind (shown in these photos) is made of two blocks of wood, and is easier to build.

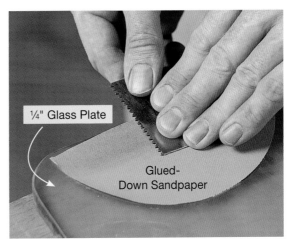

¼" Glass Plate

Glued-
Down Sandpaper

1 Saw a cutter blank from an old handsaw blade using a good-quality, 32-tpi hacksaw blade. Clamp the handsaw down to the benchtop so the blade doesn't vibrate when you cut it. You can make a cutter from other material, such as a reciprocating saw blade, but the steel may be so hard that you'll have to cut and shape it with a grinder.

2 Polish the blank on fine sandpaper the same way you would lap the back of a new chisel. Start with 120 grit and finish with 220 grit. Sand until the metal is completely smooth. Then draw a profile on the blank with a soft lead pencil.

Choose any wood that suits your fancy to make the body. It doesn't have to be as hard as maple. After all, the only wear surface on a scratch stock is the end grain in the notch of the tool.

Make your scratch stock any size that is comfortable to hold. Ours is made from two pieces of mahogany ½" thick by 2½" wide by 8" long. The notch is 1¼" wide by 5" long.

Our scratch stock uses machine screws and nuts to clamp the body around the cutter. (A simpler scratch stock would use wood screws, but they eventually strip out.) To fit the nuts into the body, drill shallow ⅜"-dia. holes. Then drill the rest of the way through with a ³⁄₁₆" bit. Thread one of the nuts onto the end of a screw. Seat the nut into its hole by hitting the head of the screw with a hammer.

Fig. A
Scrape any shape you want with a scratch stock. You'll use a lot of elbow grease, but it's a quick way to reproduce a short length of molding. Use two small cutters instead of one large cutter to make a wide molding. Make a straight cutter for a piece of inlay that isn't a standard width. File scoring tips at the corners for a clean cut across the grain. Where grooves meet, chisel the corners square and flatten the bottom with a router.

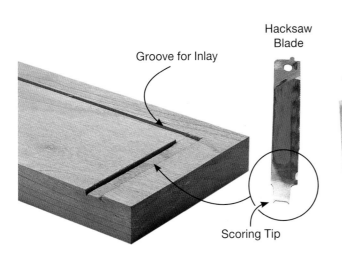

Groove for Inlay

Hacksaw Blade

Scoring Tip

Old Card Scraper

Use Two Blades for a Wide Molding

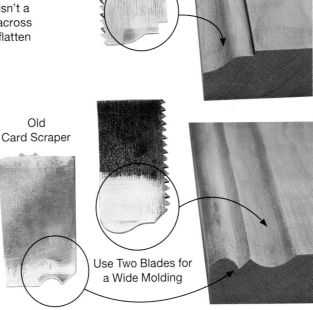

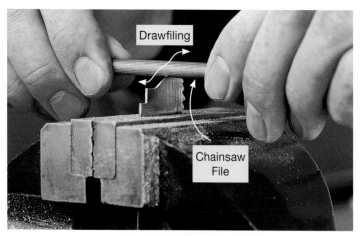

3 File the profile with sharp, new files. Hold the file at 90 degrees to the face of the blank. Use a fine chain saw file for round sections. Push the file across the cutter for initial shaping, then move the file along the cutter to polish the edge. This is called drawfiling. Remove the burr with sandpaper.

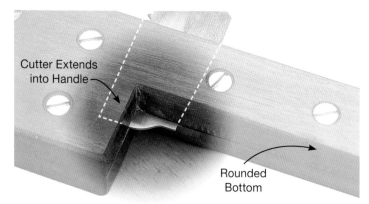

4 Install the cutter in the scratch stock body. The blade should extend a bit farther than the depth of the molding profile. For deep molding shapes, like this one, the cutter should be wide enough to extend into the handle. This cuts down on chatter.

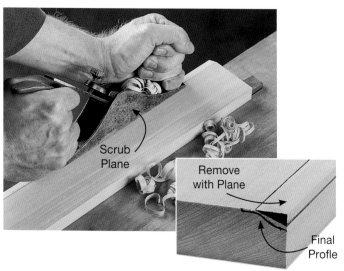

5 Remove most of the waste before using a scratch stock. Draw the molding profile on the end of the board and shade in a triangle of waste. Then extend pencil lines from the triangle's corners down the length of the board. Cut to the lines with a scrub plane or smooth plane.

Bolt the two halves together, then cut the notch and round all the edges so your tool is comfortable to hold. You must also round over the entire bottom side of the arm, in order to properly control your scratch stock (see Photo 4).

Material for Cutters

The traditional source for scratch stock cutters (and scrapers in general) is the blade of an old handsaw. You can easily find one at a yard sale or antique store. It's okay if the saw is bent or slightly rusted. Look for a saw with good-quality steel, like a Disston. You'll get at least a dozen cutters and some large pieces for hand scrapers from one saw blade.

However, any piece of steel that can hold an edge will make a good cutter for a scratch stock—an old hacksaw blade, scraper blade, bandsaw blade, or a reciprocating saw blade. Most of this steel is so hard that it can't be cut with a hacksaw or worked with files. Hacksaw blades, for example, must be broken off in a vise and shaped with a bench grinder or small rotary grinder, like a Dremel.

It's a good idea to make a cutter that's wider than the profile of your molding. If you're making a deep molding, the cutter should be wide enough to extend sideways into the handle of the tool. This prevents the cutter from chattering.

Making the Cutter

Clamp your old handsaw down to a bench and cut it with a hacksaw (Photo 1). You should use a brand-new, good-quality, 32-tpi hacksaw blade. If your hacksaw blade doesn't work, try a carbidegrit blade made for cutting tile.

Lap both faces of the cutter blank. Rub them back and forth on sandpaper glued to glass to remove rust pits and milling marks (Photo 2). Scrapers should have smooth faces, with no visible scratches.

Draw a profile on the cutter with a soft lead pencil, or coat the cutter with layout fluid or marker ink and scratch in the profile. If you have a grinder, belt sander, or disc sander, use it to remove most of the waste.

Cut to the line with a sharp file. Keep the edge square to the face. A scratch stock is one of the few woodworking tools with a 90-degree cutting edge, or arris. An 8- or 10" single-cut, smooth mill file works well. (The shorter the file, the finer the teeth.) Use chain saw files for the curves. If you're making a beading cutter in soft steel, drill a series of holes and cut across their centers.

The smoother the edge, the better the cutter will work. Finish up the edge by drawfiling (Photo 3). Diamond hones make the edge smoother yet. Remove the burr by sanding both faces again. You can burnish a hook on your cutter, the same way as you would sharpen a card scraper, but most users don't bother.

Using Your Scratch Stock

Loosen all the screws of the scratch stock to install the cutter. Wiggle it into the right position. Extend the cutter down a bit farther than the depth of the molding profile (Photo 4). Tighten up all the screws starting with the ones farthest away from the cutter.

Using a scratch stock is harder work than planing. Planes slice through wood fibers. Scratch stocks, with their upright cutting angle, push wood fibers apart. Pushing takes more effort. Remove most of the waste with a plane or router before using the scratch stock (Photo 5).

A scratch stock cuts forward or backward—you can push or pull it. That's why the edge is sharpened at 90-degrees. You have to lean the tool in the direction of the cut, so there's clearance behind the blade (Photo 6). That's why the underside of the arm is rounded. The scratch stock won't cut if it's held upright.

Inevitably your scratch stock will chatter a bit here and there, leaving a surface that looks like a washboard road. Use light (instead of heavy) pressure to smooth out the ripples. This might not work, but you could end up liking the uneven surface. It's the handmade look. You can hand sand your molding with a contoured sanding block if you want to level all the ripples.

When your cutter gets dull, you can sharpen it in one of two ways—file the edge or lap both faces on sandpaper. Simple shapes are best sharpened with a file. Complicated or precise shapes, like beading cutters, are best sharpened by lapping the faces.

Scratch stocks are venerable tools. They've been made and used by woodworkers for centuries. Now you can join their ranks.

6 Push or pull the scratch stock—it cuts in either direction. Push the fence hard against the edge of the board. Lean the tool in the direction of the cut. Clean out crumbs that accumulate at the base of the cutter after a few strokes. It's hard to control a scratch stock at the ends of a board. The best strategy is to cut your board a few inches too long, start and stop the scratched molding 1" in from each end, then cut the board to length.

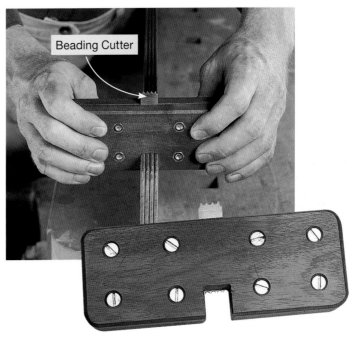

7 Prevent wandering of a scratch stock by making a body that surrounds the work. The notch should fit loosely around the edge of the board. This beading cutter is available from Lie-Nielsen.

by Tom Caspar

Japanese Dozuki Saws

THIN BLADES CUT ON THE PULL STROKE

What's the point of a handsaw in a shop full of power tools? If the saw doesn't cut worth a darn, not much at all. But if it's a Japanese dozuki saw, you'll wonder how you ever got along without one. Dozukis are hand-powered cutting machines. They cost an average of $40 to $50.

Handsaws go where machines can't. Sometimes a cut is awkward or time-consuming to set up with a machine, but a good handsaw can do it lickety-split. I used to be a big fan of English-style handsaws, but when I tried a dozuki saw, there was no turning back.

Let's first take a look at the differences between Japanese and Western joinery saws and what makes Japanese saws so good. Then we'll look at the general types of dozuki saws, and finally recommend some specific tips for using them.

Japanese and Western Saws

All Japanese saws cut on the pull stroke; Western saws, as we all know, cut on the push stroke. Once you've made the switch, you'll find the pull stroke quite natural. It has two overwhelming benefits: following a line is much easier, and that makes sawing far less fatiguing, both physically and mentally.

Japanese saws designed for cutting joints are called dozuki saws. (The word dozuki refers to the shoulder of a tenon.) Dozuki blades are very thin because they're pulled taut as you cut. All dozuki saws have a blade stiffener, or spine, that runs most of the length of the blade and into the handle. The handle itself is always long, narrow and generally wrapped with rattan to improve its grip. It can be held with one hand or with two for additional control. The entire saw is very lightweight.

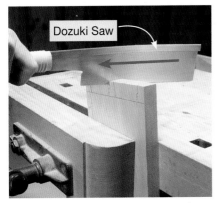

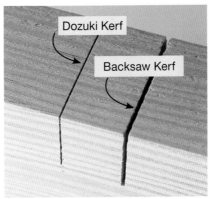

1 A Japanese dozuki saw is ideal for precision work because it's so easy to control. It cuts on the pull stroke. An English-style backsaw, of course, is just the opposite; it cuts on the push stroke. The dozuki saw blade is very thin and makes a much narrower kerf. The less wood you remove, the easier it is to guide the saw.

A Western-style saw for cutting joints also has a blade stiffener, or back, and so it's usually referred to as a backsaw. A backsaw's blade must be relatively thick so it doesn't buckle when pushed. The backsaw's handle can be an elaborately shaped grip or a simple turned knob. Both styles are held with one hand. Most backsaws are heavier than dozuki saws.

The dozuki saw's thin blade cuts an extremely narrow kerf (Photo 1). A backsaw's kerf is often twice as wide, or more. That means you're removing half as much wood with a dozuki and exerting half as much effort. Your muscles can relax, so you can concentrate on following the line (Photo 2). A backsaw requires much more effort and mental anguish, particularly when it's dull.

Dozuki saws stay sharp for a very long time. Most saws have tempered teeth so hard they can't be sharpened with a file. When the saw gets dull, you pop in a new blade. Backsaws generally have softer teeth. When they get dull, you can file and set them yourself. Backsaw teeth are so small, however, that sharpening can be a real challenge. Most woodworkers don't bother and simply continue to use a dull saw, with disappointing results.

Dozuki Teeth: Crosscut and Rip

Dozuki saws excel at sawing across the grain (Photo 3). Most dozuki saws in American catalogs have crosscut teeth.

Crosscut dozukis also cut quite well with the grain. Rip cuts for tenons and dovetails are no problem as long as they don't go more than an inch deep. (The saw may bind if your cut isn't dead straight.) In fact, it's when cutting dovetails that most woodworkers really fall in love with their dozuki saws.

Dozuki saws designed specifically for ripping are just making their way to our shores. These

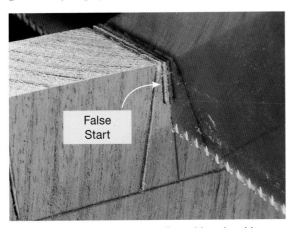

2 It's easy to cut right on the line with a dozuki saw because its tempered blade stays extremely sharp for a very long time. Even if you miss the line, you can start over again a hair breadth's away.

3 Cutting small parts is safe and easy with a dozuki saw. Dozukis are designed to make splinter-free crosscuts that are as smooth as glass. Make your own miter box to guide the cut.

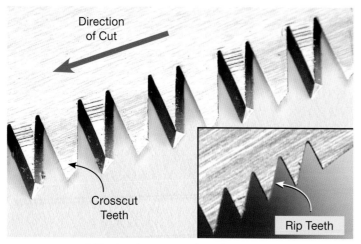

Direction of Cut

Crosscut Teeth

Rip Teeth

4 The teeth on most dozuki saws are designed for crosscutting. They have small, angled tips that score the wood like the blade of a knife. These teeth do a fine job with short rip cuts, such as dovetails, but some specialized dozuki saws have teeth designed primarily for ripping.

Each replacement blade is specifically made to (Photo 4). Rip-cut saws work across the grain fairly well, too. They're more expensive than crosscut saws.

If you've never used a dozuki, start with a standard crosscut saw. It's better for general-purpose work than a rip-cut saw. A crosscut saw is less aggressive, so learning to use one is easier.

Replaceable Blades

Most dozuki saws have replaceable blades (Photo 5). A second blade usually costs about half as much as the saw itself.

Each replacement blade is specifically made to fit only one brand of saw. When you find a saw you like, it's a good idea to buy a second blade before the first gets dull. Reserve the fresh blade for the cuts that really matter.

Teeth Per Inch

Dozuki saws have three different ranges of teeth size. Most saws have 22 to 27 teeth per inch (tpi). They work well in pieces from ⅛" to 1" thick. Saws with large teeth have 13 to 18 tpi. They cut very aggressively and are best suited for stock that's at least ¾" thick. Getting started on the first cut, without bouncing, takes some practice.

A few dozuki saws have incredibly small teeth (32 tpi). They're extremely easy to start without bouncing. They're not for beginners, however, because the blades are so thin and flexible.

Blade Length

Dozuki saws have blades of two different lengths: short (6" to 8") or long (9½" to 10½"). Length doesn't determine the size of the teeth. Two blades of different lengths by the same maker usually have the same number of teeth per inch.

A saw with a long blade is best for most work. You can take a long stroke and cut fairly deep each time you pull the saw. Short blades are best suited for small work or shallow cuts, when fewer strokes are needed.

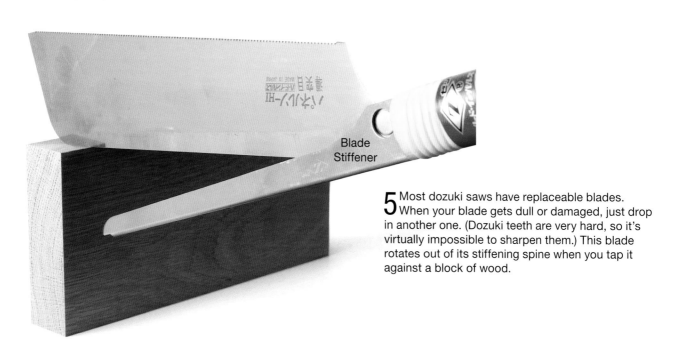

Blade Stiffener

5 Most dozuki saws have replaceable blades. When your blade gets dull or damaged, just drop in another one. (Dozuki teeth are very hard, so it's virtually impossible to sharpen them.) This blade rotates out of its stiffening spine when you tap it against a block of wood.

How to Use a Dozuki Saw

If you're 10 years old and have never used any kind of handsaw before, learning to use a Japanese dozuki pull saw should be a breeze. For the rest of us, forget everything you know about saws. Dozukis are that different.

First, you have to get used to cutting on the pull stroke. The trick to doing this may seem silly, but it's very effective. Wear a blindfold. Don't worry about following a line. Just feel the saw cut.

Pull with your elbow, not your wrist. Steady the saw by locking your wrist in position.

Don't press down hard. Let the saw do the work. Dozuki saws cut so effortlessly that the weight of the saw itself is almost enough to get it through the cut. Pushing down too hard on a saw can make it bind or, in the worst case, break off some of the saw's teeth. (A dozuki will work OK with a few missing teeth, however.)

You can take off the blindfold now. Always start your cut on the far side of the workpiece. Take long strokes, but don't pull the blade out of the cut. Short strokes invite more error.

On crosscuts, tilt the blade up about 10 degrees. This is the ideal angle of attack for the blade's teeth.

Try sawing with two hands. Square yourself to the workpiece and pull the saw toward your belt buckle. Put one hand in front of the other, or hold them side by side, as though you're praying for a good cut. Your plea will be answered! This stance makes it easier to steady the saw and stay on a line, but it's perfectly reasonable to stand to one side and saw Western-style.

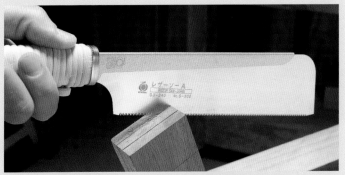

Start your cut on the far side of the workpiece. Dozuki saws cut on the pull stroke, so this rip cut is actually going downhill, with the grain. Lean the workpiece toward you for a better angle.

Hold your dozuki saw with two hands and pull it square to your body. Holding the saw with one hand, Western-style, works OK, but this method gives you even better control.

by Alan Lacer

Turning an Heirloom Awl

HARDEN AND TEMPER THE STEEL BY HEAT-TREATING

Metal and wood are the basic ingredients in most woodworking tools. As woodworkers, we're familiar with working wood, but what about metal? Actually, the level of metal working required to make some woodworking tools is pretty basic. If you've never made your own tools, give this project a try. There's something enormously satisfying about using a tool you made yourself.

We chose the scratch awl for this article because it's an everyday tool that's easy to make. Making an awl will teach you the basic principles of heat-treating steel and turning a wood handle with a metal ferrule. Perhaps this project will be the first milestone on your custom tool-making journey.

Note: This project involves metal grinding and working with an open flame, so be sure to follow these basic safety guidelines:

- Thoroughly clean the work area of all wood shavings and dust before using the torch or grinding the steel.
- Keep a fire extinguisher on hand for emergencies.
- If possible, do the heat-treating outside.
- Wear eye protection for all grinding operations.
- Never use motor oil for the heat-treating process.

What you will need:
- Fire extinguisher
- ⅛", ³⁄₁₆" or ¼", diameter drill rod in oil hardening steel
- Propane or Mapp gas torch
- Pint of olive oil and a can to pour it in
- Locking pliers
- 8" or 10" mill file
- Electric drill

- 10" grinding disc (120-grit) mounted on ¾" plywood or MDF backing.
- 2" x 2" x 4" piece of dry hardwood
- Copper plumbing coupling, brass or copper pipe, brass nut, or brass compression nut for the ferrule material
- Metal can with a lid
- Lathe tools: roughing gouge, detail gouge, parting tool, and optional skew chisel
- Scroll chuck
- Sandpaper (usually 100-, 150-, 180- and 220-grit)
- Jacobs style chuck for your lathe's tailstock
- A drill bit that's ⅟₆₄" larger than the drill rod
- Epoxy
- Optional: Tempilstik in 450–500 degrees range

Turn The Handle

Pick any strong hardwood for the handle: cherry, hard maple, oak, walnut, hickory, ash, rosewood, goncalo alves, purpleheart, etc. (Now, aren't you glad you saved those little pieces of really cool wood?) Determine the desired diameter and length of the handle. Be sure to allow for the length of the ferrule.

Mount the wood into the scroll chuck and create a cylinder with the roughing gouge.

With the parting tool, cut a small cylinder on the end to fit the metal ferrule (Photo 1). Take care to achieve a tight fit. The ferrule stock can be a copper coupling (¼" to ½", depending on the look you desire), brass nuts, brass or copper pipe. If you're using a brass nut, simply thread it onto the wood.

Shape the handle with the detail gouge or skew chisel (Photo 2). The possibilities are endless and depend on the handle style, the size of your hands, and whether the tool is meant for delicate or heavy service. I seldom make any two the same. Take the opportunity to add your own fine detailing to distinguish your awl from production versions. When satisfied with the shape, finish sand to 220-grit.

Shape the ferrule with the gouge (Photo 3).

Use a Jacobs chuck to drill a 1½" (minimum) deep hole for the steel shaft (Photo 4).

Part the handle off the chuck and hand- sand the end. You can leave the handle unfinished or use a drying oil.

Brass Nut Ferrule

1 Round the handle blank and fit the ferrule on the end. You can use different materials for a ferrule; this one is a solid-brass nut with a tapered end section.

2 Rough in the basic shape of the handle with the detailing gouge. The shape and size of the handle is up to you.

3 Turn away the flats of the nut and shape the ferrule with a detailing gouge. Cutting brass and copper on the lathe is similar to cutting wood. However, take light cuts.

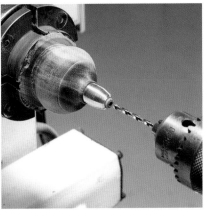

4 Drill the hole to accept the steel drill rod. Use bits ⅟₆₄" larger in diameter than the drill rod to allow room for the epoxy.

5 Cut a length of drill rod with a hacksaw for the awl's steel shaft.

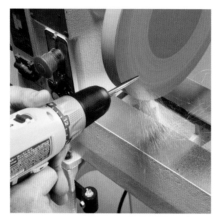

6 Shape a tapered point on the shaft using a drill and a lathe mounted abrasive disc. With the drill running, grind the point on the near lower quadrant of the spinning disc. Wear eye protection!

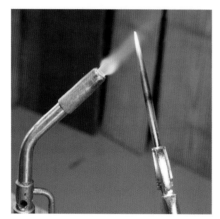

7 Harden the shaft by heating the pointed half to an even cherry-red color. Hold the shaft in a pair of locking pliers.

8 When the steel is evenly bright red from the point to the middle, quickly quench and stir it in a can of olive oil.

Make the Steel Shaft

The drill rod is annealed, which means it's too soft for use as an awl. On the other hand, soft steel is easy to work so we'll leave it that way for now and do the hardening later.

Cut the drill rod with a hacksaw to the desired length of the awl shaft (Photo 5). I normally use 3" to 6" lengths. Choose a length and diameter that fits the desired look and function of the awl.

To shape the point on the business end of the shaft, first chuck it in a drill. Then, run the drill as you hold the shaft against a spinning lathe-mounted grinding disc (Photo 6). Run the lathe at low to medium speed (400 to 800 rpm). Don't try and put a delicate point on the steel at the stage. It will just get burned off in the heat-treating process. And don't worry if you "blue" the steel at this juncture as overheating is only a concern once the steel is heat-treated.

Get the torch and pour some olive oil in a can. With the shank held in a pair of locking pliers, fire-up the torch and apply heat to the steel. Twirl the rod as if you were slow cooking a marshmallow (Photo 7). Try for an even, bright cherry-red color from the middle to the point, then quickly dunk the hot steel into the olive oil and agitate rapidly for about 30 seconds (Photo 8).

Note: Never use motor oil for this as it gives off noxious fumes and can even ignite.

Use a mill file to test the shank tip hardness (Photo 9). If the steel does not pass the file test, reheat and quench again.

Hand-sand the shaft to achieve a clean bright surface (Photo 10).

The second phase of heat-treating is called tempering. This is where the degree of final hardness is established. Tempering involves reheating the hardened area to a specific temperature, then quenching it immediately in water. The higher the temperature the softer the shaft will be. As the end user, you are free to determine the degree of hardness you want in your tool. You may want an awl that is very hard and can scratch deep lines in hard wood. The down side is a very hard shaft will have a brittle point that's prone to breaking. At the other extreme you can temper the shaft so the point won't break but it may bend so easily that the awl becomes useless. I suggest making a couple of awls, each tempered to different temperatures to see what best fits your needs.

The tempered "sweet spot" for my awls is a temperature around 450 to 500-degrees. There are three ways to achieve this:

A. Heat the steel slowly with a torch just back of the hardened area (Photo 11). When the hardened area turns a gold or bronze color, quench immediately in water to stop the process.

B. Use a temperature-indicating substance such as Tempilstik. Choose a Tempilstik that fits your desired heat range. Rub the area around the point with the wax-like stick. Then, heat the shaft as described in option A. When the steel reaches the desired temperature, the Tempilstik will smoke and liquefy. At this point, quickly quench the shaft in water.

C. The easiest, but slowest method is to bake the steel in a conventional oven for about 30 minutes at 450-degrees. Be sure to preheat the oven and place the steel on a cookie sheet. Elevate the steel with rolled up pieces of aluminum foil so it will heat evenly. Remove the steel from the oven and let it cool. There's no need to quench a shaft that's been cooked in an oven.

Wood + Steel = Awl Done

If you need a sharper point on the awl, place it back in the drill and lightly shape the tapered area on the disc mounted on the lathe (use a finer grit for this, such as a 150-grit or finer). Do this slowly, as bluing the point may make the tool too soft for your purposes.

Mount the steel in the handle (Photo 12). I put a small amount of epoxy down in the hole, and then push the handle down over the steel with the point in a scrap piece of wood. Use the awl for a while; you may find you want one harder or one more flexible—you decide based on your tempering temperatures.

9 Test the hardness of the shaft by running it along a file. The hardened part should skate off the file, not bite in.

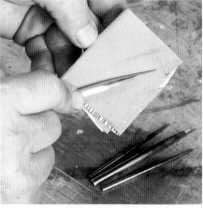

10 Sand the steel to a bright, clean surface with 220-grit paper. Wash it with soap and water to remove oil residue first.

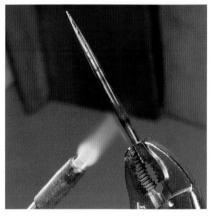

11 Temper the shaft with a torch held just below the heat-treated area. Keep the flame there and rotate the shaft until the hardened area is a uniform dark gold or bronze color. Then, quickly quench it in water.

12 Set the shaft in the handle using a bit of slow-set epoxy. Put the epoxy in the hole with a toothpick. Rotate the shaft a bit as you push it in to evenly distribute the epoxy.

by Allen Finch

Make a Leg Vise

DEEP REACH AT THE RIGHT HEIGHT

This simple leg vise is based on a traditional design still favored by many woodworkers. My version is built with inexpensive parts you can buy from any hardware store or home center.

Every bench should have a good vise. Why use a leg vise, rather than a commercial face vise? Aside from its low cost, this leg vise has three major benefits:

- Huge capacity. Many commercial vises don't open very far, but a leg vise can extend up to 2' or more. To keep the jaws roughly parallel, you change the position of the bolt in the adjustment arm.
- Deep reach. Inexpensive commercial vises are very shallow, offering only a small amount of surface area. When you tighten a vise, you want a lot of surface area to contact the workpiece, to prevent the piece from moving. You can make the faces of this vise as deep and wide as you wish.
- Convenient height. Commercial vises are mounted flush with the top of a bench. For some work, it's better to elevate the vise. A tall vise helps prevent chatter when sawing, for example. A leg vise can be mounted at any height.

Building the Vise

Cut the leg, front jaw (traditionally called a "chop") and adjustment arm to suit your bench. Use a stiff hardwood, such as 6/4 maple or hickory. Douglas fir or Southern yellow pine are good alternatives.

Make the adjustment arm 1½" square. Cut a 1½" x 1½" notch in the chop's bottom end. Cut a corresponding 1½" x 2" mortise in the leg. (The extra height allows the arm to pivot.) Drill ½" dia. holes in the front jaw and leg. Drill a series of corresponding holes in the adjustment arm, spaced 2" apart.

Shopping List

- Douglas fir 2x6, 8' long
- ⅝" x 24" threaded rod
- ⅝" x 2" coupler nut
- Two ½" x 5" bolts
- Two 1" x 6" mending plates
- Two ³⁄₁₆" x 1¼" roll pins
- Two ¾" O-rings
- ½" floor flange
- ½" x 1½" pipe nipple
- ½" x 10" pipe nipple
- ¾" x ½" tee
- Two ½" caps

The vise's threaded rod goes through a coupler nut in the leg. To capture the nut, drill a 1" dia. hole, 1" deep, in the leg's back. Continue drilling a ⅝" dia. hole through the leg. In line with this hole, cut a 1" wide x 1½" tall mortise in the front jaw. (The extra room in this mortise allows the front jaw to pivot.) Bandsaw the leg and jaw's shape and chamfer the edges.

To assemble the vise (Fig. A), pound the coupler nut into the leg. It doesn't have to be epoxied—a tight fit will keep the nut from spinning. Thread the short pipe nipple into the tee and the floor flange onto the nipple's other end. Insert the threaded rod all the way through the nipple. (You may have to file the rod's threads a bit to make it fit.) Drill two holes for roll pins (Photo 1). One goes through the tee, nipple, and threaded rod. The other goes through the floor flange, nipple, and threaded rod. Go slow and use cutting oil. Tap in the roll pins (Photo 2). Pass the long pipe nipple (the vise's handle) through the tee and add the O-rings and caps. When you rotate the handle, the threaded rod and flange will turn with it. Fasten the mending plates to the chop alongside the mortise—the flange bears against them when you tighten the vise. For additional support, you could cut a third mending plate in half and mount the two pieces between the plates shown here.

Fasten the leg to your bench. Mount the adjustment arm on the chop and pass the handle assembly through the chop's mortise. Slide the adjustment arm through the leg and thread the screw through the coupler. The vise is easy to remove if it occasionally gets in your way.

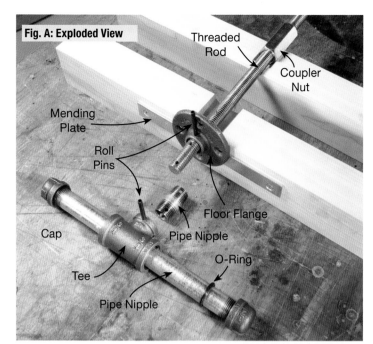

Fig. A: Exploded View

Threaded Rod
Coupler Nut
Mending Plate
Roll Pins
Floor Flange
Cap
Pipe Nipple
Tee
O-Ring
Pipe Nipple

1 Drill holes for the roll pins. The pins fasten the handle assembly to the screw. To steady the work, use a utility knife to carve a "nest" in a piece of 2" foam insulation.

2 Tap in the roll pins. They're split down the middle, to fit tight in the hole. Use wood blocks to support the screw and the tee.

The Benefits of a Leg Vise

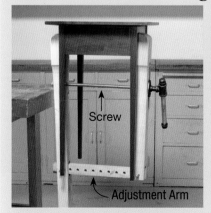

Screw
Adjustment Arm

Huge capacity. Make the vise as deep as you want—the length of the screw and adjustment arm determine how far the vise can open.

Chop

Deep reach. You can position the screw at almost any height. The chop on this vise has a much greater vertical depth than you'll find on a commercial vise.

Leg

Convenient height. You can make the vise's leg tall enough to raise the chop to chest height, placing your work at a more convenient level.

by Steve Bunn

Make a Tail Vise

CLASSIC VISE UPGRADES YOUR WORKBENCH

You can do without a tail vise. But you can do much more with one. That's why woodworkers have depended on tail vises for over 400 years. A tail vise can be used to clamp boards of all sizes horizontally or vertically for planing, sanding, carving, routing, gluing, etc. Modern versions employ metal screws and guide plates, but I prefer the traditional all-wood construction shown here, partially because it's beautiful in both form and function, and partially because you don't have to buy any vise hardware, only a thread box and tap, which can be used over and over.

This vise can be mounted on virtually any workbench, although modifying the base is almost sure to be a part of the project. A bench with a trestle-style base and a top that extends beyond it at the front and on the right side, as shown here, is ideal.

Clamp horizontally
Clamp long and short boards on top of the bench, fully supported for planing.

Clamp for work
Hold furniture parts for chopping, carving and routing. Hold jigs and fixtures, too.

Clamp vertically
Clamp freely between the jaws. Unlike a face vise, there are no screws or guide bars to get in the way.

Like any clamping devise, a tail vise has two main components, a fixed jaw and an adjustable jaw. Both jaws accept bench dogs, so that in addition to clamping between the jaws, a tail vise can also clamp above them. This dual capability is the key to a tail vise's versatility.

The fixed jaw is a laminated beam that's glued and screwed to the front of the bench top and reinforced by a solid beam—called an end cap—that's attached to the end of the top. The adjustable jaw opposes the fixed jaw. It's a complex rectangular frame that mounts against and underneath the bench top, supported and guided by another end cap. The screw that operates this jaw threads through the same end cap.

Start with the End Caps

The end caps (A and B, Fig. A) anchor both jaws. They also keep the bench top flat. Start with two 1¾" x 3¾" maple blanks that are about 6" longer than the width of the bench top. Use the tablesaw to cut a ⅞" wide dovetail-shaped groove on the inside face of each end cap blank, starting ⅝" from the top edge. Tilt the blade 9° to cut the angled shoulders. Then install a dado set to remove the waste. Clean up each channel and drill a single countersunk shank hole for a ⅜" x 6" lag bolt.

The end caps must be wide at the front to support the vise jaws, but they can be narrower at the back. Cut notches on the bandsaw or by making a series of stopped cuts on the jointer.

Dovetail-shaped keys (C, Fig. A) simultaneously hold each end cap tightly against the bench top, yet still allow seasonal movement. Make two key blanks on the tablesaw with the blade tilted 9° and set at 1" height. Stand a 1" x 4" x 24" blank on its edge and make two passes, resetting the fence between passes to determine the key's width. Make a third pass with the blank on its side to cut out each key. Each key blank should tightly fit the end cap's grooves, but slide without binding. It must also sit flush with or slightly below the cap's face.

Cut the blanks into 4" long keys and use a jig to screw them to the bench top (Photo 1). The jig is simply a 2" wide offcut from one of the end beams with a fence glued on top. Slide a key into the jig and position the jig on the bench. Drill a countersunk pilot hole through one end of the key and into the end of the bench. Install a screw. Repeat the process on the other end of the

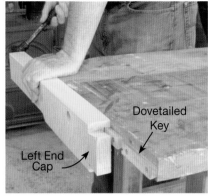

1 Start by installing end caps on both ends of the bench. They mount on dovetailed keys that are located using a jig made from an offcut.

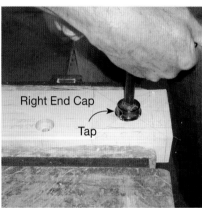

2 The right end cap contains a threaded hole for the vise's wooden screw. A woodthreading kit contains a tap to thread this hole and a thread box to cut threads on the screw.

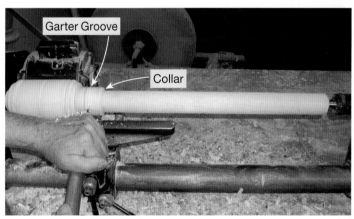

3 Turn the wooden screw. Finish by cutting a groove for the garter in the collar. The garter locks the screw in the vise's adjustable jaw, but allows it to revolve freely.

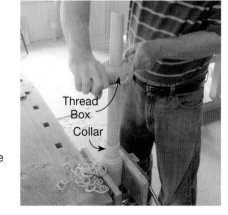

4 Use the thread box to thread the shaft of the wooden screw all the way to the collar. These threads fit the threaded hole in the end cap.

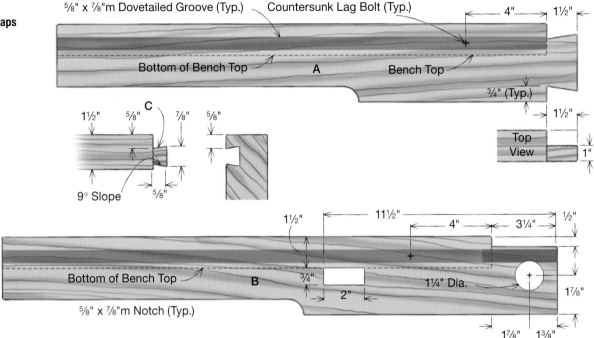

Fig. A: The End Caps

⅝" x ⅞"m Dovetailed Groove (Typ.) Countersunk Lag Bolt (Typ.)

4" 1½"

Bottom of Bench Top A Bench Top

¾" (Typ.)

C

1½" ⅝" ⅞" ⅝"

9° Slope ⅝"

1½"

Top View

1"

1½" 11½" 4" 3¼" ½"

Bottom of Bench Top B

¾"

5⁄8" x ⅞"m Notch (Typ.)

2" 1¼" Dia.

1⅞"

1⅞" 1⅜"

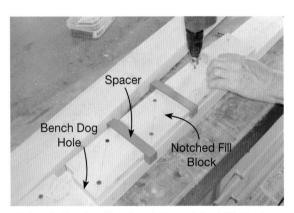

5 Create the fixed jaw by gluing notched fill blocks between two rails. Use screws instead of clamps to streamline the process. The spaces between the segments become holes for bench dogs.

Spacer

Bench Dog Hole

Notched Fill Block

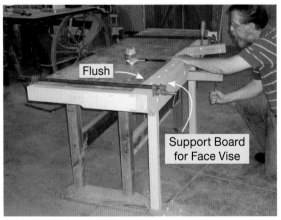

Flush

Support Board for Face Vise

6 Install the fixed jaw with glue and lag bolts, making sure it's flush with the existing bench top. The board glued on the bottom of the fixed jaw supports the Federal-style double-screw face vise.

key. Then remove the jig. Space the keys about an inch apart, starting 1" from the front of the bench top.

Finish and install the end caps one at a time. The left end cap (A) extends 1½" beyond the bench top and is dovetailed to the fixed jaw. Lay out and cut this lapped dovetail on the front of the cap. Rub paraffin in the cap's dovetailed groove and then drive it onto the keys and into position on the bench top. Install the lag bolt and finish by trimming the back end flush.

The right end cap (B) extends 3¼" beyond the bench top to support the sliding jaw and anchor the wooden screw. Use one of the keys to fill the front end of the dovetailed groove. Mark the center point of the screw and drill a 1¼" dia. pilot hole. Lay out and cut the notch at the front and the mortise. The notch allows the adjustable jaw to ride over the end cap as it's opened and closed. Similarly, the mortise accommodates the adjustable jaw's guide bar, which slides under the bench top. Make this mortise large enough for the guide bar to freely slide through. Use a 1½" dia. threaded tap to cut the threads in the bench-screw pilot hole (Photo 2). Then follow the procedure described earlier to install this end cap.

The Wooden Screw

Make the screw (D, Fig. B) from a 24" long maple blank turned to a 3" dia. cylinder (Photo 3). Lay out and turn the head and the 2" dia. x 1¾" collar. Turn the shaft to 1¹⁵⁄₃₂" dia. and finish by cutting a ¼" deep groove in the collar for the garter.

Clamp the turned screw in a vise (the vise on your other workbench) and use a 1½" thread box to cut the threads into the shaft (Photo 4). Turning the shaft to just under 1½" dia. keeps the shaft from binding in the thread box as the threads are cut.

Use a V-block and a drill press with a fence to drill a centered ⅞" dia. hole in the head of the screw for the handle

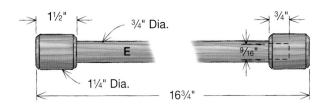

(E). Turn the handle from an 18" long maple blank turned to a 1¼" dia. Turn the shaft to ¾" dia., with a knob on each end. On one end, next to the knob, turn the shaft down to a 9/16" dia. tenon. Remove the handle from the lathe and cut off the knob that's next to the tenon. Clamp this knob in a hand screw and drill a 9/16" dia. stopped hole for the tenon. Slide the shaft of the handle through the hole in the head of the screw and then glue on the knob.

The Fixed Jaw

Determine the fixed jaw's length by subtracting 16" (the length required by the adjustable jaw) from the overall length of your bench, including the two end caps. For the 80½" long bench shown here, the fixed jaw measures 64½". This jaw contains equally spaced holes for bench dogs (Fig. C). It consists of notched, angled fill blocks (F) that are sandwiched between two rails (G). Make sure to have your bench dogs in hand before you build, so you can size the dog holes to fit.

Mill blanks for the two 1½" thick rails and the ¾" thick fill blocks. Cut the blanks 3 13/16" wide and allow extra length for trimming. Set the miter fence to 5° and use the tablesaw to cut the fill-block blank into nine 4¾" long blocks and two extra-long blocks to go on the ends of the assembly. Cut a ¼" x 1¼" notch in each fill block to allow the head of the bench dog to seat below the top surface. Drill a pair of countersunk pilot holes in each fill block and glue them on one of the rails, using spacers to create 1" gaps (Photo 5). Make sure all the notches face up and to the right. Clamp each block until you drive in the screws; then remove the clamps. After all the blocks are fastened, remove the screws. Then glue and clamp the remaining rail. When the glue is dry, level the top of the laminated jaw and mill it to final 3¾" width.

Square the jaw's right end 4½" from the first dog hole. Then square the left end at the assembly's final length (flush with the outside edge of the left end beam). Clamp the jaw to the front of the bench, level with the top and snug against the end beam's dovetail. Transfer the dovetail onto the end of the jaw. Then remove the jaw and cut the dovetail socket in the end. Drill countersunk holes for the three ⅜" x 6" lag bolts that anchor the jaw to the bench, in the middle and 3" from each end.

Install the fixed jaw (Photo 6). Apply glue to the edge of the bench top and to the end cap's dovetail. Lightly clamp the assembly in position. Then use a dead blow mallet to seat the

7 Modify the bench base by cutting off the fronts of both top rails. This allows moving the base forward to center it under the widened top. You'll also have to cut a notch for the adjustable jaw's guide bar.

8 Make the adjustable jaw's front block in two pieces to create its angled dog hole. Cut a shallow groove across the grain in each piece. Then saw the angled shoulders and clear the waste.

Fig. C: The Fixed Jaw

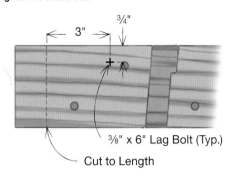

3"   ¾"

⅜" x 6" Lag Bolt (Typ.)

Cut to Length

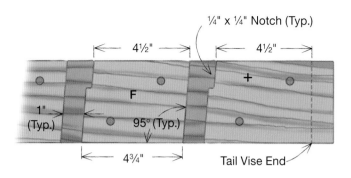

¼" x ¼" Notch (Typ.)

4½"   4½"

1" (Typ.)

F

95° (Typ.)

4¾"

Tail Vise End

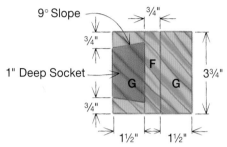

9° Slope   ¾"

¾"

1" Deep Socket

F

G   G

¾"

1½"   1½"

3¾"

Dog Hole

9 Glue the front block together to create the dog hole. Then drill it to house the wooden screw, dovetail it to fit the side and top pieces and mortise it for the cross brace.

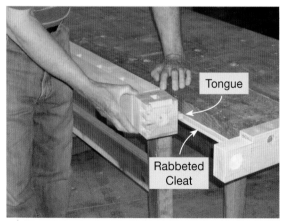

Tongue

Rabbeted Cleat

10 The front block slides in a groove created by attaching a rabbeted cleat to the bench. A tongue fastened to the jaw fits the groove and keeps the jaw flush with the bench top as it slides.

dovetail joint. Level the assembly with the front of the bench and then tighten the clamps. Drill pilot holes through the three counter-sunk holes in the jaw and then install the lag bolts.

Modify the Base

Adding the two jaws makes the top front-heavy. To keep the bench from tipping forward, you'll probably have to modify the base. On the trestle base shown here, the solution is to shorten the top rails (Photo 7). This allows moving the base forward under the top until it butts against the fixed jaw. You'll also have to cut a slot for the adjustable jaw's guide bar. It's best to make this cut later, when you're installing the adjustable jaw.

The Adjustable Jaw

The adjustable jaw (Figs. D–G) looks like a narrow box, but it's actually a rectangular frame consisting of a front block (H), a rear rail (J), side and top pieces (K and L), a guide bar (M) and a cross brace (N). The front block, rear rail, side and top form the box that's the business end of the jaw: It houses a bench dog and the wooden screw that applies the clamping pressure. This box is supported by the right end cap and kept level with the bench top by a tongue (P) that's attached to the front block. The guide bar and cross brace slide under the bench top. The guide bar, mortised into the rear rail, housed in the end cap and supported by a rub rail (Q), holds the adjustable jaw against the front of the bench as it slides. The cross brace completes the frame by connecting the guide bar to the front block.

The biggest challenge in building the adjustable jaw is cutting the angled dog hole in the center of the front block (Fig. E). The trick is to make this block in two pieces (Photo 8). Cut a pair of identical 1⅞" x 3¾" x 3¾" blocks. Then cut a precisely centered ¼" deep x 3¾" wide dado across the grain in each block, using a dado set and a miter gauge with a fence and a stop block. Clamp the blocks together with the dadoes facing each other and lay out the ends of the angled dog hole on the top and bottom faces of both blocks. Use these depth marks and a hand saw to cut the angled shoulders. Clear the waste with a chisel and cut the notch on one end. Then carefully glue the two blocks together, using a spacer to precisely align the dadoes.

Cut dovetails on both ends of the adjustable jaw's side (K) and top (L). (Note that the side's front-block dovetails are longer than its rear-rail dovetails.) Transfer the dovetail locations to the front jaw. Then cut the sockets and fit the joints (Photo 9).

Fig. D: The Adjustable Jaw

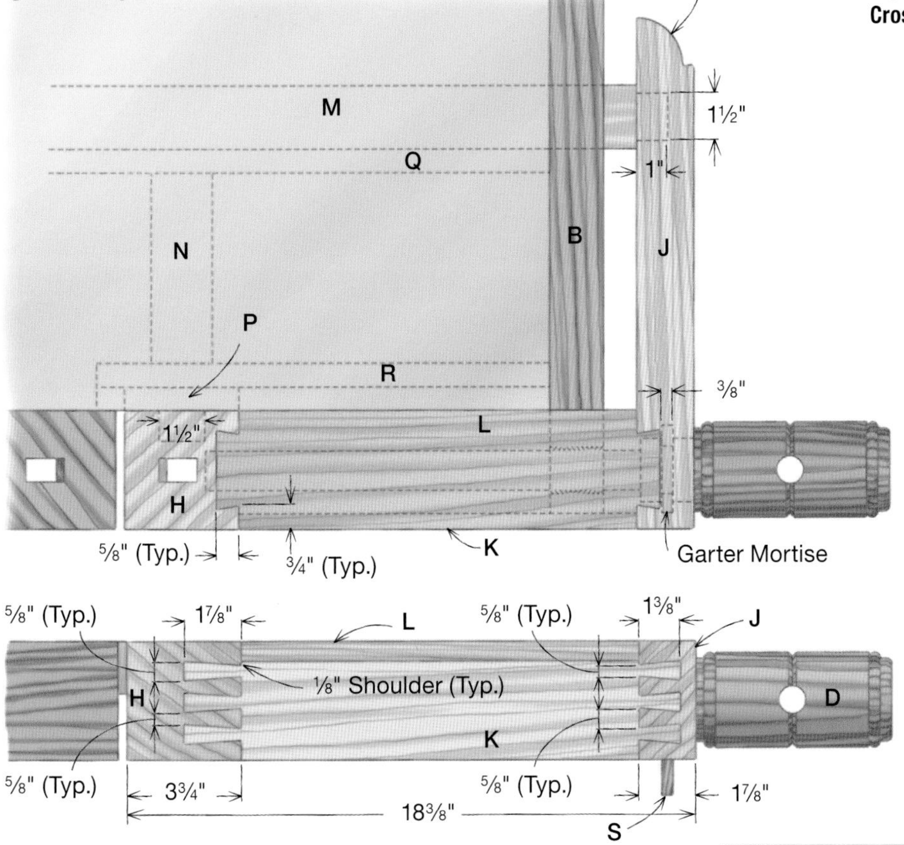
1½" R.
M
1½"
Q
1"
N
B
J
P
R
3/8"
L
1½"
H
5/8" (Typ.)
¾" (Typ.)
K
Garter Mortise
5/8" (Typ.)
1⅞"
L
5/8" (Typ.)
1⅜"
J
⅛" Shoulder (Typ.)
H
D
K
5/8" (Typ.)
3¾"
5/8" (Typ.)
1⅞"
18⅜"
S

Fig. E: Front Block Cross-Section

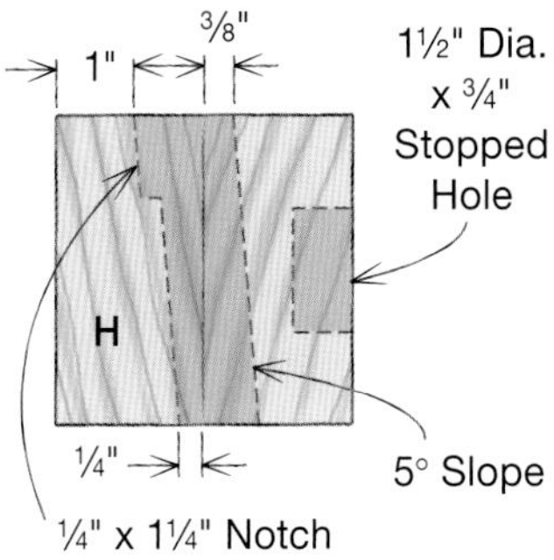
3/8"
1"
1½" Dia.
x ¾"
Stopped
Hole
H
¼"
5° Slope
¼" x 1¼" Notch

The front block's back face has a tongue and a mortise (Fig. F). The tongue (P) holds the block level with the bench top as the ajdustable jaw opens and closes (Photo 10). It slides in a groove created by a rabbeted cleat (R) that's attached to the bottom of the bench top. The mortise in the front block houses a tenon on the cross brace (N). Fasten the rabbeted cleat under the bench top and then attach the tongue with glue and screws and chop the mortise.

Cut the rear rail (J, Fig. G) to length and width. Routing a profile on its back end is optional—a matter of taste. Lay out and cut the dovetail sockets on its top and front end and chop the stopped mortise for the guide bar (M) on its inside face. Cut the guide bar and fit its tenon to the mortise in the rear rail. Cut and fit the cross brace (N). Note that it's rabbeted to fit around the rabbeted cleat (R).

Lay out and drill holes for the wooden screw in the front block and rear rail. To make sure these holes align with the threaded hole in the end cap, dry-assemble the adjustable jaw's side, front block and rear rail and position the assembly on the bench. Mark the hole in the rear rail after butting it against the end cap. To mark the hole in the front block, slide the assembly back until the block butts against the end cap. Before marking each hole, make sure the top edges of both pieces are flush. Drill a 1½" dia. x ¾" stopped hole in the front block and a 2" dia. through hole in the rear rail. Re-assemble the adjustable jaw, add the guide bar and cross brace, and test its operation on the bench (Photo 11). Make sure there's a small gap between

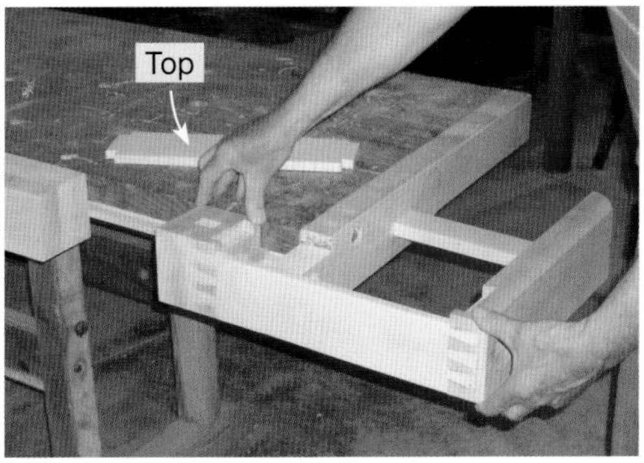
Top

11 Install the partially assembled adjustable jaw to check the alignment of the three holes for the wooden screw. Then install the top and test the jaw to make sure it slides smoothly.

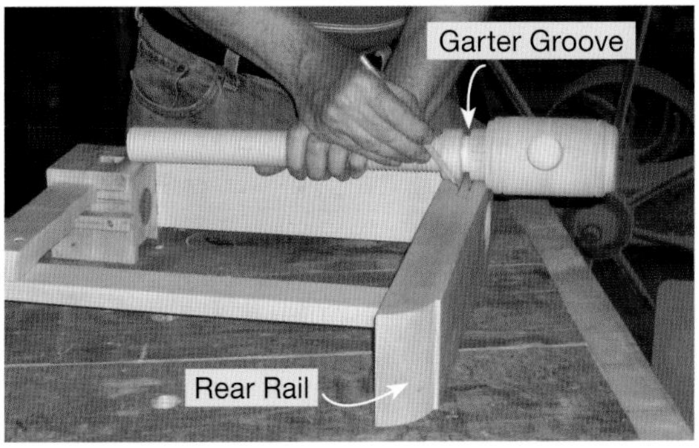
Garter Groove
Rear Rail

12 Locate the mortise for the garter that secures the wooden screw in the adjustable jaw. Position the screw with its head snug against the jaw's rear rail. Then transfer the garter groove's location.

Fig. F: Bench Top Cross-Section at Front Block

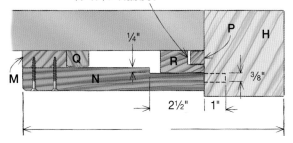

⅝" x ¾" Rabbet

¼"

P   H

Q   R

M   N

⅜"

2½"   1"

Fig. G: Rear Rail

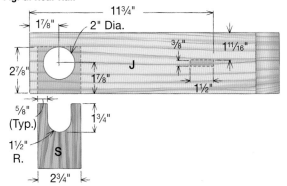

11¾"

1⅞"   2" Dia.

⅜"   1¹¹⁄₁₆"

2⅞"   J

1⅞"

1½"

⅝"
(Typ.)

1¾"

1½"
R.   S

2¾"

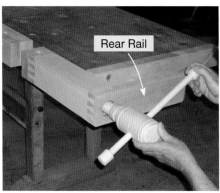

13 Mount the adjustable jaw and thread in the screw until its head seats against the rear rail. Install the garter and then test for smooth operation.

Guide Bar

Rub Rail

14 Flip over the bench top and install a rub rail against the guide bar to ensure the adjustable jaw remains parallel to the front of the bench top as it opens and closes.

the right end cap (B) and the real rail (J) when the jaws are tightly closed.

Final Assembly and Mounting

Turn the adjustable jaw upside down to locate the mortise for the garter that holds the wooden screw (Photo 12 and Fig. G). Butt the head of the screw against the rear rail and center its collar over the hole. Transfer the locations of both garter groove shoulders to the jaw and use these marks to chop the mortise. Make the garter (S).

Glue the adjustable jaw together in stages. Start by gluing the dovetailed side, top, front block and rear rail to create the body. Mount the body on the bench. Then work from underneath to glue and attach the guide bar and cross brace. Install the wooden screw by threading it through the hole in the end cap until it seats against the jaw's rear rail (Photo 13). At the other end, the screw will be housed in the hole in the front block. Tap in the garter to lock the screw in position. Finish by fastening the rub rail (Q) to track the guide bar as the vise opens and closes (Photo 14). On this bench, the rub rail reinforces the notch in the base that houses the guide rail. If your installation doesn't allow notching the base, this rub rail is essential for the vise to track properly.

Cutting List

Section	Part	Name	Qty.	Material	Th x W x L
End Beam	A	Left end beam	1	Maple	1¾" x 3¾" x 25½" (a)
	B	Right end beam	1	Maple	1¾" x 3¾" x 27¼" (b)
	C	Dovetailed key	10	Maple	⅝" x ⅞" x 4" (c)
Wooden Screw	D	Screw	1	Maple	3" dia. x 20¼"
	E	Handle	1	Maple	1¼" dia. x 16¾"
Fixed Jaw	F	Fill block	11	Maple	¾" x 3¾" x 4¾" (d)
	G	Rail	2	Maple	1½" x 3¾" x 64½" (e)
Adjustable Jaw	H	Front block	1	Maple	3¾" x 3¾" x 3¾" (f)
	J	Rear rail	1	Maple	1⅞" x 3¾" x 16"
	K	Side	1	Maple	½" x 3¼" x 16" (g)
	L	Top	1	Maple	½" x 3¾" x 14" (h)
	M	Guide bar	1	Maple	¾" x 2" x 33" (j)
	N	Cross brace	1	Maple	1" x 2" x 9¼" (k)
	P	Tongue	1	Maple	⁹⁄₁₆" x ⅝" x 3½"
	Q	Rub rail	1	Maple	¹¹⁄₁₆" x 1½" x 24"
	R	Rabbeted cleat	1	Maple	1" x 2" x 15" (l)
	S	Garter	1	Maple	⅜" x 2¾" x 4" (m)

Notes:
a. For 24" wide bench top; extends 1½" beyond front edge of bench top.
b. For 24" wide bench top; extends 3¼" beyond front edge of bench top.
c. Sides slope at 9°.
d. Ends slope at 5°; ¼" x 1¼" notch at one end. Make two of the fill blocks 8" long.
e. For 80½" long bench, including end caps. Start with 67" long blank.
f. Create by gluing together two 1⅞" x 3¾" x 3¾" blocks.

g. Dovetails are 1⅞" long on one end and 1⅜" long on the other end.
h. Cut ⅝" long dovetail on both ends.
j. Cut ⅜" x 1½" x 1" tenon on one end. Trim length as necessary
k. Cut ⅜" x 1½" x 1" tenon on one end with adjacent ¼" x 2½" rabbet.
l. Cut ⅝" x ¾" rabbet on one edge.
m. On one end, cut a centered 1½" x 1¾" slot with a round bottom.

Rock Solid Bench Support

The face vise on my workbench didn't hold long boards rigidly enough until I added this adjustable "bench slave."

First I milled a board to attach to the leg, making sure it was thick enough to fit flush with the front edge of the benchtop. Then I cut a dado right down the middle of the board, to house a piece of T-track (slotted aluminum track that accepts T-bolts). When I installed the T-track, I left a gap at the top for installing and removing the support block.

Next I drilled two centered holes in the support block, one large enough for the T-bolt to slide through freely, the other small enough for the T-bolt to thread into. I attached a T-style knob to the free-sliding bolt and fastened a toggle clamp over the threaded-in T-bolt.
—*Dave McNeely*

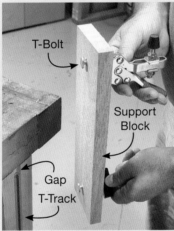

Installing and removing the support block is easy, thanks to a small gap for the T-bolts at the top of the T-track.

T-Bolt

Support Block

Gap
T-Track

Bench Helper

I use this simple device when planing the edges of long boards. It's especially useful when the board is too springy to be clamped between a bench dog and a tail vise. I hold the board in the v-shaped notch with my left hand and plane with my right. Use ½" or ¾" plywood so it doesn't split.
—*Ping Sing Li*

by Richard Tendick

Precision Squares

ESSENTIAL SETUP AND LAYOUT AIDS

Every woodworker falls in love with some favorite tools now and then. I count on my faithful set of precision squares every day, from milling the first rough board to installing the last brass hinge. They're the solid foundation of every successful project.

When I was a young woodworker, though, my first affair with an attractive square ended in bittersweet disappointment. This tool was a real beauty. It had a rosewood handle inlaid with brass and a blued steel blade.

As I gained experience, however, I realized my parts weren't truly square. I blamed everything but the tool itself. One day I compared it to a friend's square. He was a fussy machinist, so his square was true. Mine was way off! My tool was too inaccurate for critical work but too beautiful to throw away.

My pal clued me in to the best features of a good square, how to test it and how to use it— hard-earned know-ledge I'll now share with you.

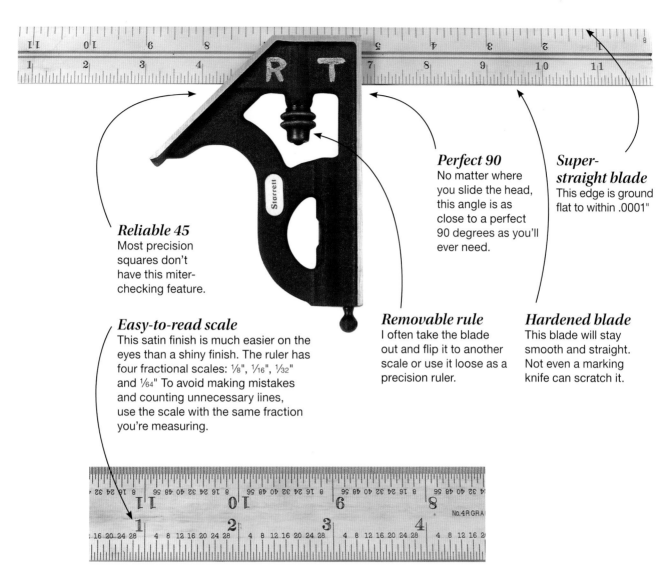

Reliable 45
Most precision squares don't have this miter-checking feature.

Easy-to-read scale
This satin finish is much easier on the eyes than a shiny finish. The ruler has four fractional scales: ⅛", ¹⁄₁₆", ¹⁄₃₂" and ¹⁄₆₄" To avoid making mistakes and counting unnecessary lines, use the scale with the same fraction you're measuring.

Perfect 90
No matter where you slide the head, this angle is as close to a perfect 90 degrees as you'll ever need.

Super-straight blade
This edge is ground flat to within .0001"

Removable rule
I often take the blade out and flip it to another scale or use it loose as a precision ruler.

Hardened blade
This blade will stay smooth and straight. Not even a marking knife can scratch it.

A Classic Precision Square

The most reliable and useful precision square in my shop is a Starrett 12" combination square. Many other finicky woodworkers have told me that they, too, treasure one of these tools. I put my initials on my square and keep it safe in its own special drawer compartment.

Many combination squares aren't very accurate, but this one is made to extremely precise tolerances and is individually checked before it leaves the factory. A good 12" square, like this one, should be no more than .002" out of square at the end of the blade (for comparison, a piece of paper is about .003" thick). Look for a published tolerance this small when you shop for any type of precision square.

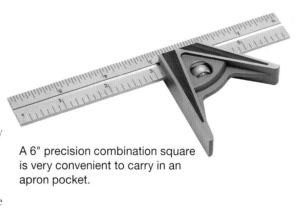

A 6" precision combination square is very convenient to carry in an apron pocket.

How Square Is Your Square?

No matter how fancy a square looks, when it comes to accuracy, I've got to see it to believe it. Inexpensive models, like a 12" fixed-blade machinist's square, should *always* be tested. Here's a new variation on an old method of testing any square.

1 Cut a line down the middle of a piece of tape attached to a melamine board. The bottom edge of the board must be absolutely straight. Check the board's edge against the top of your tablesaw.

2 Peel off the right-hand side of the tape. The contrast between the blue tape and bright white melamine makes the precisely cut edge easy to see.

3 Flip the square and butt it against the tape. They should match perfectly. A gap at top or bottom shows you twice the amount that the square is in error.

How To Check an Edge for Square

Accurately setting up your machines is only half the battle. The acid test comes when you actually test the boards themselves. I always use my 12" square for checking boards that I've crosscut on the tablesaw. For checking a jointed edge, I pull out a smaller square.

The easiest method is to look for light between the square's blade and a jointed edge. Sometimes this isn't practical, though. It's hard to hold a long or heavy board so that there's a good light source behind the square. I really can't trust what I can barely see, so I rely on a feel test with a small, lightweight square that's easy to balance.

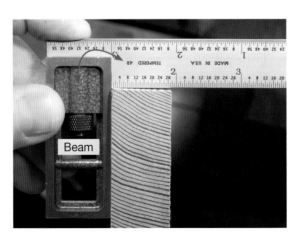

1 Firmly rest the square's beam against the board's left face. Lower the blade to the jointed edge. When it contacts the edge, try to rock the square. It should nest perfectly. If it doesn't, you'll know the left side is high.

2 Rock the square on the other side of the board. Now, you can tell whether the right side is high. I always check both sides before I'm satisfied that my boards are perfectly square.

by Tom Caspar

Make a Shaving Horse

HYBRID DESIGN MAKES SHORT WORK OF GREEN WOOD

Few woodworking experiences are as sweet as working wood that's just been split from a recently felled tree. Green wood is much easier to shape with hand tools than wood that's been dried. It has a pungent odor and soft texture that make it all the more pleasurable to handle. Simple utilitarian items, such as chairs, benches, rakes and so on, have long been made from green wood. All you need are a few basic tools and one essential device for holding the work: a shaving horse.

When I started thinking about how to make one I turned to Drew Langsner, who runs Country Workshops, a school in North Carolina. Drew introduced me to Tom Donahey, who has created an elegant design. "When I got into green woodworking, I already had a shaving horse," Tom said. "It was the old style, big and clunky. I took a class from Brian Boggs, the well-known chairmaker from Berea, Kentucky, and he had brought along his own shaving horse. It was much better than mine. With Brian's permission, I took photos of that horse, went home, and studied its construction."

Brian had developed a new feature: an adjustable, ratcheting work support. Drew suggested a futher change: use a treadle instead of the traditional cross bar for applying foot pressure. "It's much more comfortable," he said. Tom built a few horses, with Brian's permission, and started refining the design. Over the years, Tom has built more than 100 horses and streamlined their production. Tom has graciously allowed us to publish his design.

Choose Your Wood

You can make this shaving horse out of any strong wood, such as oak, ash, hard maple or Douglas fir. Tom Donahey uses southern yellow pine construction lumber because it's economical, strong and relatively lightweight. He's figured out a way to get virtually all the parts of a shaving horse from one 10 ft.-long 2x10 (Photo 1, and Fig. L). Tom selects clear, straight-grained stock for maximum strength.

1 All of the parts for this shaving horse can be cut from southern yellow pine construction lumber. It's a durable, strong wood that's relatively inexpensive, but you could substitute many other hardwoods, such as maple or oak.

Southern yellow pine isn't his top choice for the horse's ratcheting mechanism, however. These pieces take a lot of stress, so he uses hard maple for the pivot piece (K) and sycamore for the ratchet (F). Any wood that's hard to split is suitable for these pieces, though. A wood that's hard to dent, such as maple or white oak, is preferable for the rotating jaw (L), which clamps down on a workpiece.

You'll need a small amount of ¾" Baltic birch plywood for the work support (Q), seat (R), treadle (S) and treadle cleat (T).

Start With the Back Legs

If you're making the horse from a 2x10, it into three pieces: 4 ft., 4 ft. and 2 ft. long (Fig. L). As with any project, parts are easier to mill and join if the wood is flat and straight. If you use southern yellow pine construction lumber, chances are that it's neither flat nor straight. Run these pieces through a planer or drum sander before making any further cuts. It's OK if they end up less than 1½" thick, as specified

2 Cut both back legs from one long blank. Adjust your miter saw to a 15-15 compound angle, then place the blank to the left of the blade and cut the right end. Slide the piece over to cut the middle, then cut the left end.

in the cutting list, as long as they're all the same thickness.

Lay out and cut all the solid-wood pieces to size. The back legs (C) require special attention. It's a good idea to make a couple practice ones

How It Works

A shaving horse is a workbench, vise and chair all rolled into one. It's primarily used to work green wood with a drawknife, which cuts on the pull stroke, or a spokeshave, which you can push or pull. The design of this shaving horse is rather unusual, mixing traditional elements and modern engineering. Here's how it works:

To set up the horse, place your workpiece on the work support. Then, raise the work support up to the clamping jaw, which is free to rotate. The work support will click into one of eight different height positions, to accommodate thick or thin work. It's locked by a pivot that engages a series of ratchets on the work support's column. To clamp your workpiece, push the treadle forward with your foot. This swings the lever arms, squeezing the clamping jaw against the workpiece.

first to get the hang of it. Make both legs from one blank (Photo 2). On your miter saw, tilt the blade to 15 degrees and rotate the table to 15 degrees (Fig. D). Make three cuts at this setting to obtain both legs.

Stand both of the legs together and orient them so they make a matched pair (Photo 3). In order to make the legs splay out and rake back, you'll saw off a wedge-shaped piece from one side of a leg and glue it back to the opposite side. The cutting is easy–it's the layout that's hard. Draw the wedge all around the left leg, as shown in Fig. D, then draw the right leg as a mirror image.

Saw the legs (Photo 4). It's fast using a bandsaw, but you could also use a handsaw. If you orient each leg so that its angled top end leans forward, all you have to do to make the cut using a bandsaw is to follow the one line on the board's top edge. There's no need to tilt the bandsaw table, even though the layout lines seem to call for it. It's a 90-degree cut.

If the wedge-shaped cutoffs cup or distort, sand them until they're flat. Glue the pieces to the opposite sides of the legs they came from (Photo 5). To prevent the pieces from slipping when you clamp, nail some short brads into one piece and clip off their heads near the surface. Press the pieces together by hand, to drive in the brads, before applying clamps.

Drill Holes

Temporarily screw the two rails (A) together. If your stock is a full 1½" thick, plan on drilling shallow holes on both rails to accommodate washers for the bolts that hold on the front leg (B, Fig. B). Without these holes, the bolts will be too short to fully thread through the nuts (although you could use longer bolts and skip the washer holes). Lay out these washer holes on both rails and drill them before drilling the smaller dia. bolt-holes completely through the rails. If, after planing, your stock is 1⅜" thick or so, you can omit the large dia. washer holes. Lay out and drill all the ½" holes for bolts and ⅝" holes for dowels all the way through both rails (Photo 6).

Separate the rails, then clamp each back leg to the appropriate rail and drill through the leg, using the holes in the rail as a guide (Photo 7). Use the same method to drill holes through the rear spacer (M) and front leg. Temporarily assemble the horse and test the fit of the backup bar (H) between the rails. Glue the backup together (H, J, Fig. F), clamp it to one rail, and

3 Stand the two back legs together as a mating pair, then lay out the same cut on each leg, going in opposite directions.

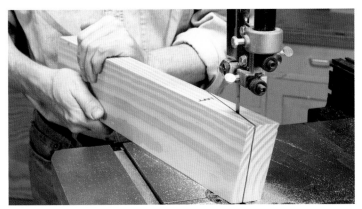

4 Turn over the legs and bandsaw them. This is a simple, straight cut, with the table set at 90°. It looks odd from this angle because the end of the leg is a compound miter.

5 Glue the offcut onto the opposite side of the leg it came from, and you're all set.

drill the dowel holes through it. Use a drill press to make the ⅜" bolt hole that passes through all three pieces of the back-up.

Rout a 5/16"-wide chamfer on all the exposed edges of the rails and legs.

Begin Assembly

Support the rails with boxes or blocks and assemble the rear end of the horse. Install the backup (Photo 8). Note that it's not glued, so you may remove it later for modifications, if necessary.

6 The main body of the shaving horse is composed of two rails running side-by-side. Temporarily screw these boards together, then drill holes for the leg-mounting bolts and other parts.

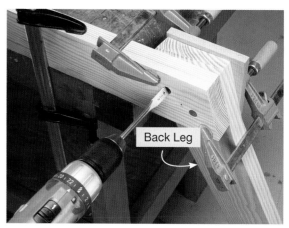

7 Separate the boards, then use the holes as guides. Drill through the rails and into the legs to complete the leg-mounting holes. This horse is easy to disassemble and store when not in use, as all the parts just bolt together.

Back Leg

Back Up

8 After attaching the rear legs, install the "backup" piece with large dowels, but no glue. This part prevents the work support from tipping forward when you apply clamping pressure.

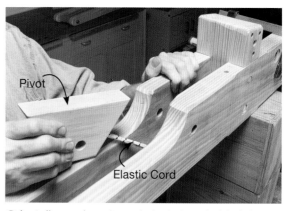

Pivot

Elastic Cord

9 Install a wedge-shaped pivot piece behind the backup. It rotates on a dowel passing through the rails; an elastic cord provides spring tension, allowing the pivot to click into the ratchets on the work support column.

Make the pivot (K and Fig. E). It should be ⅛" thinner than the front leg and rear spacer, so it may swing freely. Drill its hole using the drill press. The pivot is spring-loaded with an elastic shock or bungee cord so that it will automatically tip forward into the ratchets (Photo 9). Attach a 6"-long cord halfway up the pivot's front face using a large electrician's staple. Place the pivot between the rails and pound in the dowel on which it rotates. Clamp the pivot in a horizontal position. Grip the free end of the cord and stretch it back underneath the pivot an extra inch or so to some point on the underside of one rail. Mark the point, then release the cord and remove the dowel and pivot. Fasten the other end of the cord to the rail, then re-install the pivot. Make sure the pivot rotates easily; you may have to sand the middle of its dowel to achieve the proper fit.

Make the Lever Arms

Drill holes in the levers (D) and notch their bottom ends to receive the treadle support (N). Chamfer all four sides of both levers. Note that the distance between the levers is about ¼" greater than the width of the horse's body, so the levers are free to swing without binding. In addition, note that the length of the rotating jaw is about ¼" shorter than the distance between the levers, so it, too, is free to swing. Glue a piece of thick leather to one side of the rotating jaw to help it grip a workpiece. The rotating jaw may be placed in one of three positions; install it in the upper position for now. You may move it later, as needed, without taking the horse apart. The treadle (S) slides in between the treadle support (N) and the treadle cleats (T). To fasten the treadle in place, just use a loose-fitting duplex head nail in a pre-drilled hole or a screw (Fig. A). This arrangement makes the treadle easy to remove.

Bolt together the lever arm assembly. There are two washers that act as spacers between the lever arms and the backup. To install these washers, tape them to the inside faces of the lever arm assembly. Slide the assembly over the horse's front end (Photo 10). Install the bolt through the levers and backup, then remove the tape. Bolt on the horse's front leg.

Build the Work Support

Glue together the ratchet bar (E) and ratchet (F). Plane them 1/16" to 1/8" thinner than the space between the horse's rails. Test the fit of this assembly between the horse's rails. It should easily slide up and down. Lay out the ratchets (Fig. G) and cut them on the bandsaw (Photo 11).

Screw and glue the ratchet cheeks (G) to the ratchet bar. Glue and screw the lower part of the work support to this assembly. Saw a v-shaped notch in the upper half of the work support, then glue and screw it to the lower half. The notch will help hold rounded workpieces.

To install the work support, tilt the lever arm assembly forward. Push down on the pivot's back end and slide the support down between the horse's rails (Photo 12). When you release the pivot, it will spring into one of the ratchets and secure the work support in position.

Add the Seat

Build the seat using plywood, foam rubber and leather or other durable upholstery material (Photo 13). Make the cleat (P) 1/16" thinner than the distance between the rails, so the seat is free to slide back and forth. You're ready to make shavings!

Design Alternatives

These plans are easy to modify to suit your needs or style of work. The seat is about 20" high, so you may want to change the length of the legs if you're tall or short.

Tom Donahey uses bolts and dowels to fasten together the major parts of the horse, which allows the user to take it apart for storage, transportation, modification or maintenance. Alternatively, you could glue the parts together for a classier look, but that would limit your options for making modifications.

Washer

Bolt Hole

10 Install the lever-arm assembly. It swings on a bolt that passes through the backup piece. There's a washer between each lever arm and the back-up, so the arms will swing free. Tape these washers in place beforehand.

11 Saw ratchets on the column that holds the work support. It's made from two pieces glued together. Use a hardwood that's hard to split, such as sycamore or hard maple, for the piece that receives the ratchets.

12 Assemble the work support, then install it by tipping back the spring-loaded pivot piece.

13 When all is assembled, add the seat. It's not fastened down, but slides between the horse's rails. This way, you can easily adjust the seat's position to a comfortable distance from your workpiece.

Fig. A: Exploded View

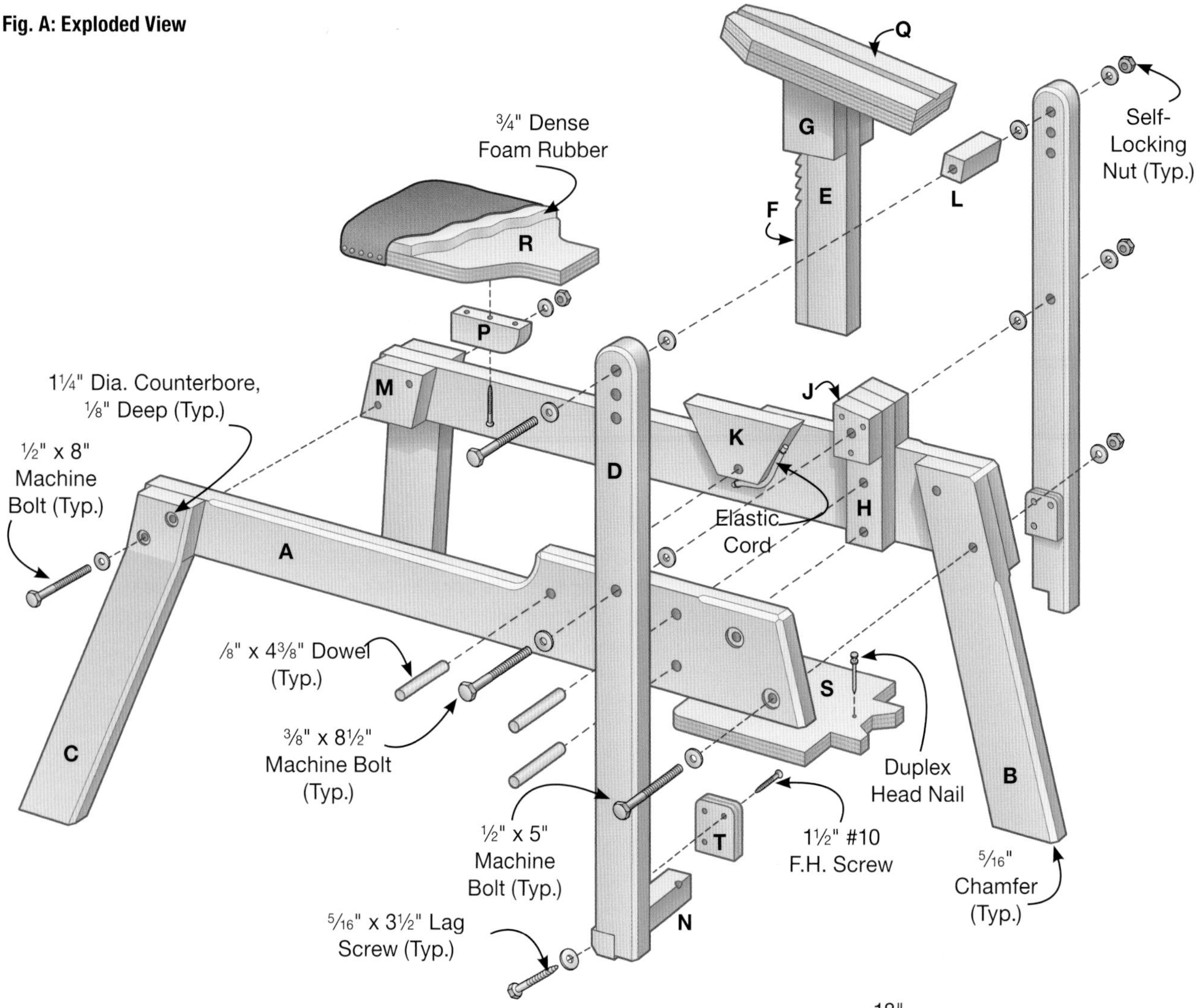
Q
G
E
F
L
Self-Locking Nut (Typ.)
¾" Dense Foam Rubber
R
P
M
1¼" Dia. Counterbore, ⅛" Deep (Typ.)
½" x 8" Machine Bolt (Typ.)
A
C
D
K
J
Elastic Cord
H
B
/8" x 4⅜" Dowel (Typ.)
⅜" x 8½" Machine Bolt (Typ.)
S
Duplex Head Nail
½" x 5" Machine Bolt (Typ.)
T
1½" #10 F.H. Screw
5/16" Chamfer (Typ.)
5/16" x 3½" Lag Screw (Typ.)
N

Fig. B: Rail

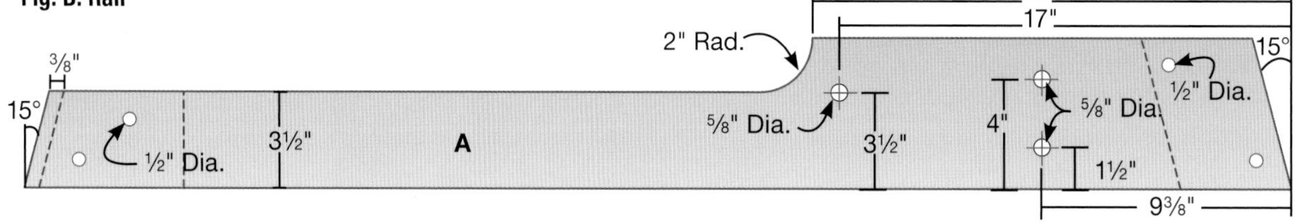
18"
17"
2" Rad.
15°
⅜"
15°
½" Dia.
3½"
A
⅝" Dia.
3½"
4"
⅝" Dia.
½" Dia.
1½"
9⅜"

Fig. C: Front Leg

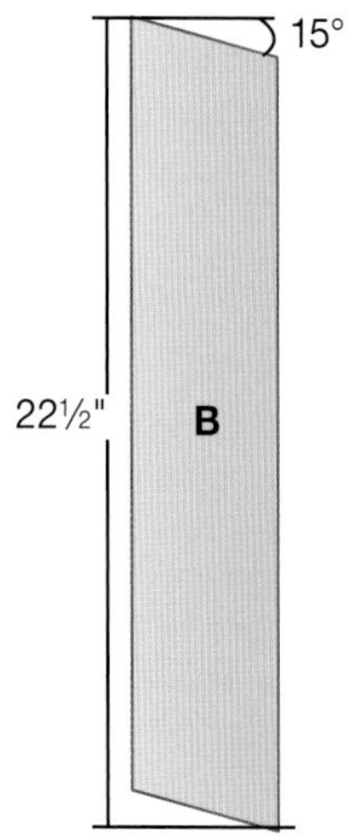
15°
22½"
B

Fig. D: Back Leg

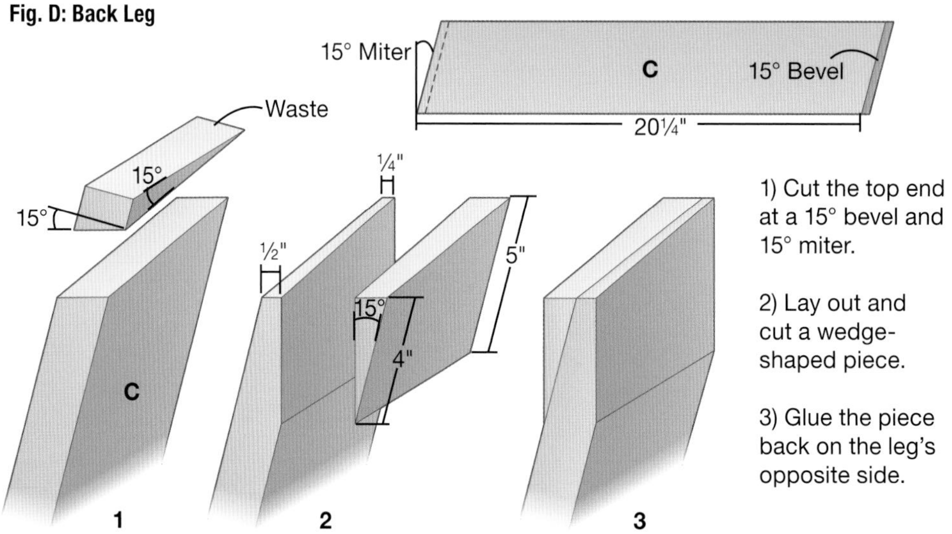
15° Miter
C
15° Bevel
20¼"
Waste
15°
15°
¼"
½"
5"
15°
4"
C
1
2
3
1) Cut the top end at a 15° bevel and 15° miter.
2) Lay out and cut a wedge-shaped piece.
3) Glue the piece back on the leg's opposite side.

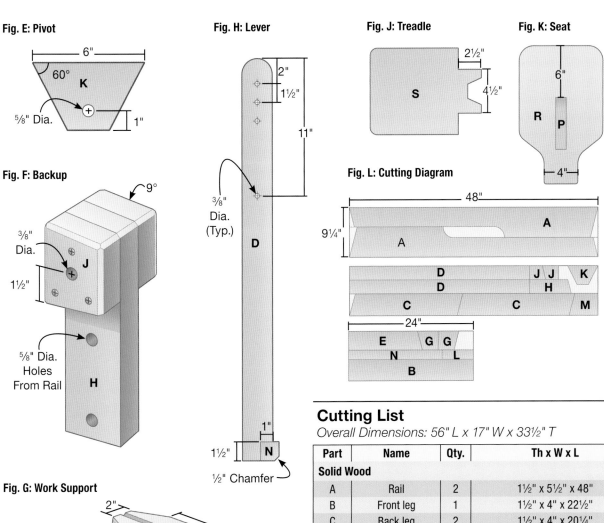

Fig. E: Pivot

6"
60°
K
⁵⁄₈" Dia.
1"

Fig. F: Backup

9°
³⁄₈" Dia.
J
1½"
⁵⁄₈" Dia. Holes From Rail
H

Fig. H: Lever

2"
1½"
³⁄₈" Dia. (Typ.)
D
11"
1"
1½"
N
½" Chamfer

Fig. J: Treadle

2½"
S
4½"

Fig. K: Seat

6"
R P
4"

Fig. L: Cutting Diagram

48"
9¼"
A
A

D   J J   K
D   H
C   C   M

24"
E   G G
N   L
B

Fig. G: Work Support

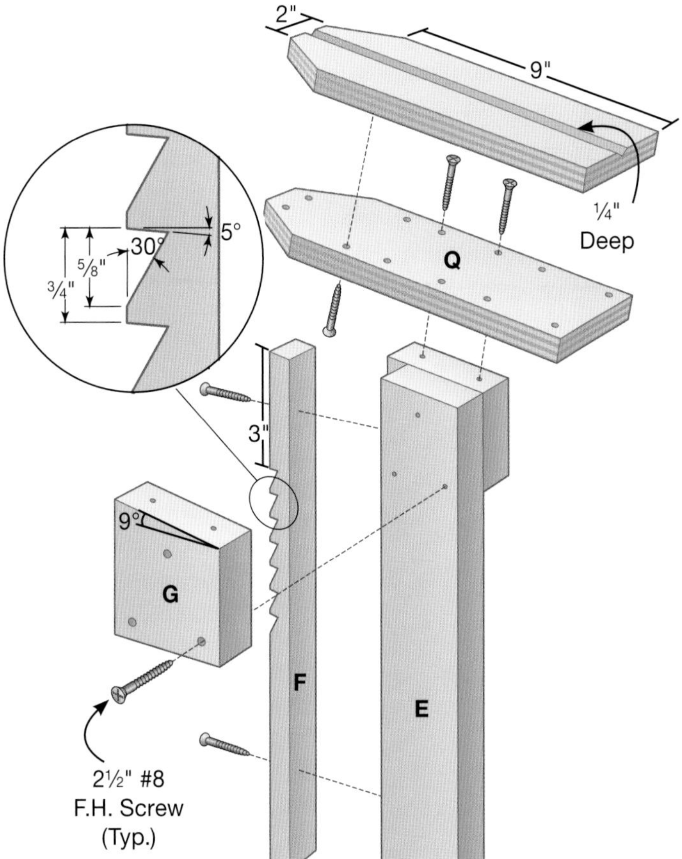

2"
9"
¼" Deep
Q
5°
30°
⁵⁄₈"
¾"
9°
3"
G
F
E
2½" #8 F.H. Screw (Typ.)

Cutting List

Overall Dimensions: 56" L x 17" W x 33½" T

Part	Name	Qty.	Th x W x L
Solid Wood			
A	Rail	2	1½" x 5½" x 48"
B	Front leg	1	1½" x 4" x 22½"
C	Back leg	2	1½" x 4" x 20¼"
D	Lever	2	1½" x 2½" x 32"
E	Ratchet bar	1	1⅜" x 2¾" x 16"
F	Ratchet	1	1⅜" x ¾" x 16" (a)
G	Ratchet cheek	2	1½" x 3½" x 3½"
H	Backup bar	1	1½" x 2½" x 8½"
J	Backup cheek	2	1½" x 2½" x 3"
K	Pivot	1	1⅜" x 3½" x 6" (b)
L	Rotating jaw	1	1½" x 1½" x 4½" (c)
M	Rear spacer	1	1½" x 3½" x 5½"
N	Treadle support	1	1½" x 1½" x 7⅝"
P	Seat cleat	1	1⁷⁄₁₆" x 1¾" x 6"
Plywood			
Q	Work support	2	¾" x 4½" x 11½"
R	Seat	1	¾" x 10" x 16"
S	Treadle	1	¾" x 9" x 12"
T	Treadle cleat	2	¾" x 2½" x 3"
Hardware			
Front leg bolts		2	½" x 5" with 2 SAE washers and a nut
Rear leg bolts		2	½" x 8" with 2 SAE washers and a nut
Lever arm and jaw bolts		2	⅜" x 8½" with 4 washers and a nut
Treadle support lag bolts		2	⁵⁄₁₆" x 3½" with 2 washers
Backup and pivot dowels		3	⁵⁄₈" x 4⅜"
Shock cord		1	⅜" x 6"

(a) Hard maple or sycamore
(b) Hard maple
(c) Hard maple or white oak

by David Pickard

Tool Rack Holds Everything

SLAT CONSTRUCTION MAKES IT EASY AND VERSATILE

Whether you have an exquisite collection of antique tools or the latest in high-tech gear, this versatile wall rack stores them all within easy reach. It's easy to build and adapts to fit virtually any wall space. The 48" by 48" rack shown here is made from poplar, but any hardwood or combination of hardwoods will work. Each tool hanger has a bottom groove that allows it to slip snugly onto any of the slats. This nifty feature makes the hangers easy to move, so you can rearrange your rack to accommodate newly acquired tools.

The biggest—and most fun—challenge this rack presents is figuring out how to modify the hangers to display your unique collection of tools.

Build the Rack

Cut and plane stiles and rails for the rack's frame to 1" thick and 1¼" wide. Their lengths depend on the size of the rack you plan to build. Internal stiles can be spaced up to 24" on center. Dry-assemble the frame and drill pilot holes through the rails and into the end-grain of the stiles. Then screw the frame together (Photo 1).

Plane and cut the horizontal slats to ½" thick and 2⁷⁄₁₆" wide. Leave one slat about ½" oversize in width—plan to attach this slat last. Cut the slats to length to fit your frame.

Make a jig to assure that the slats are consistently spaced, so the ¾" thick hangers will easily slip between them: Simply glue ¹³⁄₁₆" thick spacer blocks flush with the edge of a straight 2" wide board.

With the frame squared and clamped to your bench, align the first slat with the bottom and sides. Pre-dill pilot holes and then fasten this slat with #6 by 1¼" screws. Use your L-shaped spacer jig to position rest of the slats (Photo 2). Regularly check the frame with a square (Photo 3).

Mark the width of the last slat and cut it to fit (Photo 4).

Apply an oil finish and set the rack aside to dry. Finish seals the wood so the rack is less likely to get dirty or stained.

Mount your rack on the wall. The method you use depends on your situation. My shop has wood framing, so I could drill holes through the rack's frame and screw it directly to the studs. If you have concrete block or brick, you'll need to use wall anchors.

Create Custom Tool Hangers

The hangers are nothing more than pieces of ¾" thick hardwood with a bottom groove cut to fit snugly over the ½" thick slats. Use spacers with your dado set, if necessary, to achieve the desired friction fit. Cut the grooves about ⁷⁄₁₆" deep. Most of the hangers you'll make will be less than 2¾" wide, so you can harvest a pair of long slotted blanks from a 6" wide board (Photo 5). I made all the hangers for this rack from an 8' length of 1x6 poplar.

Cutting List

Overall Dimension: 1½" x 48" x 48"

Name	Qty.	Th x W x L
Rail	2	1" x 1¼" x 48"
Stile	3	1" x 1¼" x 45½"
Slats	15	½" x 2⁷⁄₁₆" x 48"

1 The rack consists of slats fastened to a frame. Assemble the frame with one screw at each joint. Clamps hold the frame square during assembly.

13/16"
Spacer Blocks

2 Use an L-shaped jig to assure uniform spacing when you screw the slats to the frame.

3 Check periodicaly to make sure the assembly remains square. Each added slat stiffens the frame.

4 Leave the last slat oversize. Mark the edge and trim the slat to width. This method is easier than trying to exactly size all the parts.

To create custom-fit hangers, lay all your tools onto a large table, then group them according to the types of notches you think they'll require. Sawing slots, installing dowels, drilling holes, chopping mortises or adding lipped edging will accommodate most tools. Rounding the corners makes the hangers more user-friendly. Calculate the spacing for multiple tools such as chisels or wrenches before you start drilling or sawing. You'll find yourself using Forstner bits, files and all kinds of saws to create suitable notches. Don't be afraid to experiment: I even ripped blanks in half, cut notches and then glued the halves back together. Once you've created a couple hangers, you'll get all sorts of ideas.

5 Cut grooves in a long, wide board to make tool hanger blanks. Make the grooves a hair wider than the slats.

A

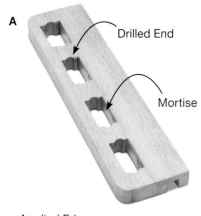

Drilled End

Mortise

Applied Edge

B

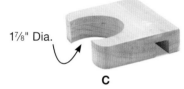

Dado

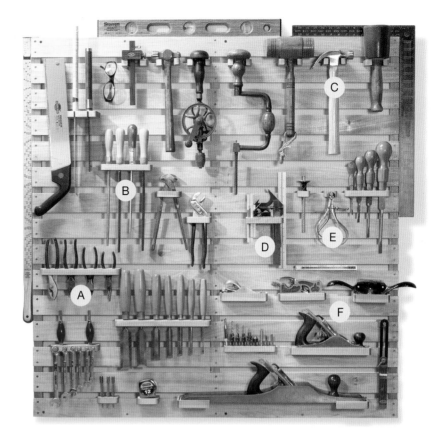

C

B

D

E

A

F

C

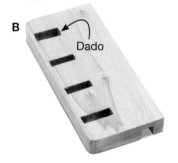

$1\frac{7}{8}$" Dia.

D

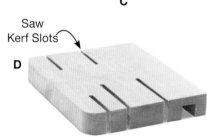

Saw
Kerf Slots

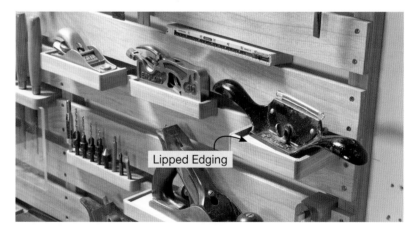

Lipped Edging

E

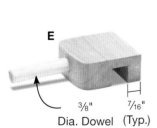

$\frac{3}{8}$"
Dia. Dowel

$\frac{7}{16}$"
(Typ.)

Lipped edging keeps planes
in place. Acrylic shields glued
into grooves protect hands
from sharp edges.

F

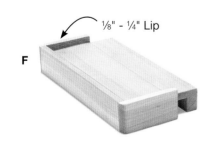

$\frac{1}{8}$" – $\frac{1}{4}$" Lip

Acrylic
Shield

TOOL RACK HOLDS EVERYTHING   95

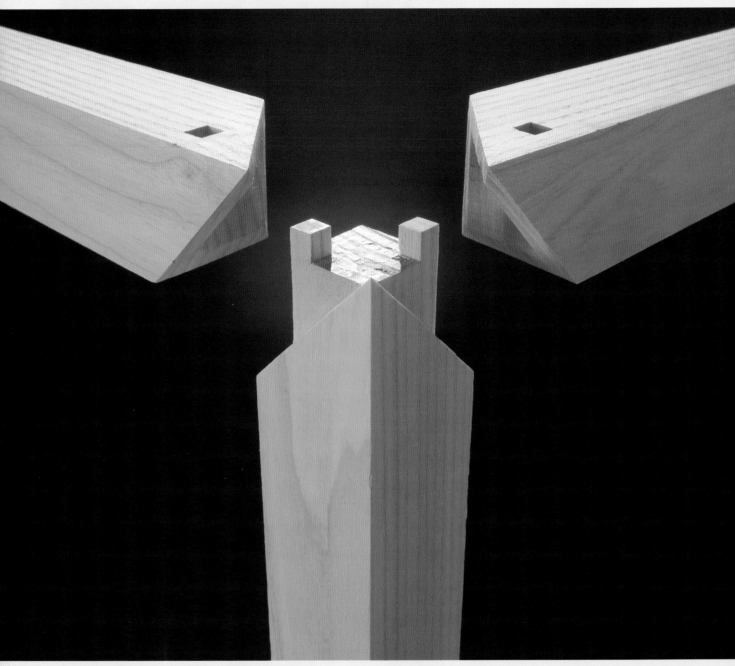

By working with hand tools, you can cut the most
intricate joints, like this three-way locking miter,
which machines simply cannot do.

Joinery Tools
and Techniques

by Tom Caspar

Measuring and Marking

14 TIPS TO MAKE LAYOUT EASIER

Write with Chalk

Lay out "cut here" marks on rough lumber with chalk. Chalk marks are easy to read, even on the scruffiest surface. Unlike ink, pencil or crayon, chalk marks are easy to erase if you change your mind. Just scrub the marks with a stiff wire or bristle brush.

Circle Template

Setting a compass to draw small arcs or circles can be a royal pain, so I cheat and use a plastic template instead. You can generally find one at an office supply store.

Shop-Made Straightedge

Every shop should have a long wooden straightedge. It's got a hundred and one uses, but I primarily use mine for checking jointed and sawn edges, and for guiding my router.

This 4-ft. one is pretty fancy, I admit, but there are good reasons for going to the extra trouble. Most of it is pine, so it's lightweight. It's laminated from strips, so it will stay straight for years. I added a hardwood strip to the bottom to prevent dings. The holes are for hanging this beautiful tool on my wall.

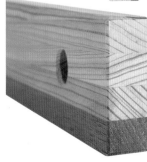

Frame Your Wood

When I lay out door panels, drawer fronts or other highly visible parts, I want to see what they'll look like before I cut. I make a window from two L-shaped pieces of cardboard taped together to find the perfect grain pattern. It's easy to re-adjust for different sized parts.

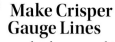

Make Crisper Gauge Lines

I love a wheel-type marking gauge for laying out tenons and dovetails. Its round cutting wheel must be super-sharp to make fine lines across the grain. Sharpening this tiny object looks nearly impossible, but it's really quite easy.

First, unscrew the cutter from the gauge. Place a piece of 320-grit or finer sandpaper on a flat surface, such as ¼" thick glass. Place the cutter on the sandpaper, flat side down, and push it around in circles. This is hard to do with your finger, but it's a cinch when you use the eraser end of a pencil. Don't mess with the cutter's bevel side. Install the cutter in the gauge and make a line across the grain. It should be as crisp as one made by a razor-sharp knife or chisel.

Cutting Wheel

Cutting Wheel

Glass

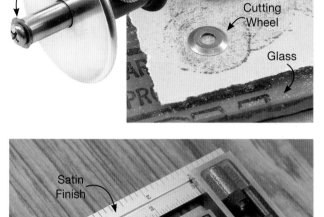

Satin Finish

Bright Finish

Satin Rules Are Easier to Read

If you're thinking about buying a precision rule or square, check its luster first. Tools with a satin or matte finish are much easier to read under all light conditions, especially their teeny-tiny ¹⁄₆₄" divisions. Glare is a big problem with brightly-finished rules. The light must be just right to easily read them.

Mark With A Chisel

A sharp chisel makes an excellent marking knife because it has a single bevel. Double-beveled knives have to be held just so in order for one bevel to snug up against a square. A chisel has to be handled the right way, though. Pull the chisel towards you, with the handle leaning away. If the handle leans toward you, you'll get a ragged line.

Bent-Stick Arcs

Bending a thin stick is a quick way to lay out an arc. Trouble is, it takes two hands to bend the stick. How are you going to draw a line around it?
The answer is to use two thin sticks, taped together at the ends. (My sticks are ⅛" thick and ¾" wide.) Place a spacer of any length between the sticks at their centerpoints. Now your hands are free to draw the arc. Adjust the spacer's length to make arcs of different curvature. Shifting the spacer off the centerpoints creates asymmetrical arcs.

Center Point

Duct Tape

Use A Pen On Dark Wood

Use a blue ballpoint pen to mark dark woods, such as walnut. Its ink is far easier to read than a pencil line.

Customary Marks

These furnituremaker's symbols are an international language. They've been used for generations because they're easy to make and easy to understand.

A board's working face and edge are the surfaces that all measurements are taken from. This dates back to when boards were planed by hand. You couldn't count on every side to be strictly parallel, so two were designated as reference surfaces. It's still a good idea. These marks can mean front and top, too.

The cabinetmaker's triangle is a straightforward method of marking boards to be joined together. Imagine an old-time shop. The master carefully arranges the boards to make the most pleasing pattern, then scrawls this triangle across the boards and hands them off to an apprentice to glue up. These days, this mark is just a handy reminder of what our intentions were when we laid out the boards last weekend!

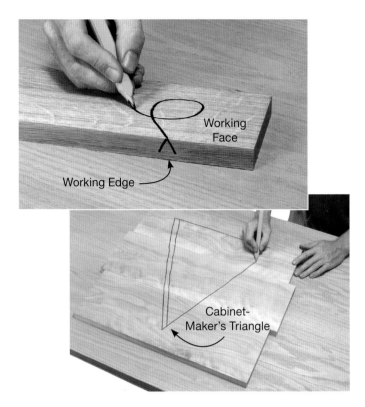

Working Face

Working Edge

Cabinet-Maker's Triangle

Quickie Center Finder

Woodworkers are both cursed and blessed with our hopelessly archaic system of measuring. When it comes time to divide any distance in half, like marking the center of a board's edge for resawing, it's best to avoid arithmetic altogether. A combination square will do the trick; just ignore the numbers.

Finding the center takes no time at all. Set the square to project an amount that appears to be about halfway across the edge of the board. Then draw two lines, one from either side of the board. No matter whether you've guessed too long or too short, the middle of the board lies exactly halfway between the two lines.

For resawing, you can probably just follow a path right between your lines. If you must know the precise center, slightly readjust your square and repeat the process. Chances are you'll be right on.

Center is Halfway Between Pencil Lines

Layout on Metal

A permanent marker works well for laying out marks on machines or tools. Rub the felt-tip marker over the whole area where you need to scribe a mark, let it dry for 30 seconds, and scribe into the ink. The extra ink can be removed with rubbing alcohol or steel wool.

Precision Gauge Lines

Draw a cutting gauge across a board and you should get a razor-sharp line that will become the precise shoulder of a handmade dovetail or tenon. But that's not the kind of line you get with a new gauge, right out of the box. A new gauge makes a pretty wretched line that skips and jumps, with fuzzy, torn edges.

An effective marking gauge knife should have a single bevel and a slightly rounded tip. A single-bevel edge starts the joint off on the right foot. It cuts a groove with one vertical wall and one sloped wall. The vertical wall is the beginning of the joint's square shoulder. The sloped wall goes on the waste side of the joint. (A double-bevel knife makes two sloped walls.) A rounded, fingernail-shaped tip stays sharp longer than a standard triangular point because there's lots more wear surface. You'll rarely have to resharpen it.

Here's how to reshape a new cutting gauge knife on a grinder or belt sander:

1. Remove the knife from the gauge.
2. Bandsaw a 1"-long slot on a 6"-long piece of ⅜" dowel.
3. Insert the knife in the slot. Wrap masking tape around the dowel to hold the knife in place.
4. Grind the knife past the existing bevels. It's only a thin piece of steel, so quench often to avoid bluing.
5. Rotate the dowel on the tool rest to create a rounded bevel. Remove the burr by honing.

Dividing a Board

This one is a chestnut, but everyone ought to know it: You can quickly divide a board into equal widths without complex fractions. Place a ruler diagonally across the surface so you can mark off the number of segments in whole numbers. For example, to divide a board into seven equal parts, place the zero mark on one edge, and place the 7" mark on the other edge. Make a pencil mark at each 1" mark to divide the board.

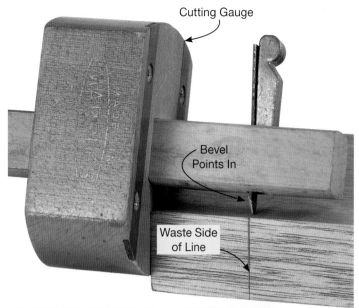

Cutting Gauge

Bevel Points In

Waste Side of Line

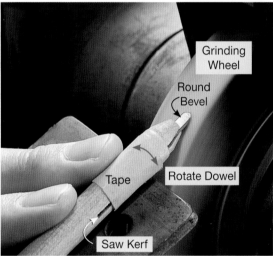

Grinding Wheel

Round Bevel

Rotate Dowel

Tape

Saw Kerf

For Sevenths Place 7 on Edge

by Tom Caspar

Tools for Dovetailing

CHOOSING, MODIFYING AND USING

Cutting dovetails by hand is one of the most satisfying jobs a woodworker can do. Sure, it can be frustrating, because mastering the art requires patience and experience—plus a nice set of tools.

Here's mine. I wouldn't claim that they're the best set for everyone, but they've served me well. I keep them in a box that also functions as a stand.

Layout Tools

A) Square. A 4" to 6" square works best because it's easy to balance. A plain engineer's square can work fine, but when you must mark the same measurement many times over, a square with a sliding blade and rule is handier.

B) Sliding T-bevel. This tool is for laying out dovetail angles. Some people prefer small T-bevels, but I prefer a large one. A large bevel allows me to draw long layout lines, which are easier to sight along than short ones.

C) Saddle square. This tool is a nice luxury—it allows you to draw a line across the end of a board and a mating line down its face at the same time. The two lines will always meet. Of course, you can draw these two lines in separate steps using a regular square, but sometimes you'll make a mistake and they won't line up. A saddle square takes the risk out of the operation.

D) Cutting gauge. This tool is used for scoring the baselines of a dovetail joint across the grain. When sharp, it should make a line as fine as one made by a surgeon's knife. Most cutting gauges come with knives that are sharpened to a point. I modified mine to have a round profile by rotating it along its axis on a grinder. A round profile will stay sharp much longer because it has more points of contact with the wood. A point only has one.

E) Striking knife. This tool is used for laying out very fine lines. I prefer a knife with a flat side and a beveled side, rather than two beveled sides (like a utility knife). Bearing the flat side against a square or a dovetail makes it easier to draw an accurate, unwavering line.

F) Pencils. Mechanical pencils never need sharpening, right? I use two—one with a .5mm lead, for drawing layout lines, and the other with a .7mm lead, for shading in waste.

Cutting and Chopping Tools

G) Dozuki saw. A Japanese-style pull saw takes a little getting used to, but it's an awesome tool. It requires very little effort to cut, so you can concentrate on following a line rather than fighting the saw. I've got nothing against a good Western-style saw, which cuts on the push stroke, but it will require occasional sharpening and setting. Both operations can be quite difficult. Most Japanese saws don't need to be sharpened—ever. When a blade gets dull, you replace it with a new one. Japanese saws come with short or long blades; I prefer a long blade because it requires fewer strokes to cut to the same depth. Each stroke introduces the possibility of error, so the fewer strokes you make, the straighter your cut will be.

H) Coping saw. This saw is used to remove the bulk of the waste from a joint before the remainder is chopped away. A fancy model certainly isn't necessary, but you should use a high-quality blade with the appropriate number of teeth for the work at hand. I prefer a blade with 15 teeth per inch—not too fine, but not too aggressive, either.

I) Chisels. I use two sets of chisels. One set has square sides, while the other has sides that taper to a sharp point. I use the first set for paring and hone them at 25°. (A low angle makes a chisel easier to push.) I use the second set for chopping and hone them at 30°. (The steeper the angle, the longer an edge will last.) The tapered edges of the second set allow me to get into angled corners, so I rarely have to use a skew chisel to clean out a dovetail. The tapers are angled at 12° and run back about

¾". I created the tapers by using a grinder.

J) Mallet. I prefer a round mallet to one with a square head. Both will work fine, of course, but you have to pay more attention to how you hold a square mallet to avoid a glancing blow. A round mallet is more forgiving. I like a mallet with some heft—about 16 to 20 oz. The extra weight means you don't have to strike a chisel with so much force. Just dropping a heavier mallet on a chisel often does the job.

K) Strop. Stropping a chisel renews its edge in just a few seconds. Stropping is easiest when a chisel's edge is hollow-ground—you just balance the edge on heel and toe and go for it. I hone my dovetail chisels the same way, without a jig, to make them easier to strop.

L) Thin blades. I use these blades for paring the sides of skinny sockets. One of the blades is just a block-plane iron; I made the other from a broken-off power hacksaw blade, wrapping tape around one end to make it more comfortable to hold.

M) Shims. These are the set of playing cards below, in case you were wondering. Years ago, while in business, I made dovetails by the artisan's quick method of sawing and chopping to a line. These days, I slow down. I saw and chop away from a line, then pare to a line using a guide block and shims. The block is clamped right on the line. I place a few shims against the block and remove one after each shaving. My rule of thumb: The thinner the shaving, the more accurate the paring.

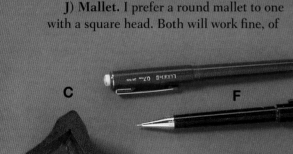

by Tom Caspar

Half-Blind Dovetails

NEW APPROACH ENSURES A PRECISION FIT

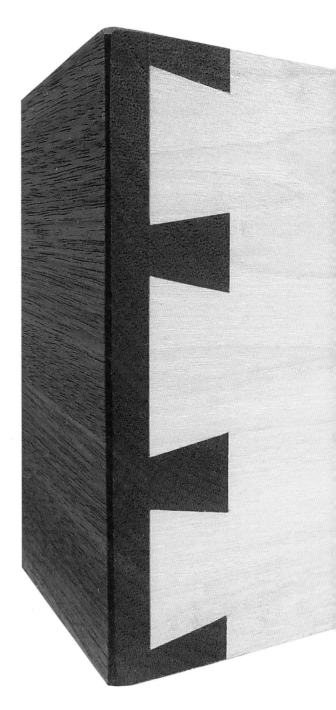

The handmade half-blind dovetail joint is an enduring symbol of fine craftsmanship. Every proud woodworker who has conquered the dovetail wants to show it off. In the old days, when every piece of wood was worked by hand, mastering this joint took lots of practice. But not today. Using machined parts and my new method, you can make perfect half-blind joints the very first time you try. There's no fussy trial-and-error fitting.

Generally, a woodworker can follow one of two paths to make dovetails by hand. The classic artisan's method requires going for broke and sawing precisely on a line. It's fast and rewarding, but it takes a sure eye and a steady hand. The second, more cautious, approach allows you to saw away from a line, then pare to the line using a chisel. It's slower, but by guiding the chisel with a jig, anyone can do it. That's the method I'll show you here. The secret is to use very sharp chisels with specially ground sides (Photo 16), and stick to the directions.

My method relies on a few simple jigs to guide your chisel. Every paring cut is straight and square. It's not the fastest way to cut dovetails, but when you use it, I can promise you precise joints, even your first time.

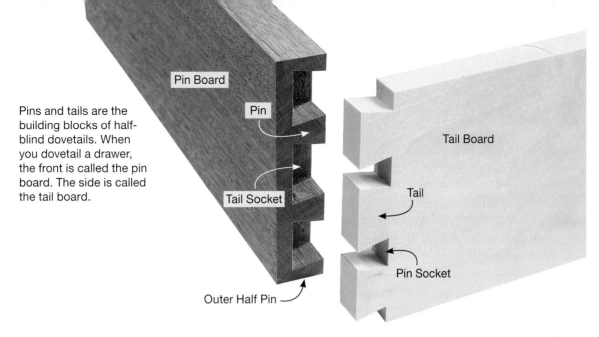

Pins and tails are the building blocks of half-blind dovetails. When you dovetail a drawer, the front is called the pin board. The side is called the tail board.

Pin Board

Pin

Tail Socket

Outer Half Pin

Tail Board

Tail

Pin Socket

Tools and Materials

You'll use ⅜" (10-mm) and 1" (26-mm) chisels for paring. These should be high-quality tools, so their edges stay razor-sharp. For chopping end grain, it's best to use a ½" firmer chisel, but a bench chisel will do. For paring into corners, grind a 12-degree skew angle on a ⅜" or ½" standard bench chisel (Photo 36). You only need a left or a right skew, not both. You'll also need a sliding bevel gauge, a small square, a Japanese dozuki saw or a dovetail saw, a coping saw with a 10-tpi blade and a mallet or hammer.

Wood selection is important. For easy paring, the drawer front, or pin board, should be straight-grained and moderately dense. Walnut, cherry and mahogany are excellent choices. The drawer side, or tail board, should be light in color and also easy to pare. Basswood is the best choice, but white pine and yellow poplar are good, too.

To start, machine each piece flat and square. Make the three guide jigs (Figs. A, B and C). Orient the drawer side so the grain on its face runs toward the back. This makes the completed joint easier to plane flush. Sharpen your chisel, and let's begin.

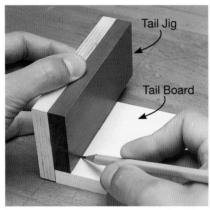

1 Draw a pencil line across the tail board to indicate the dovetails lengths. Here, you'll use the first of three simple jigs (Fig. A). This is the tail jig. I've painted its components so they're easy to see.

Tail Jig

Tail Board

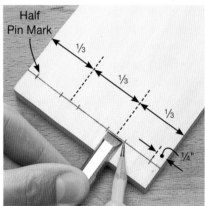

2 Draw a pair of marks for each pin socket. Evenly space the sockets by eye. Make each mark 1/32" on either side of a ⅜" chisel. This ensures that the chisel will fit inside a completed socket. Draw marks for the outer half-pins.

Half Pin Mark

⅓   ⅓   ⅓   ¼"

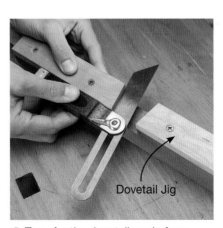

3 Transfer the dovetail angle from a jig to a sliding bevel gauge. The dovetail jig has two equal angles precisely cut on the tablesaw (Fig. C). This jig will guide your paring cuts in the final steps.

Dovetail Jig

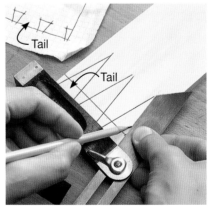

4 Lay out the tails. Draw long, fine lines through each pin mark to make triangles. Each one forms a tail. Refer to a sketch so the lines angle the right way. Flip the square as needed, so most of its handle always butts against the board's end.

Tail

Tail

5 Draw square lines across the board's end to complete the tails. Shade the pin sockets between the tails to clearly indicate the waste areas you'll remove.

Tail

6 Clamp a thick, wide board to the tail board. Position it 1/16" above the pencil line you drew in the first step (Photo 1). Use a small square to check the distance. Raise the boards to a comfortable sawing height.

7 Rough-cut the tails. Saw 1/32" inside each pencil line, within the darkened waste area. Keep the saw level and stop when you reach the guide board.

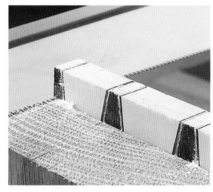

8 Remove the half-pin waste pieces at both ends of the tail board. Like the last saw cuts, these cuts are approximate. Saw level along the top of the guide board, being careful not to cut into the tails.

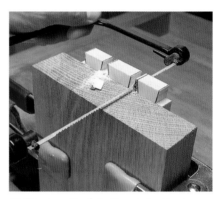

9 Remove the full-pin waste pieces with a coping saw. First, make one diagonal cut. Then come back across, flush with the guide board, to release the waste piece. Now you're ready to pare the tails exactly on the layout lines.

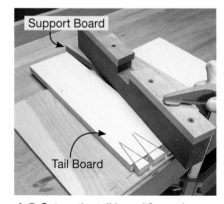

Support Board

Tail Board

10 Set up the tail board for paring. Place a piece of scrap plywood under it to protect the bench. Clamp the dovetail jig precisely along one of the angled layout lines. Support the jig, if needed, with another piece that is the same thickness as the tail board.

11 Pare the tail using a 1" chisel. It's easy to balance along the jig's side. The thinner the shaving, the better. To control each shaving's thickness, begin with one or more playing cards against the jig. Remove one card after each stroke.

12 Pare the last shaving with the chisel against the jig. For a super-smooth cut, work your way in from the end of the tail, taking one-third of a full shaving's width at a time. Reposition the dovetail jig on the other layout lines to pare both sides of each tail.

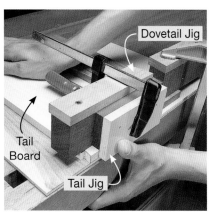

13 Set up the jig to pare each socket's end grain. First, loosely clamp the dovetail jig on top of the support board.

14 Clamp the tail jig to the dovetail jig. Slide the tail board to butt up against the tail jig. Place and tighten a clamp to the left of the tail board and remove the tail jig. Tighten the support board clamp.

15 Pare the end grain. Use playing cards again to minimize each shaving's thickness. You may have to start with three or four cards. Drive the chisel with a mallet, if necessary.

16 Bear against the jig on the last cut. To pare into these acute corners, grind 12-degree bevels on both sides of your chisel. Extend the bevels back ¾" A 12-degree bevel is slightly steeper than the 10-degree dovetail angle.

17 Clean the corners by paring from the end. Then pare from above, as in the last step, to release the shaving. Your tails are now perfectly straight, smooth and square to the board's face. They almost look machine-made!

18 Prepare the pin board to make very fine layout lines easier to see. Coat its end with a primer coat of shellac or varnish, followed by white correction fluid. Primer prevents the white fluid from penetrating into the end grain.

19 Clamp a third jig, the pin jig (Fig. B), to the pin board's outside face. Score a fine line across the board's end with the corner of the wide chisel. One light pass will do it. This is the baseline for the tail sockets.

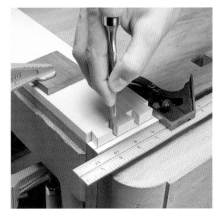

20 Clamp the pin board level with the support board from Photo 10. The pin board must be rock-solid for laying out the pins. Prevent the vise from racking by inserting a spacer that's the same thickness as the pin board.

21 Mark the pin board by lightly pushing on a chisel butted to the side of each tail. This leaves a distinct, super-thin line. Butt the tail board's end to the scribed line (Photo 19). Use a square to align the pin and tail boards.

22 Clamp the tail jig to the pin board's inside face and scribe another line with your chisel. This line indicates the pins' depth. After assembly, the pins will be flush with the tails, which makes gluing and clamping easier.

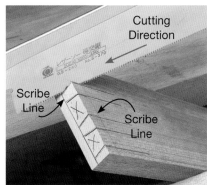

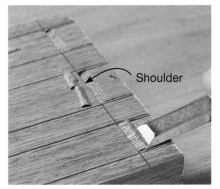

23 Draw the pins on the board's inside face. Go well beyond the scribe line. The longer the lines, the easier they will be to follow when you saw. Shade or mark Xs in the waste areas, or tail sockets, between the pins.

24 Saw the pins. Stay 1/32" inside the lines. Stop short of both scribe lines. Clamp the pin board diagonally in the vise so you can see both faces. This enables a pull saw to cut smoothly, because it's cutting with the grain.

25 Pare at a shallow angle to create small shoulders in each tail socket. Clamp the board down, push almost to the scribe line, twist and lift out a thin chip. These shoulders will guide the chisel in future paring cuts.

26 Chop the tail sockets. Hit the chisel once, straight down, 1/32" away from the shoulders. Switch to a 1/2" firmer chisel for this heavy-duty work. Reserve your bench chisels for paring. Sharpen the firmer chisel at a durable 35-degree angle.

27 Make chips! After each downward chop, lower the chisel, bevel down and split off a thick chip with a single blow into the end grain. Twist the chip to pry it loose. Continue chopping downward and sideways until you're within 1/16" of the lower scribe line.

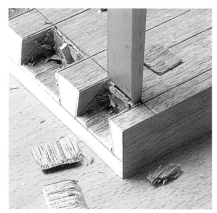  

28 Finish chopping the shoulders right on the scribe line. Rest the chisel against the small shoulder (Photo 25), hold it plumb and strike one blow. By taking a thin shaving, you'll make a crisp, clean, deep shoulder.

29 Lean the chisel a few degrees on the second blow; continue at that angle to the bottom of the tail socket. This traditional undercut ensures the joint goes together without any gaps along the scribed line.

30 Pare to the scribe line. Clamp the pin jig to the pin board once more, and use the playing card technique to remove thin shavings. Pare into the corners with the bevel-sided chisel.

 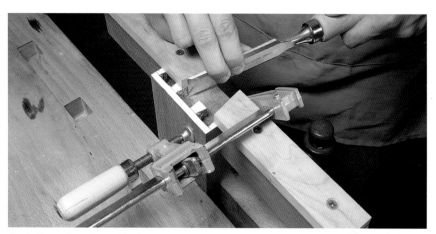

31 Remove the shavings by cutting them off at the base. Push hard and give a little twist; they'll pop right out. Don't bother for now with the shavings stuck in the corners.

32 Pare the pins with the dovetail jig. Clamp it to the pin board. Align one side of its notch with one of the saw cuts to remove a thin shaving with the wide chisel. This will be a sneak-up-to-the-line approach, without using playing cards.

33 Tap the dovetail jig after each shaving to shift the notch closer to the pin layout line. Pare again. Each shaving should be very thin, so you can easily make an accurate cut. You don't have to loosen the clamp, because the jig shifts so little.

34 Make the last paring cut right on the layout line. This method is so precise that you can split a hair, which is about the thickness each of these layout lines cut into the paint. Pare all the pins this way.

35 Pare the corners from above. The chisel's beveled edge lets you get right into this tight angle.

36 Clean out the corners with a homemade skew chisel. Push the chisel into the corner, twist it and pop out the shavings. For a right corner, flip over the chisel and use it bevel down. This tool does the job very quickly.

37 Test the joint's fit. The pin and tail boards should go together without any additional work and end up flush. If seating the joint requires more than light hammer taps, use the dovetail jig to pare the pins that are tight.

38 Even up the joint after it's glued. It only takes a light sanding or a few plane strokes to remove the white paint and make the pins flush with the tails. Now you'll see how tight the fit really is!

Fig A: Tail Jig

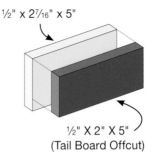

½" x 2⁷⁄₁₆" x 5"

½" X 2" X 5" (Tail Board Offcut)

The secret to success with these jigs is to use actual pieces from your drawer. The blue piece below is an offcut from a drawer side, or tail board. In drawer making, a tail board is typically ½" thick, but any thickness will work with this system. Glue or nail the pieces together with brads.

Fig. B: Pin Jig

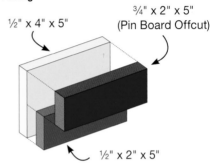

¾" x 2" x 5" (Pin Board Offcut)

½" x 4" x 5"

½" x 2" x 5"

The accuracy of this jig is also based on using offcuts. The red piece is an offcut from a drawer front, or pin board. In drawer making, a pin board is typically ¾" thick, but any thickness will work. The blue piece is a second offcut from a tail board.

Fig. C: Dovetail Jig

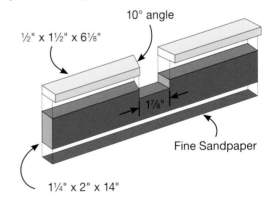

10° angle

½" x 1½" x 6⅛"

1⅞"

Fine Sandpaper

1¼" x 2" x 14"

After gluing the parts together, cut the angles in this jig on the tablesaw. Check the cuts with a sliding bevel gauge to make sure the angles are exactly the same. Glue a piece of sandpaper to the jig's bottom. This prevents the jig from moving when you clamp it to a workpiece.

Sawing Tips

Pull Saw Miter Box

Short lengths of molding can be awkward—and sometimes dangerous—to cut with power tools. It's better to cut them by hand, using a Japanese pull saw and a shop-made miter box.

Make the two guide blocks for the miter box from a 1½" x 4" x 12" blank. Crosscut the blank in half on the tablesaw or with a miter saw. Next, using paper or playing cards, make up two spacers that are exactly equal to the thickness of your saw's blade. (The blade of this saw is the same thickness as one playing card.)

To glue the blocks to a base, place the spacers between the blocks and clamp the blocks end-to-end. Next, clamp a straight, stout piece of wood across the front of the blocks to pull them into alignment. Finally, glue this assembly down to the base. Don't remove the spacers until the glue is dry.

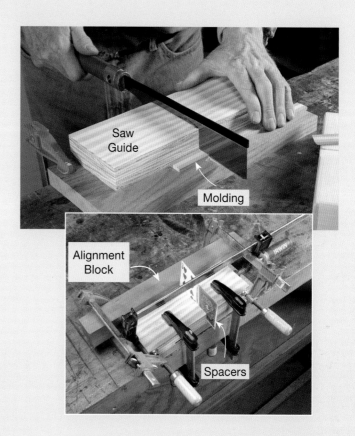

Coping Saw Blade Direction

Should the teeth of a coping saw blade point toward the handle or away from the handle?

The blade can go either way, but you'll get the best results when its teeth face towards the object that supports the workpiece. This way, the workpiece won't rattle or vibrate when you saw.

If your workpiece is supported flat on your workbench, and you pull from below, face the teeth towards the handle (top photo).

If your workpiece is supported in a vise, and the line you're cutting is close to the vise's jaws, the teeth can go either way.

If you raise the workpiece in a vise to get a better view, it's a good idea to steady it with a support block clamped from behind and out of your line of sight (bottom photo). Install the blade with the teeth pointing away from the handle. Cut on the push stroke.

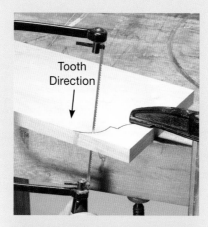

When the work is supported from below, on the handle side, the teeth should face down. You cut on the pull stroke.

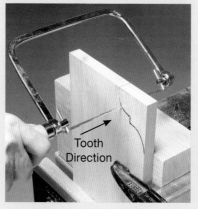

When the work is supported from behind, the teeth should face away from the handle. You cut on the push stroke.

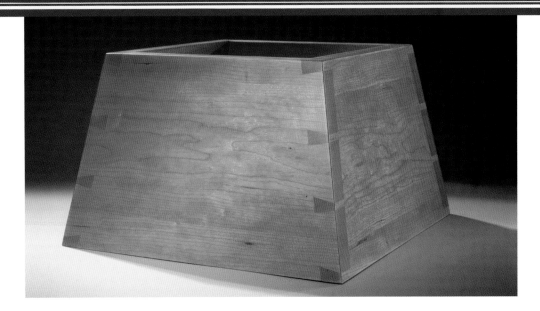

by Tom Caspar

Compound-Angle Dovetails

AN ELEGANT LAYOUT SYSTEM

Compound-angle dovetails are some of the most beguiling joints in all woodworking. But, as John Lennon once suggested, they can be as difficult to make as "fixing a hole in the ocean." Well, maybe not that hard—but it all begins with figuring out those odd angles.

I've developed a system that makes layout easy. It's based on very simple and familiar geometry (see The Basics). It's universal, too: This system works for a project with any amount of splay and for dovetails of any pitch.

Before laying out the dovetails, your boards must be cut at the correct compound angle to form tight-fitting butt joints.

We'll lay out the pins first, rather than the tails. As you follow the photos, there are a couple of small details that I'd like to emphasize. First, be sure to draw the dovetail triangles (Photo 3) on the inside face of the pin boards. (If you draw them on the outside face, the angles you transfer to the edge of the boards will come out backwards.) Second, always keep track of which side of your sliding bevel is facing up or out. I use a piece of tape to mark one side—just to be sure. Now, let's start.

Fig. 1

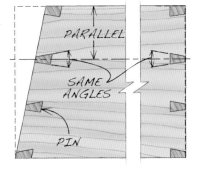

Fig. 2

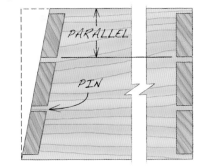

The Basics

When it comes right down to it, there are only two things you have to know about compound-angle dovetails.

First, the ends of the pins (Figure 1) slant just like standard through dovetails. It's the tapered side of the board that makes the angles look strange.

Second, the sides of the pins (Figure 2) are parallel to the top and bottom edges of the board, just like standard dovetails.

1 Draw a horizontal line across the inside face of one of the pin boards. The exact position of the line isn't important.

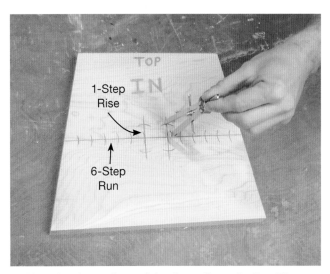

2 Mark the rise and run of the dovetails on the line. These dovetails have a pitch of 1:6, but you can use any pitch you wish.

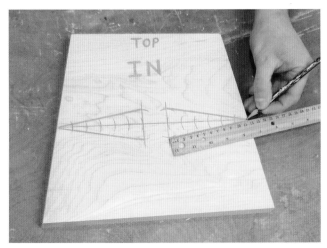

3 Draw two triangles. Think of these as representing the ends of really large pins.

4 Adjust a sliding bevel to match the right side of a triangle. Put a piece of tape on your square—this side should always face out or up in the next steps.

5 Mark the right sides of all the pins. If necessary, you can rotate the bevel to draw a line, but always keep its taped side facing up.

6 Reset the sliding bevel to the left side of the triangle.

Half Pin

7 Draw the left sides of all of the pins. Note that the line on the far right is actually the *left* side of a half pin.

8 Reset the bevel to the splay angle of the board.

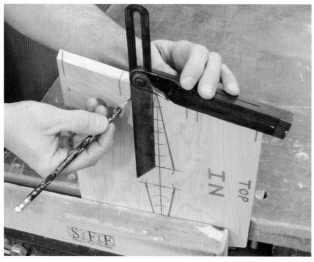

9 Draw the sides of the pins. Repeat the same process, starting with Photo 4, on the other end of the board.

10 Adjust a marking gauge to the width of one edge. Note that this is slightly longer than the thickness of the board.

11 Scribe the shoulders of the pins on both sides of the board.

12 Shade in the pins and compare opposing sides. If all the pins slant the correct way, start sawing!

by Peter Korn

Mortise and Tenon

A HAND-TOOL WORKOUT

For me hand-tool joinery is a connection to the rhythms of traditional woodworking. I enjoy the communication between the work, the tools and my hands, and I find hand-cut joints are as accurate as can be.

Mortise and tenon joints are particularly easy to cut by hand. They're simple to make and it doesn't take years of practice to produce joints that fit well.

The drawings show the technique I like to use, which is fairly conventional. But there are a few tips I'll stress that can improve accuracy.

First, use a sharp knife—not a pencil—when laying out the shoulders and mortise ends. It is easier to work to the exact edge the knife cuts than to figure out which part of a broad pencil mark indicates where to saw or chisel.

Second, I always make small cuts to the shoulder lines on the tenon and to the mortise ends. This forms a V-groove that helps guide my chisel and saw.

Finally, when making the shoulder cuts on the tenons, I first saw diagonally at each corner, using a fine-toothed backsaw that leaves a thin kerf. This makes it easy to saw across and down accurately. When I've cut all four shoulders on the diagonal, I finish with straight-across cuts down to the tenon line, using the existing kerfs to guide the saw.

Mortise

Make mortise one-third the thickness of stock.

1. Mark layout lines with square, knife and mortising gauge.

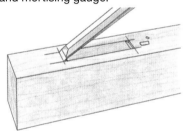

2. Cut small grooves at both ends of mortise.

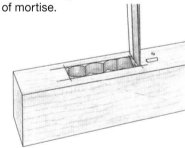

3. Drill out waste, then place chisel in groove and chop straight down to square ends of mortise.

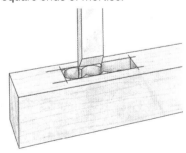

4. Square sides of mortise.

Tenon

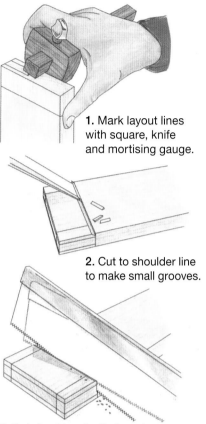

1. Mark layout lines with square, knife and mortising gauge.

2. Cut to shoulder line to make small grooves.

3. Cut shoulders by first sawing diagonally at each corner, then connecting these cuts by sawing straight across to depth of tenon.

4. Make cheek cuts by repeating technique used to cut shoulders.

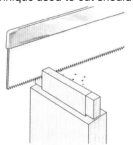

5. Re-mark shoulder lines and saw tenon to width. Then, pare tenon to fit mortise.

by Tom Caspar

Breadboard Ends

THEY'LL HOLD A SOLID-WOOD TOP FLAT

Breadboard ends are old devices for improving a solid-wood top. They act like cleats to hold the top flat, which is particularly important when there's minimal understructure, such as on a trestle table. Breadboard ends also cover end grain, which can help prevent a top from cracking. They're often used on boards for kneading dough or cutting bread (thus the name), but breadboard ends have also traditionally been used on dining tables, kitchen work tables, desks, library tables, and workbenches.

Cabinetmakers realized long ago that breadboard ends add visual interest, too. As your eye scans down the length of a top with breadboard ends, it stops at an end piece, turns, follows it, and returns down the tabletop. The ends keep your eye moving, making a top look more dynamic.

Narrow breadboard ends, like those used on cutting boards, are usually held on with a simple tongue and groove joint. Breadboard ends that are over 1½" wide or so benefit from a stronger joint. Making this joint on a big tabletop can be a bit of

Inside a Breadboard Joint

A wide breadboard end needs plenty of support, so it won't break off if somebody leans on it. That support is provided by a series of long tenons, which fit into deep mortises.

The trick in designing this joint is to accommodate wood movement. As humidity changes with the seasons, a tabletop expands and contracts across the grain. The breadboard end won't get shorter and longer, though: its length stays the same. To allow the top to move inside the breadboad end, most of the tenons are ¹⁄₁₆" to ⅛" narrower than their mortises. The center tenon is the same width as its mortise. This equalizes the amount that both sides of the top will move.

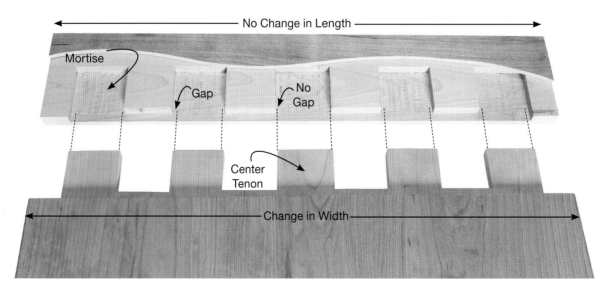

No Change in Length

Mortise

Gap

No Gap

Center Tenon

Change in Width

a problem, though. Here's a method using portable electric tools and hand tools that will work with a top of any size.

Prepare the Top

Breadboard end joints are very difficult to make if your top is slightly cupped. It pays to do whatever you can to ensure that the top is flat when you glue it up, such as clamping heavy battens across the ends. If your top is still cupped, despite your best efforts, you can clamp it flat to a workbench while you make the joints. You'll be flipping the top over now and then, though, which will be awkward.

You may also use a belt sander or a large plane, such as a No. 6 or a No. 7, to flatten a cupped top (Photo 1). This requires skill and practice, whichever tool you use. It's important to flatten both sides, because they will be reference surfaces for making the tenons. Measure the thickness of your top at both ends when you're done. It should be the same all the way across, to make the joints easier to fit. It also helps if both ends are the same thickness.

Next, make the ends straight and square. The easiest way to do this is to use a router, a wide guide board, and a top-bearing flush trim bit (Photo 2). Make the guide board from ¼"- or ½"-thick hardboard or MDF, about 12" wide and 3 to 4" longer than the width of your top. Clamp a sacrificial piece to the right side of the guide board to prevent tearout on the top's edge.

Mortise the Ends

Mill the breadboard ends the same thickness as the top. Make an extra piece to test your setups along the way. Their width is up to you; on a long or wide top, such as a dining table, ends that are 2½" to 4" wide look about right; the ends shown here are 3½" wide.

Cut a stopped groove down the length of both end pieces using a plunge router and edge guide (Photo 3). Use a bit that's about one-third the thickness of your top (a ¼" dia. bit for a ¾" top, for example). Make the groove about ⅜" deep. Center the groove as precisely as you can. Stop the groove about 1" shy of both ends. You could run the groove the full length of the pieces, but the ends of the finished joint won't look as neat.

Lay out and cut mortises in the end pieces (Photo 4). Their width and spacing is your call; just be sure to leave plenty of room between them, so as not to unduly weaken the end pieces. Make

1 Your top must be flat before cutting breadboard-end joints. If it's cupped, plane across the grain to remove the high spots. This advanced technique requires skill and practice.

2 Rout a square, straight end on the tabletop using a guide board and a top-bearing flush trim bit.

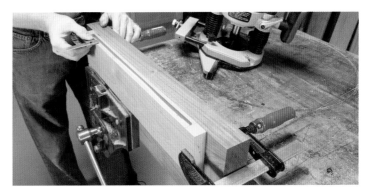

3 Make the end pieces next. Use a plunge router to cut a shallow, stopped groove down the length of each piece. Make sure the groove is centered side-to-side.

4 Cut a series of deep mortises in the end pieces using a mortising machine. The mortising bit is the same width as the groove.

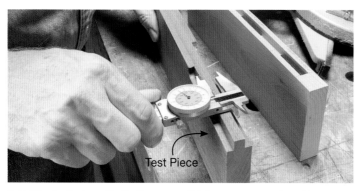

5 Mill a test piece that's the same thickness as your top. Use a router and edge guide to form a tongue on the test piece. Make the tongue the same width as the groove.

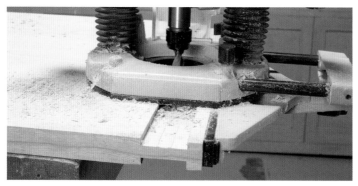

6 Rout wide dados across both sides of the top to start forming the tenons. Leave a strip of wood uncut to support the router.

7 Saw off the support piece by hand or use a jigsaw. It doesn't matter if the sawn edge is a bit uneven or out of square.

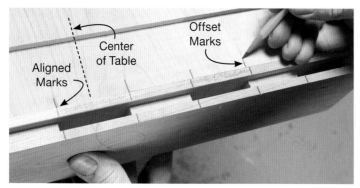

8 Place an end piece next to the top. Mark the center tenon exactly in line with its mortise. Mark the other tenons narrower than their mortises.

the mortises 1½" to 2" deep (the ones shown here are 2" deep).

Cut the Tenons

Chuck a ½" or ¾"-dia. bit in your router. Set the depth of cut equal to the distance between the face of the end piece and the groove. Place the router on the top of the test piece (not on its edge), and rout a tongue (Photo 5). Check the tongue's thickness—it should be equal to the width of the groove and mortises. If you readjust the router's depth of cut, be sure to rout from both faces of the test piece.

Rout the ends of the table top (Photo 6). This requires a series of overlapping cuts, on both sides of the top. Start with the outermost cut, then flip the top to repeat the same cut on the opposite side. Reset the edge guide and work your way in. The last cut, which creates the tenons' shoulders, must be absolutely straight. Shift the router's edge guide only ¹⁄₁₆" or so to make this cut—that should do the trick. Saw off the support piece (Photo 7). The resulting tenon should be ¹⁄₁₆" shorter than the depth of the mortises.

Lay out the individual tenons (Photo 8). Mark the center tenon the exact width of its corresponding mortise. Mark the next tenons about ¹⁄₁₆" narrower, on both sides, than their mortises. This offset should get larger as you go, depending on how wide your top is, how much your species of wood moves, the humidity range in your area, etc. As a general rule, an ⅛" offset on both sides of the tenon should be sufficient for most tops.

Draw a line across the top to lay out the haunches (the short segments between the tenons). Make the haunches ¹⁄₁₆" shorter than the depth of the grooves in the end pieces to ensure that the joint's shoulders fit tight. Saw the tenons (Photos 9 and 10). After removing the end waste pieces, pare the shoulders even using a chisel or a trim router and a flush-trim bit.

Fit the Joint

Try fitting each breadboard end onto the tabletop. Chances are that it won't go without force, and that's fine. It's better that the fit be a bit too tight than too loose at this point. (If it's too loose, you can shim the tenons with glued-on veneer.) Don't strike the end piece with a hammer; if the fit is that tight, you'll have a very hard time getting the piece off. Typically, the tenons must be shaved a bit thinner. The best way to figure out how much

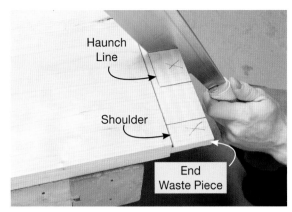

Haunch Line

Shoulder

End Waste Piece

9 Cut the tenons. Stop most of the cuts at the haunch line. At the outer ends, saw full depth, then saw near the shoulder to remove the end waste piece.

to take off, and where, is by using a short test piece (Photo 11).

Pare the tenons as needed (Photo 12). You can use an electric router, a router plane (see Sources, below), or a rabbet plane. An electric router is fast, but you must be very careful not to cut into the joint's shoulders. A rabbet plane won't harm the shoulders, but you may create another problem: inadvertently leaning a rabbet plane from side to side will cut a taper on the tenons. A router plane works best—and is a fun tool to use! You can't cut into the shoulders, and the tenons will always be parallel to the top. Shoot for a somewhat loose fit for the breadboard ends. You should be able to push them home with hand pressure alone.

Use yellow (PVA) glue to secure the breadboard ends to the top (Photo 13). In the Titebond series of glues, use Titebond Original, which may provide more stretch than Titebond II or III. If you expect a large amount of movement in your top, don't glue the outermost mortises and tenons. Even up the top and breadboard ends using a hand plane, scraper plane, or random-orbit sander.

10 Cut the waste between the tenons using a coping saw. Twist the blade so it's at a right angle to the saw's frame.

11 Test each tenon's fit using a short piece of wood that has the same groove and mortise as the end pieces. Ideally, this test piece should slip over the tenon with very little effort.

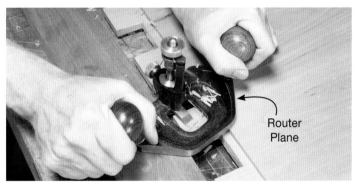

Router Plane

12 Use a router plane or rabbet plane to pare the tenons thinner, if necessary. Support the router plane with the test piece you made that's the same thickness as the top.

13 Apply yellow glue across the entire joint. When dry, this glue has enough give to allow the top to slowly expand and contract with the seasons.

by Garrett Glaser

How to Cut a 3-way Miter

CAREFUL LAYOUT, SAWING AND PARING

Admiring the complex 3-way mitered joint between the leg and aprons in an antique Chinese table is natural. But the thought of cutting and fitting this interlocking joint by hand is enough to make most woodworkers run up a white flag. However, there is a straightforward way to fashion this elegant, versatile and time-tested joint.

Most traditional Chinese 3-way miter joints consist of three (or more) interlocking pieces, each with their own configuration of tenons and mortises. I've created a simplified version that requires only two pieces, the leg and two identical but mirror-image aprons. My joint won't win awards for authentic traditional joinery, but it's a good jumping-off point. Mastering this joint develops skills that will allow you to tackle more complex versions. A good place to start looking for authentic examples is Gustav Ecke's excellent book *Chinese Domestic Furniture*.

Build a Table with 3-Way Miter Joints

The legs and aprons of tables joined with 3-way miters form an open frame whose dimensions are determined by the lengths of the three components. Adding a top can be as simple as attaching cleats inside the aprons and cutting a piece to fit.

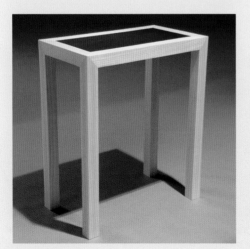

Cutting List 3-Way Miter Table
Overall Dimensions: 22" L x 14" W x 26" H

Part	Name	Qty.	Material	Th x W x L
A	Leg	4	Ash	1¾" x 1¾" x 26"
B	Short apron	2	Ash	1¾" x 1¾" x 14"
C	Long apron	2	Ash	1¾" x 1¾" x 22"
D	Loose tenon	12	Ash	⅜" x 1" x 1"
E	Short cleat	2	Ash	¾" x ¾" x 10¼"
F	Long cleat	2	Ash	¾" x ¾" x 16½"
G	Top	1	Mahogany plywood	

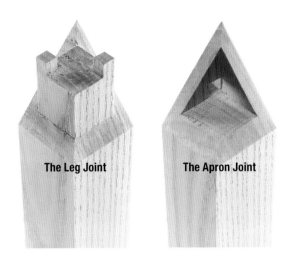

The Leg Joint

The Apron Joint

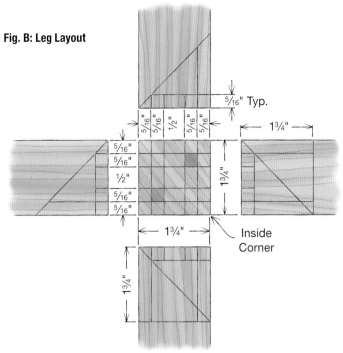

Fig. B: Leg Layout

5/16" Typ.

5/16" 5/16" 1/2" 5/16" 5/16"

1 3/4"

5/16"
5/16"
1/2"
5/16"
5/16"

1 3/4"

1 3/4"

Inside Corner

1 3/4"

Creating a 3-way miter by hand requires three skills: precise layout, sawing straight lines and accurately removing waste. No single step is especially difficult, but there are a good number of them. The order in which you complete the steps is the key to success. A fourth requirement isn't so much a skill as a personality trait: patience. Mastering this process takes practice.

Start by milling the stock. Use light-colored wood at first, so your layout lines will be easy to see and imperfections will show clearly as dark crevices in the assembled joints. In 3-way miters, the aprons and legs are squared to the same dimensions. Every piece must be straight. If one piece has a twist or bend, it won't matter how masterfully you cut and chisel—the joint will never close tightly.

Cut the aprons and legs to final length—the aprons on opposite sides must be identical (or all four aprons, if the table is square). Lay out all of the cuts on the top and all four faces of each leg (Fig. B). Use an accurate square and a sharp pencil or a knife to create the lines.

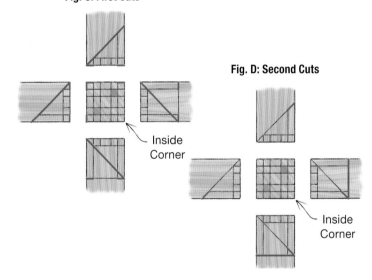

Fig. C: First Cuts

Inside Corner

Fig. D: Second Cuts

Inside Corner

Inside Corner

1 Start by sawing four diagonals on each leg, one on each face. Use a straightedge to guide the saw. Attach sandpaper to the back of the straightedge so it won't slip.

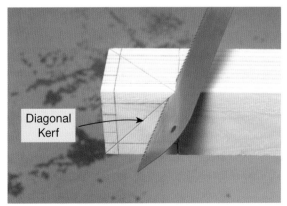

Diagonal Kerf

2 Saw the bottom edge of the miter on the two inside faces. Use the diagonal kerf from the previous step to establish the 45° slope. Then work back to the diagonal kerf on the opposite edge.

Fig. E: Third Cuts

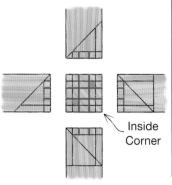

Inside Corner

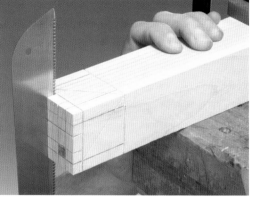

3 Create the tic-tac-toe grid on the top by making four straight cuts. Saw to the upper layout lines on the adjacent faces.

Fig. F: Fourth Cuts

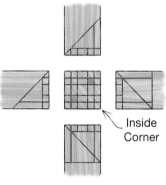

Inside Corner

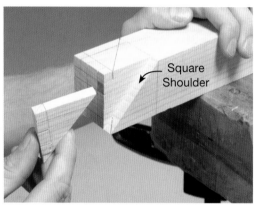

Square Shoulder

4 Create square shoulders on the two outside miters by sawing diagonally across the top and one adjacent face. Waste removal begins with these cuts.

Making a Stopped Cut

To make a stopped cut you need three lines—the line across the top and stopped lines on the opposite adjacent faces. Begin the cut as you would a through cut, creating a groove across the top and then cutting with the heel to the bottom of the first stopped line. But instead of putting pressure on the heel to continue the cut, make the toe of the saw do all the work, cutting down the line on the opposite face, slowly leveling the blade so that the teeth connect the two points where the cut should stop.

The Leg Joint

The first cuts on each leg are diagonal and stopped (Photo 1 and Fig. C). The two diagonal cuts on the outside faces are the most visible of all the cuts you will make, so use a metal straightedge to ensure clean, straight cuts. Position the straightedge so the blade will split the layout line. Hold the saw against the straightedge and flat on the workpiece. Then saw a groove just deep enough to keep the saw from jumping out as you complete the cut. Remove the straightedge. Keep the blade in the groove while using its heel to make a perpendicular cut down the adjacent side to the first stop line. Then slowly angle the blade forward and use its toe to cut down to the stop line on the opposite side.

The second cuts run across the leg's two inside faces (Photo 2 and Fig. D). They're the only cuts that aren't perpendicular to the surface. Use one of the diagonal cuts you just made to position your saw at the correct angle, then saw back across the face to the diagonal cut on the opposite side.

The third cuts form a tic-tac-toe grid across the top (Photo 3 and Fig. E). Although most of these cuts will be removed later, making them now ensures square tenons, because it's much harder to cut a perfectly true short line than a long one. These stopped cuts also act as a guide for waste removal.

The fourth cuts create shoulders for the miter joints (Photo 4 and Fig. F). Establish a straight, shallow groove and then saw diagonally until you reach the outside edge of the top and the bottom edge of the miter on the adjacent face. If the triangular waste piece doesn't come loose, make sure the diagonal cut was sawed to a uniform depth—rocking the saw from heel to toe sometimes leaves a high spot in the middle.

The fifth cuts remove waste and reveal angled shoulders on the inside faces (Photo 5 and Fig. G). Make a pair of deep stopped cuts that run across

5 Make deep stopped cuts across both inside faces to reveal the angled inside shoulders. You'll have to re-mark some of the layout lines in order to make these cuts.

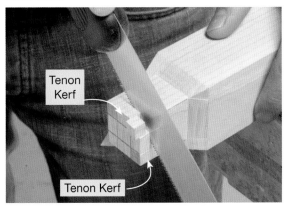

6 Complete each leg joint by removing the waste from around the two tenons. Sawing across the inside corner to the tenon kerfs creates a flat shoulder at the base of the tenons.

the top and down both adjacent faces. Be careful not to cut into the mitered shoulders on the outside faces, as doing so will leave a visible mark when the joint is assembled.

The final cut establishes the flat shoulder at the base of the tenons (Photo 6 and Fig. H). Start by marking guide lines on both inside faces, ⁵⁄₁₆" down from the top and running from the inside corner to the saw kerf that defines the tenon cheek. Use the lines to cut diagonally to the kerfs—be sure to stop before you saw into the tenons!

Use a ¼" Forstner bit to remove as much of the waste as you can (Photo 7). Then switch to a chisel (Photo 8). The shoulder's surface must be absolutely flat, so finish by paring across the grain. Be sure to remove any ragged fibers left in the corners.

Fig. G: Fifth Cuts

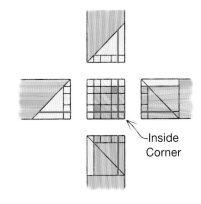

Inside Corner

Fig. H: Final Cut

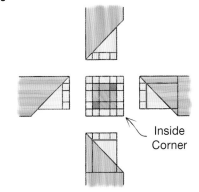

Inside Corner

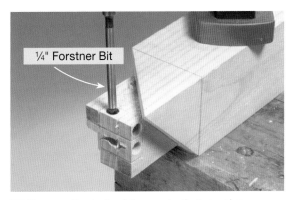

¼" Forstner Bit

7 Remove the bulk of the waste that remains between the tenons by drilling through the tic-tac-toe blocks.

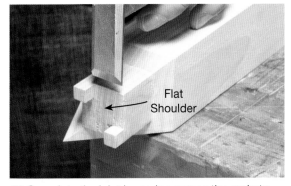

Flat Shoulder

8 Complete the joint by paring across the grain to create a flat shoulder beneath the tenons.

9 Start each apron corner by making two through diagonal cuts, one on the top and one on the outside face.

10 Square the mortise after drilling a stopped hole to remove most of the waste.

11 Hollow the inside of the joint after marking the shoulders on both mitered faces. Remove the waste with a series of shallow chisel cuts, working from front to back.

Long-Grain
Shoulder

End-Grain
Shoulder

12 Pare to the guide lines and square the end-grain shoulder. Removing the waste reveals the mortise—it's flush with the corner formed by the end-grain and long-grain shoulders.

The Apron Joint

Mark the aprons for cutting and mortising (Fig. J). The first cuts create miters on the top and outside faces (Photo 9). These diagonal cuts are just as visible as those on the leg, so start them the same way, using a straightedge. Use the heel of the blade to saw the line on the adjacent face and finish the cut by sawing at a 45° angle.

Cut the mortise in the top face. (Each apron joint houses one of the leg tenons.) Drill a ⅜" deep hole with a ¼" Forstner bit and then square the corners with a chisel (Photo 10).

Draw guide lines on the two mitered faces on the inside of the joint (Fig. J). One line is located ⁵⁄₁₆" from the outside edge and the other ⁵⁄₁₆" from the bottom of the miter—these lines align with the mortise on two sides.

When removing the waste, use one line to guide the side of the chisel and the other to establish the depth (Photo 11). Barely tap the chisel for the first cuts—the grain is so short at the front that it's easy to remove too much. You should be left with one relatively clean end-grain shoulder and two fairly ragged long-grain shoulders. Make sure the end-grain shoulder is absolutely flat. Pare the long-grain shoulders to exactly ⁵⁄₁₆" thickness (Photo 12).

Fig. J: Apron Layout

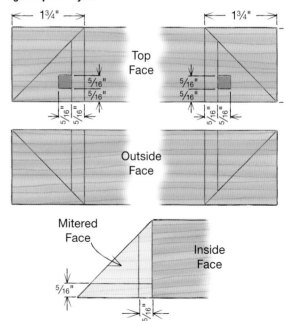

Top
Face

Outside
Face

Mitered
Face

Inside
Face

True the Fit

When you first assemble a leg and apron, don't be alarmed if the pieces don't even go together. Truing the fit requires patience and thoughtful sleuthing. Look carefully to determine what might be gumming up the works (Photo 13). Make sure the mortise fits the tenon without binding—if this joint is too tight it can keep the other parts of the joint from fitting. Once the mortise and tenon fit properly, check the other joint surfaces for irregularities.

Don't spend too much time fitting an apron and leg before adding the second apron. After all, this is a three-piece joint, and having all three parts together shows much more than two parts can show. You'll quickly learn how a small adjustment on one piece can affect the way the other two pieces fit.

In fact, because all the joints are interrelated, the best strategy is to assemble the legs and aprons as soon as possible and true each joint in stages, round-robin-style, using a rabbet plane and a chisel (Photo 14). Use the positioning jig shown earlier to keep the legs plumb while you finesse the joints. Temporarily shimming the mortises during this process can help to identify problem areas. Once all the joints have been fit, you'll probably have to permanently shim some of the mortises. That's OK; the shims will be virtually invisible after they're glued and sanded flush.

Use the assembly jig and the band clamp for glue-up. If you need to apply downward pressure on the aprons, raise the jig on blocks to provide a clamping lip.

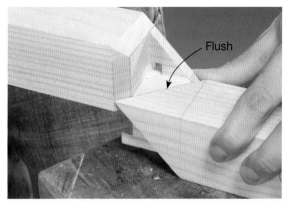

13 Fitting the joints takes time. Make sure that the shoulders of each joint are the same thickness, that all of the mating surfaces are absolutely flat and that the mortises aren't too small.

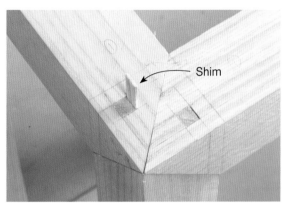

14 All of the joints are interrelated, so assemble the table as soon as you can. Then work a little on each joint in rotation. Here, a temporary shim shows high spots that require further work.

Using a Pull Saw

The art of sawing straight and square with a pull saw isn't as mysterious as you might think.

I use a fine-tooth flush-cut pull saw to cut 3-way miters. (The teeth on a flush-cut saw have no set, which means they don't flare beyond the body of the blade). You can spend a lot of money for this type of saw, but I get great results using an inexpensive version from a home improvement store—and I don't have to worry about the replacement cost if I kink the blade or break a tooth.

When you saw, the goal is to split the layout line. Don't worry—it's easier than it sounds. Just make sure that the outside edge of the blade follows the center of the line, so half of the line remains on the workpiece and the other half becomes sawdust.

To make a through cut, you follow two adjacent lines, one across the top of the piece and one continuing down the side that faces you. Focus first on the top line. Hold the blade nearly parallel to the surface, but with the heel (the end closest to the handle) raised slightly, and saw lightly along the line from the far side to the near side until you've made a shallow groove across the top. Keep the saw in the groove and switch your focus to the vertical line on the side. Using the heel of the blade, saw your way down the line until the teeth of your saw meet the ends of both lines. If you are cutting square stock, this puts your saw at a 45°angle. Keep your saw at this angle to complete the cut. The kerf you've created keeps the saw square and plumb for the rest of the cut.

by Bill McCarthy

Hand-Planed Moldings

CREATE CUSTOM PROFILES WITH PAIRS OF PLANES

A woodworker who needs a small amount of hardwood molding for a furniture or cabinet project is often out of luck. Hardwood moldings are scarce at local home centers, and most commercial shops can't economically set up a molding machine for a short run. And the typical small-shop shaper can't produce moldings wider than about 3".

Fortunately, there's a way to make your own custom moldings using traditional molding planes. In this article, I'll show you how to tune up and use a hollow plane and a round plane—two of the most versatile molding planes. The hollow plane, with its concave sole, cuts a rounded shape. The round plane has a convex sole and cuts a hollow in the workpiece. A pair of these planes with the same radius is commonly used to produce a true ogee—one whose curves mirror each other.

In this article, I'll show you how I make a 4½"-wide crown molding using a set of complementary, 1"- radius planes. Once you get the hang of working with these time-honored tools, you'll be able to make a variety of moldings (see Fig. A).

Selecting the Planes

Old hollow and round planes are often available at flea markets or from antique dealers for less than $35 apiece. Look for a pair with matching radii. When selecting a plane, make sure it is in good overall condition. It should have no cracks in the plane body and no heavy rust or deep pitting on the iron.

You'll want to tune up each plane before using it. It's best to start with the round plane. Use a reliable straightedge to check the flatness of the sole along its length. If the sole is bowed, plane it straight using a block plane set for a light cut. Take a series of light, overlapping passes to shape the cross section of the sole to the desired radius (Photo 1). You can make a cardboard template to check the radius all along the sole. Finish up by smoothing and fairing the curve of the sole with sandpaper.

Next, check the shape of the iron's cutting edge. It should conform as closely as possible to the curvature of the plane's sole. If the curve is off, you'll need to reshape it. Begin by coating the back of the iron with machinist's layout bluing. The bluing allows you to scribe a highly visible line into the iron. Insert the iron in the plane so its entire cutting edge projects about 1/16". Transfer the curvature of the sole onto the iron using a dull knife (Photo 2).

Grind the cutting edge down to your scribed line. I use a 60-grit white or pink grinding wheel. Dip the iron in water frequently to prevent overheating. After grinding, hone the bevel and the back of the iron to bring the cutter to a razor-sharp edge. Reassemble the plane, set it for a light cut, and test it on a piece of scrap. To adjust the iron for a deeper cut, tap it lightly downward with a hammer. To retract the iron slightly, tap on the rear of the plane body.

You can now use the tuned round plane to shape the sole of the hollow plane. Afterward, scribe the hollow's iron as you did the round plane's iron. I find that grinding a concave cutting edge is easier on a grinding wheel with a rounded edge.

I hone the iron (Photo 3) with a soft, aluminum oxide "roughing" stone. To hone a concave cutting edge, I grind off the stone's corners using a typical, vitrified, gray grinding wheel.

Making a Crown Molding

With your planes tuned up, you're ready to make some molding. Fig. B shows a nice molding profile that incorporates an ogee and a cove, with a shoulder separating them. To lay out the molding, first make a cardboard template of the profile. Lay out the profile on the end of a short length of 13/16"-thick by 4½"-wide straight-grain softwood. You will use this piece for practice.

Before planing, you need to do a little tablesaw work: First, saw all the 45-degree bevels on the edges of the molding stock (Fig. B). Then, saw a 45-degree V-shaped notch in the face of the stock

1 Planing the plane. The bottom of an old plane often needs to be reshaped. I used a block plane to true up the bottom of this round plane before smoothing the contour with sandpaper.

2 Scribing a round iron. To transfer the shape of the sole to the plane iron, coat the iron with machinist's bluing, then scribe it with a knife.

3 Honing a hollow iron. After grinding the iron, I bring it to final shape using a modified "roughing" stone.

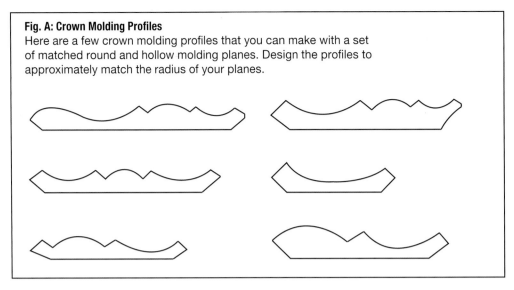

Fig. A: Crown Molding Profiles
Here are a few crown molding profiles that you can make with a set of matched round and hollow molding planes. Design the profiles to approximately match the radius of your planes.

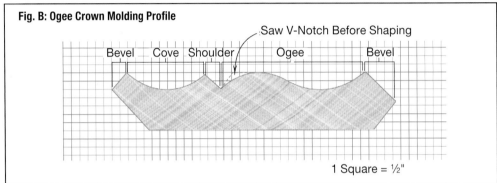

Fig. B: Ogee Crown Molding Profile

Saw V-Notch Before Shaping

Bevel | Cove | Shoulder | Ogee | Bevel

1 Square = ½"

to create the shoulder. I use a jack plane to clean up any saw marks on the four edge bevels.

Begin shaping the molding by planing the concave half of the ogee with the round plane. Make sure you're working on a firm, flat surface. I clamp a 1"-thick wooden straightedge to the molding to guide my first few strokes. I plane to about ⅛" deep. After that, I remove the straightedge and let the hollow guide the plane.

Make each planing pass with a firm, steady stroke. Each complete pass should yield one continuous shaving. If you find yourself fighting the plane, retract the iron slightly. If the plane skips over the middle of the board, try shimming under the center of the molding to raise it a bit.

As I approach the final depth of cut, I roll the plane to one side or the other as necessary to widen the hollow and match the desired profile. The outside edge of the hollow should meet the sawn bevel in a sharp edge.

After completing the hollow, I use a rabbet plane to remove any saw marks on the edge of the molding's shoulder (Photo 4).

Next, clamp your straightedge to guide the first few passes on the molding's cove (Photo 5).

Remove the straightedge as before and complete the cuts, again rolling the plane to one side or the other to create the desired profile. The cove should meet the bevel and shoulder in a sharp edge.

The last step is to plane the convex section of the ogee using the hollow plane. The V-shaped ridge on the sole of the plane rides against the molding's shoulder to guide this cut.

Place the sole's ridge into the molding's V-shaped notch and make your first cut. For each subsequent cut, tilt the plane farther into the workpiece (see lead photo). You're done when the ogee's curves meet in a smooth transition that matches your profile.

If you've done your work well, you should have a lovely molding that needs little or no sanding.

4 Planing the shoulder. A rabbet plane cleans up any saw marks left on the molding's shoulder.

5 Starting straight. Guide the first few hollowing passes with a wooden straightedge that's clamped along the workpiece.

Shaping a Grinding Wheel

The squared edge of a typical grinding wheel doesn't lend itself well to shaping the concave profiles you'll find on molding plane irons, carving tools, and turning gouges. To make grinding odd profiles much easier, it's a simple matter to reshape a wheel to suit the desired profile of the iron.

All you need is a "soft" grinding wheel and a tool to dress it. White or pink grinding wheels have a softer bond than typical gray wheels and can easily be shaped with a dressing tool. I prefer 60-grit grinding wheels.

Dressing sticks are commonly available, and work fine for rounding over a grinding wheel. But I prefer using a diamond-tipped dresser. Don't panic; they don't cost much. This dresser is simply a steel rod with an industrial diamond mounted on its end. It allows you to dress the edge of a grinding wheel to any shape you like.

When dressing a grinding wheel, adjust the grinder's rest about ½" below the center of the wheel (see photo, at right). Apply light pressure to the wheel and don't overheat the diamond. You can't cool it in water or it could break. Rotate the diamond occasionally to distribute wear.

Dressing a wheel. A diamond-point dresser will shape a soft grinding wheel to any profile you need for grinding concave plane irons.

You can't do anything with dull tools, that's why every woodworker must master the art of sharpening.

Sharpening
Hand Tools

by Tom Caspar

Sharpening Shortcuts

IT HELPS TO KNOW WHY AS WELL AS HOW

Hand tools are a pleasure to use—if they're sharp. Once you have a sharp tool in your hands, you'll begin to realize why some woodworkers are so passionate about old ways of working wood. Slow is beautiful, after all.

I've been a hand tool enthusiast for years, and I can honestly say that learning how to sharpen a tool is just as important as learning how to handle it. It's not something you master right away; sharpening is a skill that requires patience, practice, and persistence. This story is for folks who already know a bit about sharpening, and are ready to move on to the next level.

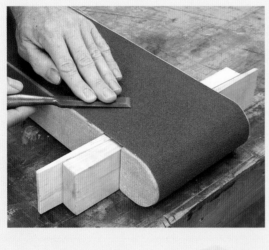

Sanding Belt Lapping Jig

You can chew up a lot of sandpaper flattening a plane iron, a large chisel or the bottom of a plane. It makes sense to use paper that lasts a long time—like a sanding belt. But, if you cut a belt to lay open, it won't sit flat, because its backing is too stiff.

To overcome this problem, I devised a jig that stretches a belt very tight. I only use it with coarse grits—60, 80, and 100—for tools that need a lot of flattening. The jig is double-sided, of course, so you'll use the whole belt. It won't slip when you're flattening, because the abrasive on the bottom grips your workbench.

I made this jig for the 6x48 belts that go on my combination disc/belt sander, but it could be any size. The body consists of three 3/4" MDF pieces laminated together. After gluing, flatten the faces by rubbing the blank on sheets of sandpaper taped to the top of a tablesaw. Round the ends by making 45° cuts on both ends of the blank, then soften the sharp corners with a file. Cut off the short end and make opposing wedges to pull the belt tight.

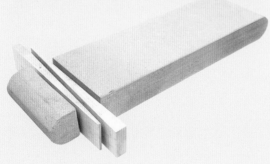

Blunt A Nicked Edge

If your chisel gets a serious nick or ding, you'll have to grind away a lot of metal to renew the edge. The best strategy for doing this is to adjust your grinder's tool rest to 90° and blunt your tool like a screwdriver. Once you've ground past the damage, reset the tool rest at the appropriate grinding angle and have at it.

Consider this as an insurance policy. You're much less likely to overheat and draw the temper out of a blunt edge than an acute edge.

Overheating an edge is all too easy to do when you're removing a lot of material. It's not pretty. The steel turns blue—a definite sign of trouble. The blued portion is softened, and will no longer hold an edge. You have to continue grinding past the blued area to get to good steel again.

Blunting the edge is just a different way to shape a new bevel. You'll have to take off all that metal anyway, so you may as well do it without risking any further damage—a nick is bad enough!

What's What With Bevels

So we're all on the same page, here's a visual guide to 5 types of bevels that are used on chisels and plane blades.

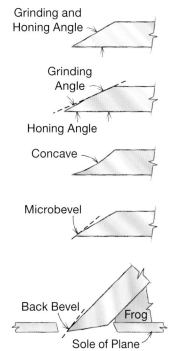

Grinding and Honing Angle

Grinding Angle

Honing Angle

Concave

Microbevel

Back Bevel — Frog

Sole of Plane

Single bevel
A blade with a single bevel is ground and honed at the same angle.

Double bevel
A blade with a double bevel is ground at a lower angle and honed at a higher angle. The difference between the ground bevel and the honed bevel is usually 5°.

Hollow ground bevel
A hollow ground bevel is made on a grinding wheel, which creates a concave shape.

Microbevel
A microbevel is a very short bevel that is one or two degrees steeper than the honing bevel. The blade may have a single bevel or a double bevel.

Back bevel
A back bevel is an optional type of microbevel for a plane blade.

What's the Deal with Microbevels?

A microbevel sounds like a pretty sophisticated concept, but the idea is really quite simple. A microbevel is just a very short bevel that's honed at a slightly steeper angle than the rest of a tool's bevel. You create it in the last stage of the honing process, using your finest stone.

Why bother? Well, a microbevel has two significant benefits. First, it gives you an extremely sharp edge with a minimum amount of effort. When you're honing on your finest stone, each stroke doesn't remove a whole lot of steel. There's no point in making the whole bevel as smooth and shiny as possible, so it makes sense to concentrate your efforts right at the business end, where it counts. And that's what happens when you raise the honing angle a degree or two.

A microbevel also makes your edge last a bit longer. Think of your blade as a wedge. A thin wedge is going to dull quicker than a thick wedge, right? A 35° edge, for example, will stay sharp longer than a 25° edge. So any increase in a bevel's angle helps an edge stay sharp, even if it's only a degree or two.

Microbevel

A Bargain Honing Jig, and How To Improve It

When I First learned how to sharpen, I bought a very simple and inexpensive honing jig made in England by Eclipse. Today, the same jig is widely available under many different brand names and still doesn't cost very much. It works quite well—I've used mine for years—but I've made a few small refinements to it. The jig's body is aluminum, so it's very easy to modify using a file or disc sander.

The jig has two positions for clamping tools: an upper ledge for plane irons and a lower pair of V-shaped grooves for chisels. To set the honing angle, you measure the distance from the tip of the blade to the body of the jig. Here's what you can do to make this good jig even better:

• **Flatten its face.** For accurate and repeatable projection measurements, the two front faces of the jig must be square and even with each other. The easiest way to flatten the faces is by placing the jig on a disc sander's worktable and gently pushing it into the disc (Photo 1).

• Widen the chisel slots. Many chisels don't fit very well in the V-shaped grooves because their sides are too thick. Clamp the jig in a vise and use the edge of a 6" or 8" mill bastard file to widen the grooves to fit your tools (Photo 2).

• **Make a projection jig.** You don't need a ruler to measure a tool's projection–use a stepped wooden jig instead (Photo 3). It's more convenient, more accurate, and easily repeatable. I use a single 30mm (about 1³⁄₁₆") projection for most chisels and plane irons. This creates a 30° bevel on a chisel and a 35° bevel on a plane iron.

• **Add a microbevel setting.** I added a second side to the projection jig that is 2mm (about ¹⁄₁₆") shorter than the first side, which increases the bevel angle by about 1°. To sharpen an edge, I use the normal 30mm projection on medium and fine stones (side #1), then reset the projection to 28mm (side #2) and hone on a superfine stone.

• **Form a back-bevel ramp.** Adding a back bevel to a plane iron makes the iron easier to sharpen. To make a back bevel using this jig, you just turn the jig over and rest its top on your stone (Photo 4). Unaltered, the jig produces a back bevel that's quite steep, so I used a disc sander to grind down the top of the jig, sloping from front to back.

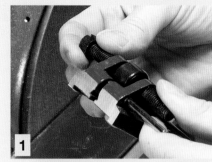

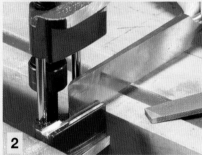

Angles to Remember

To keep things simple, burn these three numbers in your memory banks: 25°, 30° and 35°. These are the three most commonly used angles when grinding and honing chisels and plane blades.

If you prefer to grind and hone your tools with a single bevel, just remember one number for each type of tool.

If you prefer a double bevel, make the grinding angle 5° less than the honing angle. A general purpose chisel, for example, is ground at 25° and honed at 30°.

The most widely used honing angle for a bench plane's blade is 30°. I prefer 35°, because a steeper edge lasts longer.

Chisels			Plane Blades	
25°	30°	35°	25°	30° 35°
Paring	General Purpose	Mortising	Block Plane	Bench Planes

The Hollow-Ground Bevel: What's the Big Deal?

The name "hollow-ground bevel" has been widely misused. I'd like to set the record straight as to what a hollow-ground bevel is, what it's good for, and when to avoid it. It's simply a concave bevel—the natural result of using a grinding wheel. The wheel is convex, of course, so it always creates a bevel that's concave.

A tool with a hollow-ground bevel is easier to sharpen by hand, without the use of a jig. The biggest problem with honing by hand is holding the tool at the correct angle with every stroke. A hollow-ground bevel helps you find and maintain that angle, so there's no wasted effort.

With a hollow grind, you simply rock the tool up and down until it locks in place, resting on the bevel's heel and toe. Two points of support make the difference—it would be much harder to feel the correct angle if the bevel were flat, rather than concave.

That's why we have arches in our feet-they make balancing easier.

I often sharpen chisels by hand, without a jig, simply because it's so easy. Ditto for plow plane and rabbeting plane irons that are awkward or impossible to hold in a jig. I do use a jig for honing standard-thickness bench plane irons, though. Even with a hollow grind, their bevels are too narrow for me to maintain that correct angle with every pass on the stone.

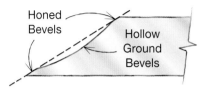

So when is a hollow-ground bevel not appropriate? Japanese tools and Western mortising chisels should not be hollow ground. Ideally, Japanese tools should be ground with a flat bevel, to maximize support of the tip. The steel of Japanese tools can be brittle; without adequate support, a tip could fracture. Mortising chisels should be flat ground, too, or made slightly convex, for the same reason. To withstand heavy blows, their tips need to be as strong as possible.

Waterstone Mat

When I switched from oilstones to waterstones back in the Paleozoic era, I thought that I could say goodbye to making a big mess while sharpening. Well, not exactly. Waterstones are messy, too, when you keep their surfaces flooded with water—as you should.

I've been looking for the best method of containing the mess for years, and modern technology has finally delivered: a rubber garden paver. It's about 16" square, ¾" thick, and made from recycled tires. Water beads up on it, and best of all, the surface is a bit rough and sticky, so stones stay put. You don't need a holder or clamps or anything—just your stones and the mat.

Similar material is used for floor underlayment for gyms, so you may be able to scrounge a mat for free, but these pavers are now available at home centers. I'll bet they'll last forever.

Waterstone Maintenance

Waterstones are renowned for cutting fast, but many require regular maintenance to stay flat. This is no small thing—a flat surface is essential for producing a straight edge and to properly remove a wire edge.

Flattening is a must-do, routine chore. How often do you have to do it? Well, ideally you'd flatten a stone each time before you use it, but that may strike you as being obsessive. Flattening after a half-dozen uses is probably more realistic. But consider this: the longer you let it go, the more dished-out a stone may become and the more work you have to do to make it flat again.

The easiest and least expensive way to flatten a waterstone is to rub it on a piece of 220 grit wet/dry sandpaper mounted on a piece of ¼" glass. The best source for this sandpaper is an automotive supply shop. Pick up a handful of sheets, because each one is only good for two or three uses.

When you flatten, use lots of water to keep the paper from loading. You don't have to adhere the paper to the glass—the water will cause the paper to stick by itself.

If you really want to get the job done in a hurry, lap your stones on a fine diamond stone under running water in a utility sink. You'll be

done before you know it. If you're really nuts about this, like I am, build a support so you don't have to lean over too far.

Hone Scrapers with Diamonds

A lot of folks use a stone to put the final edge on a scraper before turning its hook, but I prefer to use a diamond paddle. It cuts faster than most stones and obviously won't develop a rut, which is always a danger when you continually run the edge of a scraper on a stone.

I use an extra-fine diamond paddle, which is roughly equivalent to a soft Arkansas oilstone or a 1000 grit waterstone. While the diamond can't make a scraper's edge quite as sharp as a very fine stone, the edge is good enough for all but the most demanding work. I lubricate the paddle with some 3–In-One oil to float away the metal debris, so it won't clog the paddle.

To hone the scraper's edge, I position the scraper in a vise so that it's level with a small stick. Resting the paddle on the stick ensures that the scraper's edge will be exactly 90° (Photo 1). I also use the paddle to remove the wire edge formed by honing (Photo 2).

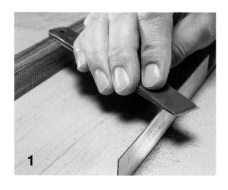

1

2

Dress Those Wheels

If your grinder shakes and vibrates, chances are that the wheels aren't round. Sure, they're more or less round, but they have to be perfectly round for your machine to run smoothly. For truing a wheel, you need a wheel dresser.

If your wheels are full of metal particles and have a glazed surface, you've got another problem. All that metal makes the wheel cut slower and build up heat faster—a surefire recipe for drawing the temper from a tool. To renew a wheel's surface, you need a wheel dresser.

You get the picture. A wheel dresser is a must-have accessory for any grinder. It removes material from the face of a grinding wheel the same way that a turning gouge shapes a spindle. As it cuts into the wheel, a dresser removes the high spots, making the wheel truly round. At the same time, it renews the surface by exposing fresh abrasive.

Before you dress your wheels, it's a good idea to mark them all around with a pencil so you know

when all the high spots are gone. To mark a wheel, rotate it by hand and hold a pencil against it.

There's more than one type of wheel dresser, but my favorite is a T-shaped tool with a diamond face. To use it, adjust the tool rest to 90°, turn on the grinder, and gently hold the dresser against the wheel. It's that easy. You'll be amazed at the difference it makes.

Accurate Paring Requires a Flat Back

Is the back of your chisel really flat? For accurate paring, it has to be as flat as flat can be, for at least 2" to 3". Even though your chisel may look like it's OK, it probably needs to be lapped to make it truly flat.

Lapping consists of two stages: flattening and polishing. First, you flatten the back by rubbing it hard on sandpaper that's adhered to a flat surface. I've used a ¼" thick piece of glass, the cast iron wing of a tablesaw, or the bed of a jointer, but my favorite lapping surface is an inexpensive granite surface plate.

Start with 220 grit paper. Take a few strokes and examine the back. If it's really bad, begin lapping in earnest with 80 grit paper. On most chisels, I start with 120 grit. If the back is pretty good, stick with the 220 grit.

On your first grit, keep sanding until the scratches go all the way from corner to corner and 2" to 3" up the length of the back. This completes the flattening stage.

In the next stage, polish the back with finer and finer grits. A complete sequence is 80, 120, 180, 220, and 320 grit paper. (You can go even further, and save wear on your stones, by using 15 micron and 5 micron 3M PSA-backed Microfinishing paper.)

When you switch to a finer grit, lap in a different direction, so the scratches make a different pattern. Keep lapping on each grit until the scratches made by the previous grit disappear.

Once you've finished with 320 grit, continue lapping on your stones—assuming they're flat.

For abrasives, I prefer 3M's PSA Gold, which is available in discs or rolls at auto supply stores. It cuts faster than any other paper commonly available and doesn't require a sprayed-on adhesive.

Plane Blade Lapping Jig

Lapping the back of a plane blade can be a lot of work. My fingers have often complained very loudly, so I've tried many ways to hold the blade comfortably. I've used a magnet, made a holder from a chunk of wood with a shallow dado in it, and worn gardener's gloves—the kind that have rubber bumps all over them. Each method worked OK, but I finally decided that the sharpening world needs another jig.

This one really does the trick. It allows you to put a lot of pressure right on top of the blade, without tipping it, and that extra pressure makes lapping go much faster. The blade is fastened directly to the jig; the knob is elevated on a stack of nylon washers to give you a roomier grip. The knob is threaded and fastened to the jig with a ⁵⁄₁₆" flat head machine bolt.

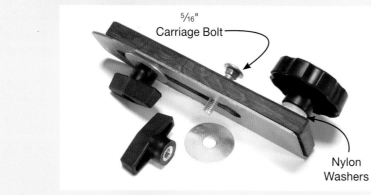

⁵⁄₁₆"
Carriage Bolt

Nylon
Washers

Vacuum Lapping Dust

The best way to keep your sandpaper clean when lapping is to vacuum it. Sandpaper is much less efficient when it clogs up with swarf (a machinist's term for metal debris). Removing the swarf every few strokes makes a tedious chore go faster. Cleaning the sandpaper with a stiff brush or an eraser works so-so, but a vacuum removes everything, almost instantly, with no mess.

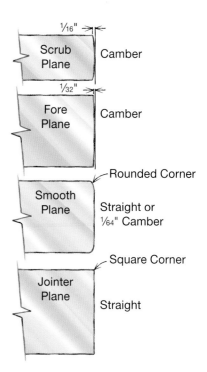

¹⁄₁₆"
Scrub Plane — Camber

¹⁄₃₂"
Fore Plane — Camber

Rounded Corner
Smooth Plane — Straight or ¹⁄₆₄" Camber

Square Corner
Jointer Plane — Straight

4 Blade Profiles

Here's a quick guide on how to sharpen the blades of four major types of bench planes.

Scrub plane. This tool is used to hog off lots of wood, fast. Its blade has a large camber, which is created on a grinder. (No honing is necessary.) The amount of camber depends on the wood's hardness and whether it's green or dry. A ¹⁄₁₆" curve will take off shavings up to ¹⁄₁₆" thick, just right for kiln-dried hardwoods.

Fore plane. This plane is used to level a large surface. (A fore plane is a 5, 5½, or 6 in the Stanley series.) Its blade has a smaller camber, made on a grinder. This camber is honed.

Smooth plane. A smoother finishes off a surface. Its blade has a very slight camber or none at all. The blade's corners are rounded to prevent them from digging into the surface and leaving a series of steps. This rounding is best done on a grinder. The camber is created by honing only, not on the grinder.

Jointer plane. A jointer is often used to flatten surfaces that will be glued together. Its blade has no camber—it's dead straight across. Block planes are sharpened with a straight profile, too.

by Mario Rodriguez

Make a Grinding Rig

SHOP-MADE TOOL RESTS ARE MORE ACCURATE

Let's face it, the tool rests on most grinders just don't cut it. They may be fine for sharpening scissors or lawnmower blades, but when it comes to woodworking tools, forget it. They're often too small and too hard to adjust. In addition, they usually have to be set at an awkward angle that's really hard on your wrists.

You're way better off making your own tool rests. I've designed a pair that will give you accurate and consistent results that can easily be repeated. Using these rests, you'll spend less time

at the grinder. You'll be able to hone your tools and get back to work much faster.

My replacement tool rests will fit almost any grinder. They're fastened to a plywood base, rather than directly to the grinder. This way, they can be positioned to accommodate almost any machine. These rests are designed to fit a 6" Delta grinder, but their dimensions are easy to change for a different model or an 8" grinder.

Chisels and Plane Irons

Making a straight edge is the biggest problem most woodworkers face when grinding chisels and plane irons. That's because most tools are wider than the grinding wheel, so you have to slide the tool from side to side to grind its whole face. That's really hard to do with a standard tool rest, but a cinch with this one.

The tool is securely clamped in a commercial tool holder, which slides back and forth on a long piece of electrical tubing. You can lift the holder off the tube at any point to inspect your progress.

The second problem most woodworkers have with a standard tool rest is fine-tuning the grinding angle. Precisely matching an existing angle saves you lots of time on the grinder. This tool rest is easy to adjust: To change the grinding angle, you just move the rest in or out.

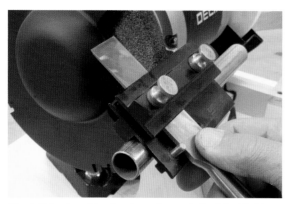

The left tool rest is simply a piece of electrical tubing mounted on a block. A Veritas tool holder fits it perfectly, and can be slid back and forth or lifted off at any time.

To adjust the angle of the tool's bevel, simply move the tool rest in or out. A knob locks it in place.

Turning and Carving Gouges

Many gouges have a bevel that's created by rotating the tool, but making a smooth, even bevel is difficult using a standard tool rest. Steadying the tool is tricky. This extension arm makes the job much easier. Just nest the end of the tool in the arm's V-shaped cradle, rotate the gouge, and you're all set.

This arm accommodates gouges of all lengths. It's hinged in two places to give you maximum flexibility in setting up your tool. Raising and lowering the cradle makes major changes to the bevel angle; to fine-tune the angle, you slide the arm in or out.

Caution: Always place the tool high up on the wheel, as shown in the photo, and use light pressure.

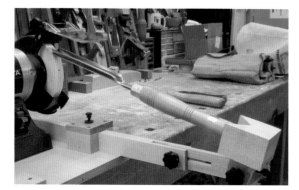

The right-hand tool rest is an articulated arm. To create a perfectly even bevel on a gouge, just rotate the tool.

The arm can be configured to handle tools of almost any length.

Exploded View

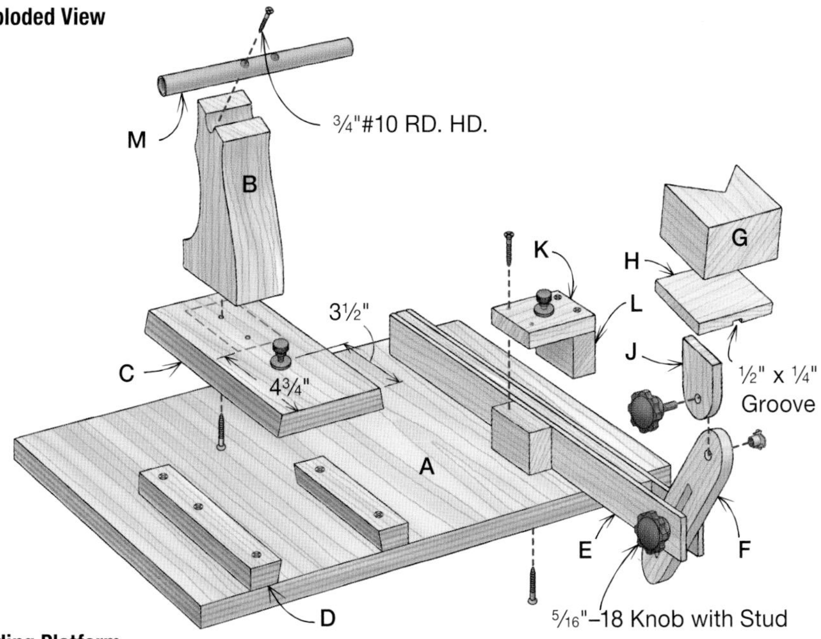

M
3/4"#10 RD. HD.
B
K
H
G
L
3 1/2"
C
4 3/4"
J
1/2" x 1/4" Groove
A
E
F
D
5/16"–18 Knob with Stud

Tower

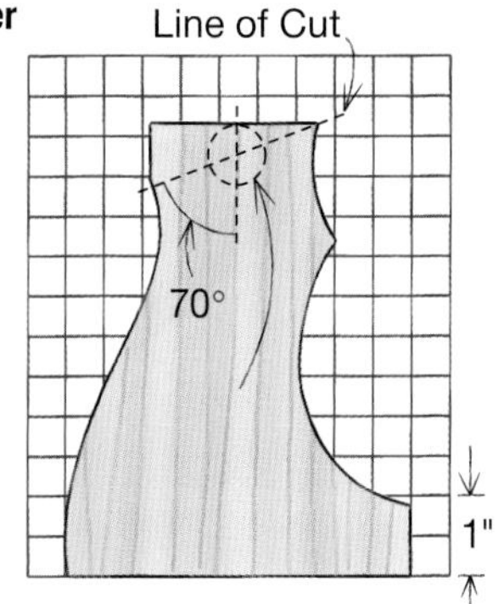

Line of Cut
70°
1"

Tool Rest Bar

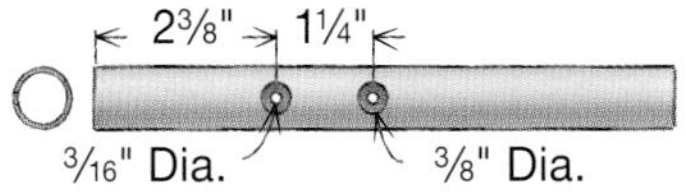

2 3/8"
1 1/4"
3/16" Dia.
3/8" Dia.

Sliding Platform and Guides

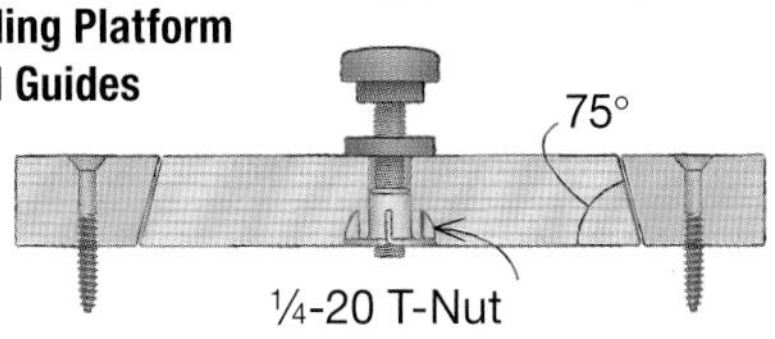

75°
1/4-20 T-Nut

Sliding Arm Lock

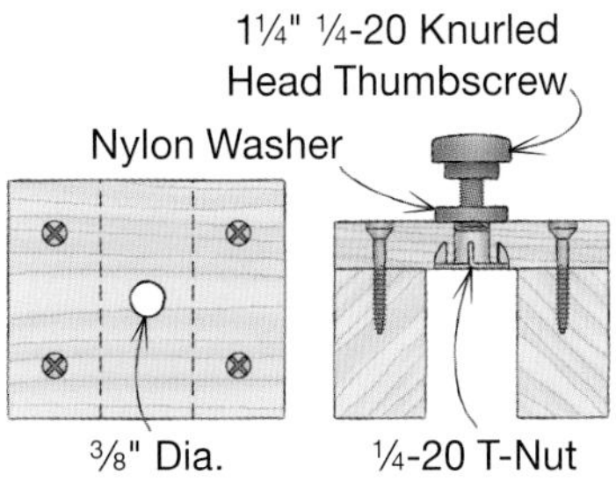

1 1/4" 1/4-20 Knurled Head Thumbscrew
Nylon Washer
3/8" Dia.
1/4-20 T-Nut

Pivot

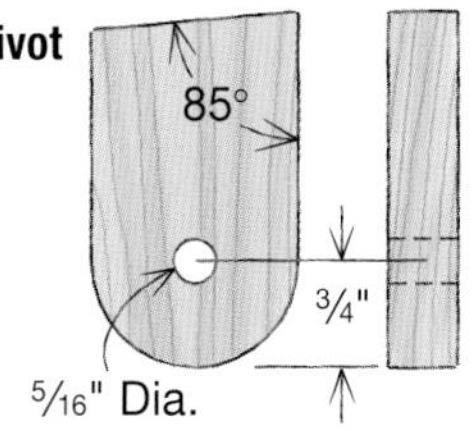

85°
3/4"
5/16" Dia.

Sliding Arm

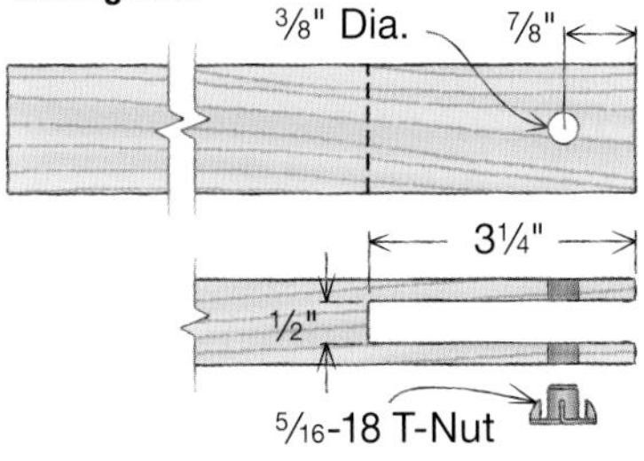

3/8" Dia.
7/8"
3 1/4"
1/2"
5/16-18 T-Nut

Articulating Arm

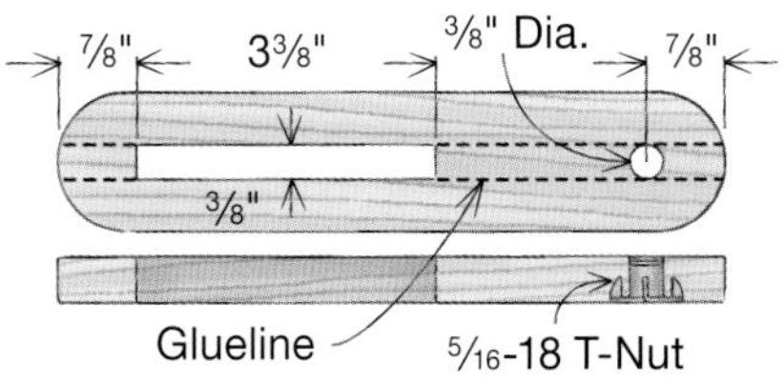

7/8"
3 3/8"
3/8" Dia.
7/8"
3/8"
Glueline
5/16-18 T-Nut

Grinding Jig Cutting List

Part	Name	Qty.	Material	Th x W x L
A	Base	1	Plywood	3/4" x 14" x 20"
B	Tower	1	Hardwood	2" x 4 1/2" x 5 5/8"
C	Sliding platform	1	Plywood	3/4" x 4 3/8" x 10"
D	Platform guide	2	Plywood	3/4" x 1 1/4" x 8" (a)
E	Sliding arm	1	Hardwood	1" x 1 1/2" x 22" (b)
F	Articulating arm	1	Hardwood	1/2" x 1 1/2" x 7 1/2"
G	"V" tool holder	1	Hardwood	1" x 2 1/2" x 3"
H	Tool holder base	1	Hardwood	1/2" x 3" x 2 1/2" (c)
J	Tool holder pivot	1	Hardwood	1/2" x 1 1/2" x 2 1/2" (d)
K	Top of sliding arm lock	1	Hardwood/plywood	1/2" x 3" x 2 1/2"
L	Side of sliding arm lock	2	Hardwood	1" x 1 9/16" x 2 1/2" (e)
M	Tool rest	1	EMT	3/4" dia. x 7 1/2" L

Notes: (a) One guide is cut down to 5 3/4" long. (b) Glue up from three pieces; the inner piece is 1/2" thick, the outer pieces are 1/4" thick. (c) Glue to tool holder. (d) Cut top end to 5°. (e) Screw to base from underneath.

Building Notes

Base (A) This is simply a piece of 3/4" veneer-core plywood. The base will be easier to pick up and move if you put feet under its corners. Leave a margin on either side of the base so you have room to grip it. Use flat-head machine screws to fasten the grinder to the base; their heads go under the base, in holes that are countersunk. Make sure the grinder is square to the base, so the tool rests will be easier to align.

Tool Rest (M) This is just a length of 3/4" electrical metal tubing (EMT). To drill holes for the mounting screws, first make a long, V-shaped cradle in a 12" long block of wood to support the tube. Drill the holes using a drill press. Drill the smaller ones first, all the way through the tube. Then, drill larger holes to accommodate the heads of the screws and your screwdriver.

Tower (B) This part supports the tool rest. Measure your grinder to determine the tower's exact height. The tower should hold the tube just above the axis of the grinding wheel. The tower's shape is designed to nest as close as possible to the grinder. You may have to alter the shape to fit your machine. The semi-circular cutout that holds the tool rest is actually the lower half of a hole. Make the tower an inch or two extra tall, as shown in the diagram. Drill the hole, then cut the top of the tower at the indicated angle.

Sliding Platform and Guides (C & D) Install the guides one at a time. Bolt the grinder to the base first, then center the sliding platform on the grinder's wheel. Make sure the platform is square to the base and clamp it in place. Fasten one guide next to the platform, then place a piece of notebook paper on the other side of the platform, to use as a temporary shim, and fasten the second guide in place.

Articulating Arm Assembly (E-L) Maple is a good choice for these parts because it's hard, strong and machines well. Glue up the articulating arm (F) from four pieces in order to create a slot.

by Tom Caspar

Choosing and Using Waterstones

FAST CUTTING AND EASY MAINTENANCE

For this woodworker, it doesn't get any better than using a sharp hand tool. Not just kind of sharp, the way new tools come out of the box. I mean really, really sharp, with an edge honed to perfection by a well-maintained set of sharpening stones. In search of that perfect edge, I've tried oil stones, diamond plates and sandpaper. With enough time, money or elbow grease, all these materials can deliver top-notch results. But none can beat waterstones, which combine fast cutting, easy maintenance and great value in one package.

Grit Guide

All manufactured waterstones are graded by grit numbers. The higher the number, the finer the grit. Roughly speaking, grits fall into five functional categories. In general, the higher the grit number, the higher the price. Within one grit category, higher-priced stones cut faster and resist wear better.

Types of Stones

Waterstones were first quarried from small mines in Japan more than 1,200 years ago. Today, most waterstones are made in a factory. They're composed of aluminum oxide, silicon carbide or chromium oxide abrasives heated at high temperature to fuse into a brick-shaped porous matrix. Many hold water just like a sponge.

Most waterstones come in two sizes: regular and large. Large stones are thicker, wider and longer, so they have more wear surface. The extra width of a large stone is handy for wide plane irons, but not essential.

Single grit
Single-grit stones are my first choice, because they have four working surfaces. I use the top and bottom for plane irons and the edges for chisels. The wider the edge, the easier it is to balance the stone.

Combination
Combination stones are the best value, because you get two grits for the price of one. However, the stone has only one working surface for each grit. Many different grit combinations are available.

Ceramic
Ceramic stones are a special type of waterstone. They're more expensive than ordinary waterstones, but save time sharpening. They cut faster and wear more slowly than other waterstones.

Natural
Quarried stones are the way to go if you use high-grade Japanese tools. They produce a softer-looking finish than manufactured stones do. Traditional artisans believe that's better for examining the edge of Japanese laminated steel.

Grit Guide

Category	Grit	Use
Extra-Coarse	80 to 700	Removes a nick, straightens an edge or renews an entire evel. A power grinder is faster, though.
Coarse	800 and 1,000	Removes metal fast without leaving deep scratches. It's the best grit to start with when sharpening a very dull edge.
Medium	1,200, 2,000 or 3,000	Quickly removes the scratches made by a coarse stone. Medium serves as the final grit for carpentry tools.
Fine	4,000, 6,000 or 8,000	Makes a super-sharp edge with a mirror polish. This is the final grit for most cabinetmaking tools.
Super-Fine'	12,000, 15,000 and higher	Super-Fine produces the ultimate edge, best suited for premium tools made of the highest-quality steel.

Recommended Sets

Best Value
The least-expensive way to get a decent edge is to buy a regular-size combination stone. Go for a 1,000/6,000 coarse/fine. A large stone requires reflattening less often. A 1,200/8,000 medium/fine stone gives you a slightly sharper edge, but requires more strokes on the medium side to prepare a very dull edge for final polishing.

More Convenience
I use a three-stone system of large single-grit stones: 800 coarse, 1,200 medium and either 6,000 or 8,000 fine. Compared with using the two sides of a combination stone, this set requires fewer strokes on each grit. That produces less wear, so keeping the stones flat is much easier. Buying this set of three adds up, but considering the dough I've spent on good hand tools, it's worth it. After all, your hand tools are only as good as the stones you sharpen with.

If your tools have very high-quality blades, such as A2 or cryogenically treated plane blades, super-fine stones with 12,000 or higher grit will produce an unbelievably sharp edge. These stones don't help very much, though, on average-quality tools, whose steel won't hold a super-sharp edge for more than a few licks.

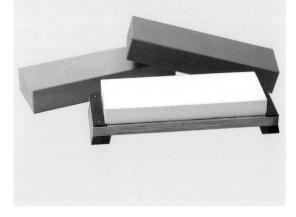

Soak 'Em

Check the directions that come with your stone; some types don't require presoaking, and others should not be soaked or they'll deteriorate.

Most coarse and medium waterstones, though, should be immersed in water when not in use. This keeps them saturated so the surface doesn't dry out quickly when you're sharpening. If you've just bought a new stone, soak it overnight before trying it out. Fine and super-fine stones don't absolutely require soaking, but if you do soak them, they'll be ready to go right away.

I keep my stones in a plastic tub with a lid. They've been soaking since 1979! I add a drop or two of bleach to keep the water free of green scum.

Use Lots of Water

Flood the top of a waterstone with water when you sharpen. This suspends the small particles of worn-off steel in the water, keeping the particles from clogging the stone's surface. You can use a cup or spray bottle or simply dip your fingers in a water container to continually keep the stone wet. I use a plastic mustard bottle.

The undeniable downside to waterstones is that they're messy—though not as messy as oil stones. Your hands will get wet and grubby. To protect my bench, I place my stones on a cookie sheet. Open-weave shelf liner below the stones and under the cookie sheet keeps everything from slipping. After sharpening, I dry my tools right away so they don't rust, place the stones back in the storage tub and wash my hands. The gunk comes off quite easily with ordinary soap.

Cookie Sheet

Water Bottle

Shelf Liner

Keep 'Em Flat

Routinely rub your waterstones with 220-grit wet-dry sandpaper placed on ordinary plate glass that's ¼" or more thick. A waterstone cuts fast because its surface wears down quickly, constantly exposing new, sharp abrasive particles. This wear eventually creates an uneven surface, which produces an undesirable curved edge on chisels and plane irons.

Make a squiggle line with a pencil down the length of a stone before you flatten it. Put a little water on the plate glass so the sandpaper sticks. Then put lots of water on the paper and go at it. When the pencil line is gone, the stone is flat. I also sand a 45-degree bevel on every edge of the stone to prevent flaking.

220-Grit Wet-Dry Sandpaper

Plate Glass

Flatten a combination waterstone with wet-dry sandpaper on glass.

Flatten single-grit stones by rubbing them against each other. Both wear down until they mate perfectly flat.

With my three-stone single-grit system, I skip the sandpaper and glass method and simply flatten all three stones against each other. The trick to avoid making concave and convex pairs is to continually alternate sides. Rubbing medium against fine does no harm to the fine stone. This is so easy that I flatten my stones before each sharpening session. It only takes a minute or so. Flattening the sides removes the inked grit numbers, so I write them in pencil on the end of each stone.

Make a Slurry

The secret to sharpening on a fine-grit stone is to build up a paste slurry before you get going. It looks like thin mud. A slurry keeps the microscopic metal particles removed from the tool's edge in suspension more effectively than water alone. That makes sharpening go faster and results in a better edge. The paste also makes the stone more slippery, which prevents the backs of your chisels and plane irons from sticking to the stone's surface. You can get by without the slurry, but sharpening will be more difficult.

Nagura Stone

To create the paste, wet the stone and vigorously rub its top with a Nagura stone. The Nagura wears away the stone to leave a chalky paste. As you sharpen, the paste will be pushed to the ends of the stone. When that happens, wet your fingers and work the paste back over the whole stone, or rub the stone with the Nagura again. When you're done, leave the paste to dry on the stone, ready for next time.

Honing Guide

Guides Are OK

Some folks claim that the wheel underneath a honing guide will quickly hollow out and ruin a stone's surface, but I disagree. You just need to use the right technique. I concentrate my finger pressure on the edge of the tool, not on the honing guide itself. The harder you press on the tool's edge, the faster the stone will cut, but there's no reason to bear down on the wheel.

Sharpening Tips

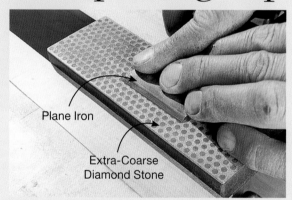

Plane Iron

Extra-Coarse Diamond Stone

Flatten Blade Backs Fast

It would be great if chisels and planes came from the factory ready to use, but they don't. A perfectly flat, mirror-like finish on the back is essential for a truly sharp edge. Flattening always requires a large dose of elbow grease and patience. The fastest method is to use an extra-coarse diamond stone. It won't dish out the way oilstones and waterstones do and it can easily be clamped in a vise.

Once you have a flat surface, move on to finer stones until your chisels and planes shine like a mirror.

3 Ways to Test for Sharpness

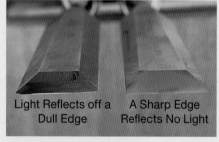

Light Reflects off a Dull Edge   A Sharp Edge Reflects No Light

1 If you can see light on the edge, it's not sharp. A sharp edge is too fine to reflect light.

2 A sharp edge catches easily on the side of a plastic pen barrel. A dull edge slides right off.

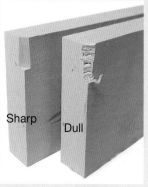

Sharp   Dull

3 A sharp blade slices softwood end grain cleanly (left). A dull blade tears the end grain (right).

by Dave Munkittrick

Water-Cooled Sharpening Machines

THERE'S NO RISK OF BURNING THE STEEL

Today's water-cooled sharpening machines, also called wet grinders for short, can reshape and sharpen almost any cutting tool you own. Like their foot-powered ancestors, they get the job done without the risks associated with a bench grinder. Overheating and blueing tool steel is impossible with a wet grinder because its slow speed and constant water bath keep the tool cool. There are no flying sparks or superfine grinding-wheel dust to worry about either.

In this article, we'll look at wet grinders that come with a leather honing wheel, making a one-stop sharpening machine. Other types of wet grinders don't have honing wheels but come with additional high-speed dry wheels, or are simply horizontal wet-wheels.

These one-stop systems are self-contained. There's no need to switch wheels to change grits. You use the wet-wheel for coarse and medium-grit grinding and the leather wheel for final honing. They're also compact and easy to store.

Wet grinders have a couple downsides, though. Wet grinding is slower than using a bench grinder when it comes to reshaping a tool or removing a nick in its edge. If you're in a hurry, you'd use a bench grinder for shaping, then move to a wet grinder for sharpening.

Like waterstones, these machines make a wet mess. Keep that in mind when you choose a place for your machine. It's best to mount it on a plywood base with a lip to capture the water. A large cookie sheet will also do the trick.

There is a vast array of accessories available for these machines that allow you to sharpen just about anything: planer and jointer blades, axes, knives, scissors, even hard-to-sharpen

carving chisels and turning tools. Most of the accessories are interchangeable between machines because all the guide bars that the accessories mount on have the same diameter.

We looked at four models: two from Tormek and one each from Grizzly and Jet. All four produced a good, sharp edge on chisels and plane irons.

The price range is pretty dramatic, but there are considerations that explain that spread. The more expensive the machine, the less hassling and tinkering around you have to do to get the job done. Things like microadjustment knobs, well-designed tool holders, and easy-to-use angle guides make setup quick and easy. Another price factor is the number of accessories included in the basic package. At the base price, some machines leave out essentials such as a wheel trueing device and a dressing stone. These are hidden costs that a buyer should be aware of.

Machines such as these come ready to go. All that's needed is to mount the wheel, add water and charge the leather honing wheel with compound, and you're ready to sharpen chisels and plane blades.

Features

The sharpening procedure is similar on the four machines we tested. The way in which the following features perform can make using the machine more of a pleasure and less of a chore.

Guide Bar

A solid bar with two posts guides the tool across the face of both wheels. Raising or lowering the guide bar changes the bevel angle of a tool. The guide bars on these machines aren't exactly the same. Three have a microadjust for setting the bar's height—one doesn't. A microadjust takes the hit or miss out of the setup and makes it easy to add a microbevel. A microbevel is a short bevel at a steeper angle that's honed only at the final grit.

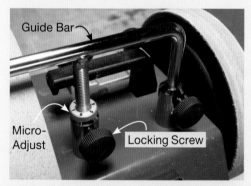

Tormek's guide bar features a calibrated micro adjust knob for accurate height adjustments in .01" increments. Tormek uses Acme threads on the guide bar to prevent damage from the locking screws.

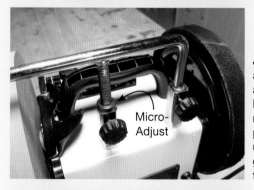

Jet's microadjust knob also simplifies height adjustment, but a larger knob with calibration would make this setup better. In place of Acme threads, Jet uses standard threads and grinds a flat on the post for the locking screws.

Grizzly has the same sturdy two-post design as the other two guide bars. This machine doesn't have a micro-adjust knob, though. The guide bar's height is a little trickier to fine-tune.

Trueing Tool

The surface of any grinding wheel eventually gets uneven. A diamond-tipped trueing tool is a must to restore the surface so that the wheel is round and flat. The most accurate way to do this is to mount the truing tool on the machine's guide bar. The Tormek T-7 comes with such a guided diamond trueing tool; the T-3 and Jet offer one as an accessory. Grizzly offers a handheld diamond trueing tool as an accessory. While you could get by with this, a guided system is much better. Fortunately, both the Tormek and Jet trueing tools fit on the Grizzly guide bar.

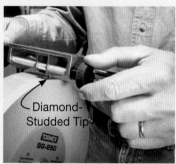

Tormek's diamond trueing tool is the best of the bunch. It uses a foolproof screw-feed system to slowly draw the diamond-studded tip across the stone. The tool's depth of cut is controlled by the guide bar's microadjust.

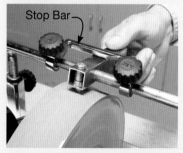

Jet's truing tool is sold as an accessory. The tool rides on the guide bar and uses a stop bar to control the depth of cut. The Jet tool relies on your hand to guide it across the stone.

Dressing Stone

A dressing stone is used by all the systems to alter the wheel's grit. This must-have tool is only included with the Jet and the Tormek T-7. The dressing stone has a smooth side and a rough side. When sharpening, the normal progression is to dress the wheel with the rough side of the stone to expose fresh grit for your initial grinding. This creates a roughly 220-grit surface. After that, the wheel is dressed with the smooth side of the stone to create a finer surface (about 1,000 grit), which puts a sharper edge on the tool. The tool is now ready for a final polish on the honing wheel.

Honing Wheel

All the wet grinders have a small leather-covered wheel for putting the final edge on a tool. It can be used freehand or with the guide bar. The leather is charged with a polishing paste that contains a very fine grit. Honing puts a mirror finish on the tool's edge. The wheel can also be used to polish the backs of chisels and plane irons.

Chisel and Plane Blade Tool Holder

When you sharpen a straight-edged chisel or plane blade, you'll clamp it in a holder. This maintains a constant angle and guides the tool across the stone.

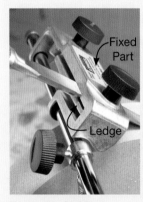

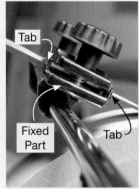

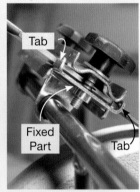

Tormek's holder eliminates the chance of clamping the tool unevenly. The back of the blade registers against the fixed upper part of the holder. An alignment ledge automatically squares the tool and accommodates short chisels.

Jet's holder works well for standard chisels and plane irons. Alignment can be a problem, though. The upper part that registers the chisel's back isn't fixed, but can rock. In addition, the holder's two small alignment tabs are spaced too far apart to easily position a chisel with a short blade.

The Grizzly holder does a fine job on standard chisels and plane irons. This holder also clamps the top of the chisel against the fixed part of the jig. This arrangement can cause misalignment of the chisel in the holder. As with the Jet holder, a two-tab design makes short chisels difficult to align.

Angle Guide

An angle guide is critical to setting the height of the guide bar. You'll use the angle guide to repeat a specific bevel angle or create a new one. The Tormek and Jet guides adjust to compensate for a shrinking diameter as the wheel wears.

by Tom Caspar

Sharpening Scrapers

NEW METHOD IS FOOLPROOF

Scraping is quiet and efficient. It's perfect for removing milling marks and shallow tear-out.

I couldn't believe my eyes the first time I saw John Erickson, the woodworker I apprenticed with, scrape a piece of walnut. How could a mere piece of steel work so quickly? John didn't have to go through five grits of sandpaper to get a smooth surface. He'd take a board right from the jointer, scrape a few strokes, lightly sand with the finest paper, and that was it!

I was only a young apprentice in his shop. When it came time for me to sharpen my own scraper, all I got was dust, not those long shavings John made. How did he do it?

Although the old man never shared his sharpening system with me, I've developed my own approach using some modern twists. The best thing about it is that anyone can get great results. Once you get the hang of it, you can put a fresh edge on a scraper in five minutes, tops. All you need is some basic sharpening equipment, the world's simplest jig (a plain stick with one beveled side), a vise on the front of your bench and the patience to take the process one step at a time.

What You Need

The Scraper

A card scraper is a rectangular piece of flat steel. Like a handsaw blade, the steel is soft enough to be filed, but hard enough to hold an edge. Scrapers have four cutting edges shaped like miniature hooks. The hooks are almost too small to see, but you can feel them with your fingers.

In the steps, we only tackle the top side of the scraper, making two cutting edges. To sharpen all four edges, flip over the scraper and repeat each step on the bottom side.

The Sharpening Kit

File. The handiest tool is a 10" combination mill file with a built-in handle. The double-cut side of the file has two crisscrossed rows of teeth for fast stock removal. The single-cut side has a single row of teeth. This side cuts slower but leaves a smoother surface. Actually, any 8- or 10" mill file will work, as long as it's sharp.

Honing Paddle. A diamond paddle cuts fast and stays flat. You can substitute a slipstone or small oilstone, but they're slower and score too easily. An extra-fine grit paddle is best, but a fine will work.

Burnisher. A burnisher is nothing more than a hardened and polished ⅜"-dia. steel rod. Most come with a handle, but you really don't need one.

File Card. A file card cleans your file. If you don't routinely clean your file, metal debris caught in the file's teeth will put deep scratches on a scraper's edge.

Oil. Honing oil lubricates the burnisher. Household oil (such as 3 IN 1) works, too, but leaves your hands smelly.

The Jig

This beveled stick is all you need to hold the file, honing paddle and burnisher at the correct angles.

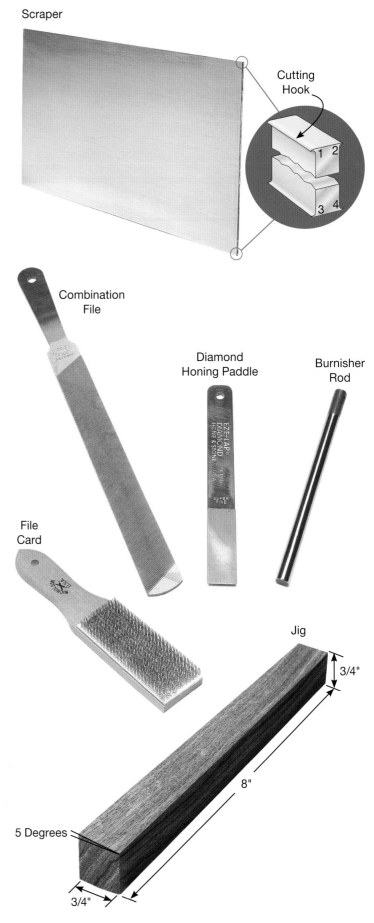

Scraper

Cutting Hook

1 2

3 4

Combination File

Diamond Honing Paddle

Burnisher Rod

File Card

Jig

3/4"

8"

5 Degrees

3/4"

1 Flatten the dull hooks. Stroke the burnisher back and forth over each edge of a dull scraper. Smear a few drops of oil on the burnisher first, then press down lightly and rub until you no longer feel a hook. Two or three passes should do it. Hold the burnisher flat on the scraper, or lean it over the edge, as shown.

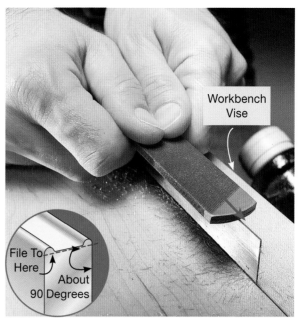

2 Remove the dull edge. Push the coarse, double-cut side of the file down the full length of the scraper. Removing lots of metal is the key to success. Hold the scraper in a vise. Ride the knuckles of your hand along the benchtop to steady the file at about 90 degrees. You don't have to be precise, just aggressive. Don't drag the file back over the scraper on the return stroke, though, or you'll prematurely dull the file.

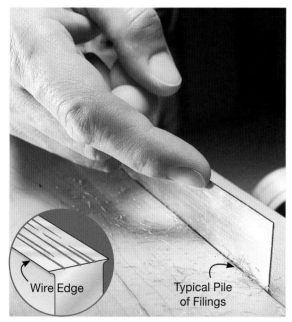

3 Test for sharpness I. Feel for a very small ridge of excess metal on both sides of the scraper. This ridge is called a wire edge. Pay special attention to the center section of the scraper, where it's the dullest. If you feel a wire edge here, move on to Step 4. If you don't, go back to Step 2.

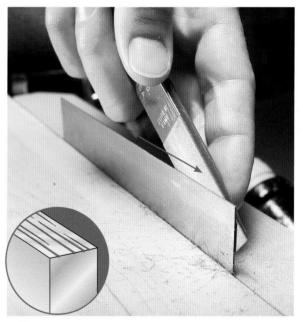

4 Remove the wire edge. Hone both sides of the scraper with the diamond paddle. Hold the paddle so most of its face is riding on the scraper's side. Hone back and forth until you no longer feel a wire edge. It should only take a few strokes. Wipe the paddle on a damp rag to keep it clean and cutting efficiently.

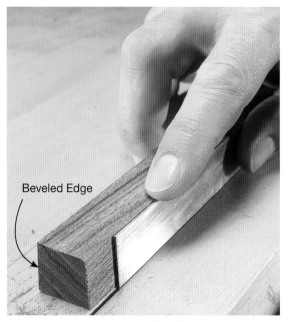

Beveled Edge

5 Level the scraper with the jig. Adjust the scraper in the vise so the full length of its top edge feels even with the jig stick. Make sure the beveled side of the stick faces away from the scraper.

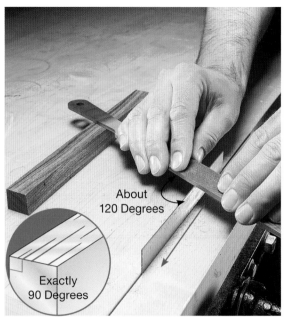

About 120 Degrees

Exactly 90 Degrees

6 File the edge square. File the edge again, this time using the finer, single-cut side. Support the end of the file with the jig stick. This guarantees that you'll make a 90-degree edge. Keep filing until you feel a faint wire edge on both sides, just like in Step 2.

Pushing the file at about 120 degrees is called draw-filing. This produces a smoother edge than pushing the file in line with the edge, as shown in Step 2.

Exactly 90 Degrees

7 Hone the edge square. Support the honing paddle with the jig stick to maintain a perfect 90-degree edge. Then hone both sides of the scraper, as shown in Step 4. Alternate honing the sides and the top four or five times. This is the only way to completely remove the wire edge.

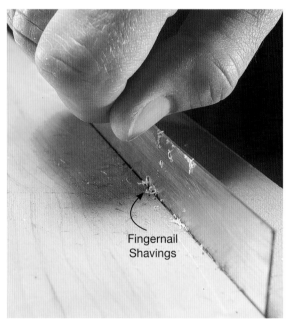

Fingernail Shavings

8 Test for sharpness II. Check the edge to make sure it's sharp. Pull your thumbnail across the center and both ends of the scraper. If you see small shavings, and the center feels as sharp as the ends, you're ready to go on to the next step. If not, repeat Step 7.

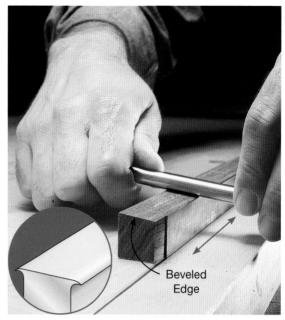

Beveled
Edge

9 Bend the hook in. Burnish the edge into a concave shape. Remove the scraper from the vise and lubricate the burnisher with a few drops of oil. Then lean the burnisher about 5 degrees and stroke it back and forth over the scraper's edge three or four times. Press hard with your thumb directly over the edge. Flip the scraper over and burnish the other side.

10 Bend the hook out. Bend the cutting hook using the jig stick as a guide. Clamp the scraper back in the vise so it's level with the lower edge of the stick's bevel. Push the burnisher back and forth four or five times, applying hard pressure.

When you're done with one hook, place the jig stick on the other side of the scraper and repeat to form the second hook. As you gain experience in burnishing, you'll find that you won't need a guide to get the angle right.

Try It Out

Bend the scraper to stiffen the cutting edge. Place your thumbs near the bottom edge and pull back the ends with your fingers. Lean the scraper forward and push with your thumbs. It may take a bit of experimentation to figure out how much lean you'll need to make full-fledged shavings.

Re-sharpening a Dull Scraper

When you've worn out all four edges of your scraper and all you get is dust, not shavings, it's time to reburnish the edges. Chances are the hooks aren't dull, but simply bent back. To re-form the hooks with your burnisher, repeat Steps 9 and 10. This usually works two or three times, but eventually the hooks get worn away and can't be re-formed. Then it's time to get out the file and start from the beginning.

by Alan Turner

Stropping on Leather

THIS TECHNIQUE CREATES THE ULTIMATE SHARP EDGE

I have a special set of chisels that I only use for paring. To do a good job, they have to be wicked sharp—and stay that way. My secret weapon isn't a fabulously expensive honing stone. It's a cheap, homemade strop.

I use these chisels a lot when I'm cutting dovetails (Photo 1). Whenever a chisel feels the least bit dull, I renew its edge on the strop. This only takes a moment, but the results are dramatic. When I pare end grain, for example, I routinely get tissue-thin shavings, not dust. I use the strop quite often, so I store it right next to my chisels (Photo 2).

A strop is a very simple device. It's just a thick piece of firm leather, about 2-3" wide, glued to a block. The leather is charged with a thin layer of 0.5 micron honing compound. A strop will serve you for many years: The leather won't wear out, and one stick of compound is probably all you'll ever need to buy.

Here's how to make one. Cut the leather about 10-12" long, then cut a board slightly wider and longer than the leather. Spread a thin layer of yellow glue onto the board and place the leather on the board (Photo 3). Clamp a second board on top of the leather to keep it flat. After the glue dries, trim the block flush with the leather. Next, apply a thin coat of mineral oil to the leather (Photo 4) and rub on some honing compound (Photo 5). Your strop is ready to go.

Before I explain how to use the strop and describe what it does to an edge, let's return to my set of paring chisels. They're made of high-quality steel, so they can hold a thin edge. (A chisel with a low-angled bevel requires less effort to push when paring than one with a steep-angled bevel.) I grind these chisels at 20°, then hone on 500, 2000 and 8000 grit Shapton waterstones. I don't use a guide. Instead, I rock the chisel on the stone until I feel both the bevel's heel and toe contact the surface. Then I start honing, maintaining that angle, until I feel a wire edge on the back of the chisel. I remove the wire edge on the 8000 stone.

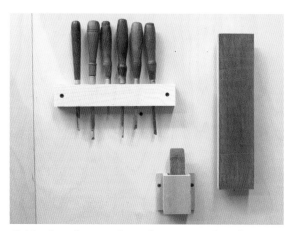

1 Paring end grain requires an extremely sharp edge. When my chisel feels a bit dull, I go right to the strop to restore its edge.

2 My strop lives on the wall next to my bench, always ready to go. Stropping a chisel takes less than a minute.

3 To make a strop, glue a thick, stiff piece of leather to a block. MDF makes an ideal block—it's very flat and stable.

4 Prepare the strop by applying a light coat of mineral oil. Work it into the leather—you only have to do this once.

5 Rub honing compound onto the strop. The compound lasts a long time—I only recharge the strop every 3 months or so.

6 Strop the back of your chisel, as well as the bevel. Hold the chisel flat on the strop, so you don't round the edge, and pull it back.

Next, I go to the strop. Again, I rock the chisel to find the bevel, press hard, then pull the chisel backwards down the strop. I repeat this process three or four times, making sure I maintain the bevel's original angle. I also strop the chisel's back (Photo 6).

What does the strop do? It polishes the edge—making it sharper; and slightly rounds over the edge—making it stronger. I'm convinced that a stropped edge lasts longer than an edge that's only been honed. It's amazing!

by Brad Holden

Sharpening Station

EVERYTHING YOU NEED IS RIGHT AT HAND

If your sharpening supplies are scattered all over your shop, here's a project designed to keep them in one place. This station holds everything you need for grinding, lapping and honing, with room to spare for storing tools.

Picture this: you're grinding at the perfect height for precision work. When you're done, you push the grinder back out of the way and vacuum or wipe off grinding dust from the cabinet's plastic laminate surface. You pull a rubber mat from its storage pocket, retrieve your stones from one of the drawers, and you're ready to hone.

That mat is really terrific. It's made from flexible but firm solid rubber. Water can't soak in; it just makes puddles. Better yet, stones stay put, as if they were locked in place.

Experiment with Heights

This project is designed for a 5'6" to 5'10" tall woodworker. If you're shorter or taller than this, you may want to alter the plans so the working surfaces are at more comfortable heights.

Experiment before you build. First, figure out the height at which you're comfortable honing (don't forget to add the thickness of the rubber mat and stones). For most folks, this is roughly equal to the height of their wrists when their arms are hanging at their sides. Use this measurement to determine the height of the cabinet.

Second, figure out the height at which you're comfortable grinding. Many woodworkers prefer elevating a grinder so its tool rests are about elbow-high. This height will vary between 6" and 8" grinders (we used an 8" grinder for our station). Use this measurement to determine the height of the shelf above the cabinet.

Build the Cabinet

Use basic plywood-construction techniques to build the base cabinet and drawers. See Fig. C for the location of the dadoes and rabbets in the cabinet's sides and Fig. B for drawer details.

Make the Top

To ensure a flat top, use MDF for the substrate (B1, Fig. A). Edgeband it with solid birch (B2 and B3), mitered at the front corners. Use an 80-grit sanding block, a plane, or a router and flush-trim bit to level the edging (Photo 1).

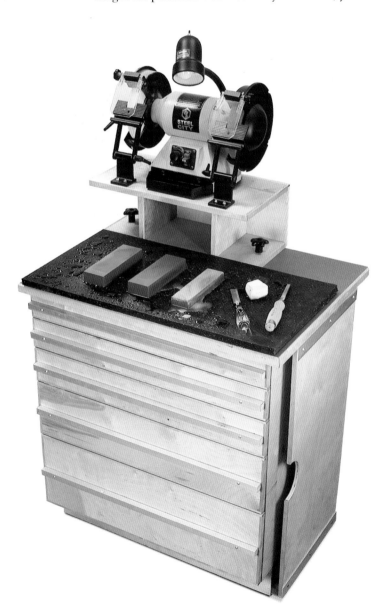

Apply the laminate (B4). Use a chamfer bit to trim the laminate and create the finished edge in one step (Photo 1).

Rout two grooves for the T-track (B5 and Fig. D). Seal the grooves with slow curing epoxy to keep water from soaking into the MDF. While the epoxy is still tacky, apply a second, thicker coat and glue in the T-track (Photo 2). Drill two holes in the top for registration pins. These keep the rubber mat from sliding back and forth. Attach the top to the cabinet. Position it flush with the back and offset on the right side, to allow for the pocket.

Add the Pocket

The pocket fastens to both the top and the cabinet. Cut two pieces of aluminum angle (D2). Drill and countersink holes in one piece for fastening it to the top. Drill the remaining holes for fastening both pieces to the pocket's side (D4). Fasten the top angle to the cabinet top, then install the side, spacer (D3), stop (D5) and bottom angle.

Cut the Mat

The rubber mat (D1) comes in a 2 ft. x 3 ft. piece. Use a straightedge and a utility knife to cut it to size. It will take a few passes to cut entirely through the rubber. Drill registration holes in the mat to correspond to the holes in the cabinet top. Use a utility knife to cut a recessed fingerhold on one side of the mat. A fingerhold makes it easier to pull the mat out of the pocket.

3 Key Features

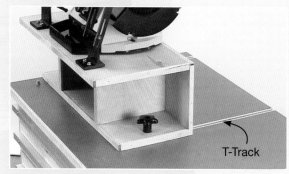

Moveable Grinder
The grinder sits on a tall shelf that slides on two T-tracks. Pull the shelf forward for grinding; push it back to make room for sharpening.

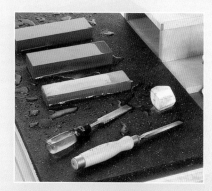

Honing Mat
Place your waterstones on this solid rubber mat. They'll stay put on its non-skid surface.

Protected Storage
Slide the mat into this side pocket to protect it from grinding dust, which you don't want on your stones.

1 The station's top is designed to survive water, grit, oil and shop dings. Begin building the top by gluing thick, solid edging to an MDF substrate. Level the edging with coarse sandpaper, then glue on an oversized piece of plastic laminate. Trim the laminate flush to the edging by forming a large chamfer.

2 Glue T-track into the slots with epoxy. Add screws to clamp the T-track in place.

Fig. A: Exploded View

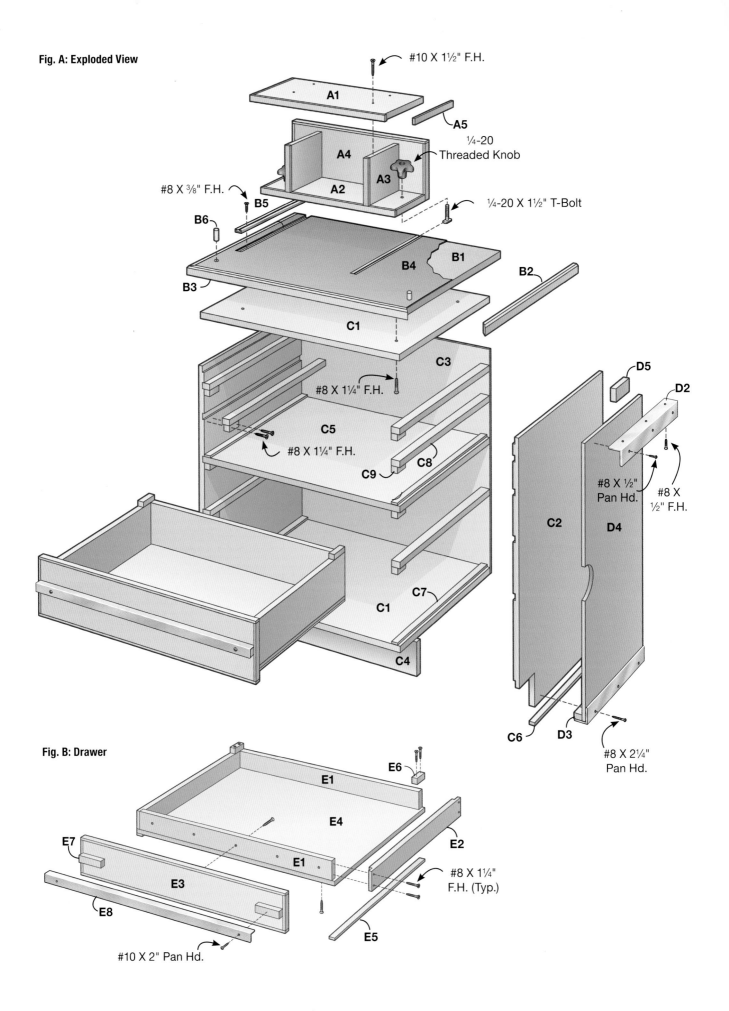

#10 X 1½" F.H.

A1

A5

A4

A2

A3

¼-20
Threaded Knob

#8 X ³⁄₈" F.H.

B5

B6

¼-20 X 1½" T-Bolt

B3

B4

B1

B2

C1

C3

#8 X 1¼" F.H.

D5

D2

C5

C8

C9

#8 X 1¼" F.H.

#8 X ½"
Pan Hd.

#8 X
½" F.H.

C2

D4

C7

C1

C4

C6

D3

#8 X 2¼"
Pan Hd.

Fig. B: Drawer

E1

E6

E4

E2

E7

E1

E3

E5

E8

#8 X 1¼"
F.H. (Typ.)

#10 X 2" Pan Hd.

Fig. C: Side Dado Layout

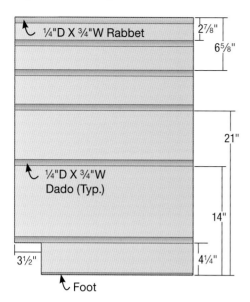

¼"D X ¾"W Rabbet

2⅞"

6⅝"

¼"D X ¾"W Dado (Typ.)

21"

14"

3½"

4¼"

Foot

Fig. D: Top Layout

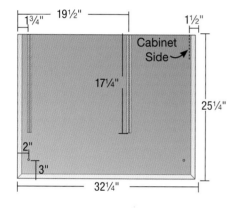

19½"

1¾"

1½"

Cabinet Side

17¼"

25¼"

2"

3"

32¼"

Cutting List Notes

* Cabinet is 33½"H
(1) Add ¼" edgebanding front and sides.
(2) Add ¼" edgebanding on front.
(3) Add ¼" edgebanding all around.

Cutting List

Overall Dimensions: 41¼" H x 32¼" L x 25¼" D*

Section	Part	Name	Qty.	Material	Th x W x L
Shelf	A1	Top	1	Birch plywood	¾" x 10¼" x 20½" (1)
	A2	Bottom	1	Birch plywood	¾" x 7-3/4" x 20½" (1)
	A3	Support	2	Birch plywood	¾" x 6¼" x 7¾" (1)
	A4	Back	1	Birch plywood	½" x 20½" x 7½" (1)
	A5	Edging		Solid birch	¼" x ¾"
Top	B1	Substrate	1	MDF	¾" x 24½" x 30¾"
	B2	Side edging	2	Solid birch	¾" x 1" x 25¼"
	B3	Front edging	1	Solid birch	¾" x 1" x 32¼"
	B4	Laminate	1		26" x 33"
	B5	T-track	2		⅜" x ¾" x 17¼"
	B6	Registration peg	2	Birch dowel	⅜" x 1¼"
Base	C1	Subtop & bottom	2	Birch plywood	¾" x 28⅞" x 23"
	C2	Side	2	Birch plywood	¾" x 23¼" x 32½"
	C3	Back	1	Birch plywood	¼" x 28½" x 29⅛"
	C4	Toe kick	1	Solid birch	¾" x 4¼" x 29¹⁵⁄₁₆"
	C5	Center support	1	Birch plywood	¾" x 28⅞" x 23"
	C6	Feet	2	Solid maple	¼" x ¾" x 19¾"
	C7	Wear strip	4	Solid maple	¼" x ¾" x 22⅞"
	C8	Drawer support	6	Solid maple	¾" x 1" x 22⅞"
	C9	Drawer stop	10	Solid maple	¾" x ¾" x 2"
Pocket	D1	Mat	1	Rubber	¾" x 16" x 31"
	D2	Bracket	2	Aluminum angle	1½" x 1½" x 16"
	D3	Spacer	1	Solid birch	¾" x 1" x 16"
	D4	Side	1	Birch plywood	½" x 15¾" x 31¾" (2)
	D5	Stop	1	Solid birch	¾" x 1½" x 3½"
Drawers					
#1	E1	Front and back	2	Birch plywood	¾" x ⅝" x 27¼"
	E2	Sides	2	Birch plywood	¾" x ⅝" x 22⅞"
	E3	Front	1	Birch plywood	¾" x 2⅝" x 29¼" (3)
#2	E1	Front and back	2	Birch plywood	¾" x 1½" x 27¼"
	E2	Sides	2	Birch plywood	¾" x 1½" x 22⅞"
	E3	Front	1	Birch plywood	¾" x 3⅛" x 29¼" (3)
#3	E1	Front and back	2	Birch plywood	¾" x 2⅛" x 27¼"
	E2	Sides	2	Birch plywood	¾" x 2⅛" x 22⅞"
	E3	Front	1	Birch plywood	¾" x 3¾" x 29¼" (3)
#4	E1	Front and back	2	Birch plywood	¾" x 4¾" x 27¼"
	E2	Sides	2	Birch plywood	¾" x 4¾" x 22⅞"
	E3	Front	1	Birch plywood	¾" x 6⅜" x 29¼" (3)
#5	E1	Front and back	2	Birch plywood	¾" x 7½" x 27¼"
	E2	Sides	2	Birch plywood	¾" x 7½" x 22⅞"
	E3	Front	1	Birch plywood	¾" x 9¼" x 29¼" (3)
All	E4	Bottom	5	Birch plywood	½" x 28¼" x 22⅞"
	E5	Runner	10	Solid maple	¼" x ¾" x 22⅞"
	E6	Stop	10	Solid maple	¾" x ¾" x 2"
	E7	Handle block	10	Birch plywood	¾" x ¾" x 4"
	E8	Handle	5	Aluminum angle	¾" x ¾" x 29¼"

AMERICAN WOODWORKER'S HAND TOOL FUNDAMENTALS

Copyright © 2014 by F+W, A Content + eCommerce Company.
Printed and bound in China. All rights reserved. No part of this
book may be reproduced in any form or by any electronic or
mechanical means, including information storage and retrieval
systems, without permission in writing from the publisher,
except by a reviewer, who may quote brief passages in a
review. Published by American Woodworker, an imprint of
F+W, 10151 Carver Rd., Suite 200, Blue Ash, Ohio, 45236.
(800) 289-0963. First edition.

Distributed in Canada by Fraser Direct
100 Armstrong Avenue
Georgetown, Ontario L7G 5S4
Canada

Distributed in the U.K. and Europe by
F&W Media International, LTD
Brunel House, Ford Close
Newton Abbot
TQ12 4PU, UK
Tel: (+44) 1626 323200; Fax: (+44) 1626 323319
E-mail: enquiries@fwmedia.com

Distributed in Australia by Capricorn Link
P.O.Box 704
Windsor, NSW 2756
Australia
Tel: (02) 4560 1600; Fax: (02) 4577 5288

Visit our consumer website at shopwoodworking.com for more
woodworking information projects.

Other fine American Woodworker publications are available
from your local bookstore or direct from the publisher.

ISBN-13: 978-1-940038-12-4

18 17 16 15 14   5 4 3 2 1

Acquistions editor: David Thiel
Editor: John Kelsey
Designer: Maura J. Zimmer
Cover Design: Daniel T. Pessell
Production Coordinator: Debbie Thomas